Class Work

Women & Social Class

Series editors: Pat Mahony and Christine Zmroczek
(Roehampton Institute, UK)

This new series aims to address a relatively neglected area of feminist theory, women and social class. The series is intended to analyze social class in relation to women's lives, to theorize it by highlighting personal experience and to understand it in ways which move beyond the macro analyses provided by male, 'left' oriented accounts. In developing feminist understandings and analyses of how class continues to operate across and within diverse contexts, the series is committed to evaluating the ways in which social class combines with other social forces to produce inequalities for women in the present and in the future.

Already published:

Class Matters: 'Working-Class' Women's Perspectives on Social Class
Edited by Pat Mahony and Christine Zmroczek

Class Work:
Mothers' Involvement in their
Children's Primary Schooling

Diane Reay

RoutledgeFalmer
Taylor & Francis Group

First published in 1998 by UCL Press

Reprinted 2003 by RoutledgeFalmer
11 New Fetter Lane
London, EC4P 4EE

RoutledgeFalmer is an imprint of the
Taylor & Francis Group

British Library Cataloguing in Publication Data
A catalogue record for this book is available from the British Library.

Library of Congress Cataloging-in-Publication data are available.

ISBNs:
1-85728-915-3 HB
1-85728-916-1 PB

Typeset in 10/12pt Times
by Best-set Typesetter Ltd, Hong Kong.

Printed and Bound by Antony Rowe Ltd

This book is dedicated to the memory of my great-grandmother, Alice Pickering who died in the workhouse at Ashby-de-la-Zouch in 1929.

Contents

Acknowledgments

I would like to thank both the mothers and teachers in the two schools where I conducted my research for their many insights and reflections. I am extremely grateful to my series editors, Pat Mahony and Christine Zmroczek. They were very generous with their time, providing encouraging as well as constructively critical comments on an earlier draft of the book. I am indebted to Miriam David, my supervisor at South Bank University, for her unfailing positive support over the period of completing a Ph.D. and since. Heidi Mirza has provided intellectual and emotional support and sustenance throughout my time in academia. Her warmth, wisdom and humanity have been a continuing source of strength.

Chapter 1

Introduction

This book's main aim is to reassert the centrality of social class, as gendered and racialized, in an explanation of the maintenance of educational differences and the reproduction of social inequality. Over the past twenty years social inequalities have increasingly become something many of us take for granted, rather than something we feel responsible for. The myth of meritocracy normalizes inequalities, converting them into individual rather than collective responsibilities. Furthermore, meritocracy sustains fictions of equal access and homogeneous provision, denying differences that count. Behind the bland rhetoric of difference as diversity lie differences that add up to social advantage for some and subtract into social disadvantage for others. Certainly there is no fair distribution of reward for the time, commitment and energy expended by the mothers in this study in support of their children's education. Time, commitment and energy all count for more if they are underpinned by material and cultural resources.

There is a long history of sociological writing which positions the educational system as instrumental in the distribution of social advantage and disadvantage within society (Jackson and Marsden, 1966; Willis, 1977; Halsey et al., 1980; Connell et al., 1982; Gewirtz et al., 1995). However, few of the studies of social class reproduction have attempted a gendered analysis, and even fewer have included 'race' within their ambit. This book attempts both through a focus on the home–school relationship as the key to social class reproduction. Much has been made of pupil–teacher interaction, and the school site as pivotal in working-class educational failure. Far less has been written of middle-class monopolization of educational markets (Cohen, 1981; Sieber, 1982; Gewirtz et al., 1995) and how mothering work in support of children's education is differentially rewarded through the operation of educational markets which privilege middle-class cultural capital. The tales mothers tell run counter to the ideology of the market and claims of neutrality and classlessness. This is a story, then, of unfair advantages and unfair disadvantages, not individual deficits. Black and white, working-class mothers were working just as hard on their children's educational attainment as the white, middle-class mothers. But as the words of the women throughout this book illustrate, it was not hard work that counted.

1

Nicos Mouzelis argues that much sociological theorizing of human inter-action continues to be conceptualized in a hierarchical vacuum (Mouzelis, 1995: 26). Hierarchies are the key to comprehending home–school relation-ships. In order to understand how parental involvement sustains rather than erodes existing social inequalities, there needs to be a recognition of *three* interrelated hierarchies. The link between the mother and children's educa-tional attainment highlights the hierarchical relations embedded in hetero-sexual relationships. Despite 30 years of second-wave feminisms, women are still the parents with the responsibility for the children. Beyond the home, class and 'race' hierarchies permeate parent–teacher interactions. Lastly, there are hierarchies of 'race' and class pervading the wider educational market-place. These result in the privileging of white, middle-class cultural capital and the monopolization of the UK state-educational market by white, middle-class parents acting on behalf of their children. As Jordan *et al.* argue in relation to white, middle-class families:

> The paradox of their lives was not the constraint associated with riches, but the self-defeating pursuit of advantage. Putting the family first implied that they had to take every step available to give their children a better chance of making something of themselves than other people's children enjoyed . . . the logic of their choices must always tend towards giving their offspring a headstart – more learn-ing capacity, greater concentration, more practice, better facilities, more resources, a favourable environment, more qualifications, more confidence, more contacts, more social skills – over others who would also be striving to make something of themselves. (Jordan *et al.*, 1994: 222)

This book is about 33 mothers living in metropolitan London. At the same time, the story that I have woven out of women's words and actions is power-fully influenced by my own history as a white, English woman from a working-class background, who has experienced periods of being a lone mother alongside longer periods of being partnered. I have written extensively else-where about reflexivity and research methods (Reay, 1995c; 1996a; 1996b). I believe all research is in one way or another autobiographical or else the avoidance of autobiography. I agree with Heidi Mirza's analysis of what happens to black women's writing. She writes of how tales from the margins are appropriated and rewritten by the dominant culture:

> In writing about our world, our place on the margin, black feminists take the risk of what happens when you expose yourself as an object of study. Laid bare in our unveiling, our inner-most life stories be-come objects for public gaze; our resistance is known. We engage in naming our subjectivity, telling our story. We undertake journeys of self-discovery, which are then appropriated and recorded as objec-

tive knowledge, 'original context' and 'specificities'. The dominant culture achieves hegemony precisely by its capacity to convert and recode for the authoritative other. (Mirza, 1997: 18)

I would contend that similar processes are at work in relation to the words of working-class women, both black and white, and to a lesser extent ex-working-class women like myself who continue to struggle with an identity as middle-class (Reay, 1997a). I have a past record of using myself and my earlier experiences in my texts, and I believe much revelation in academic texts is about a failure to fit the norm (Reay, 1996b; 1997a). Because I have written about my subjectivity as a researcher elsewhere, I only discuss briefly my own experience in the field in this book and, instead, give a conventional account of the research methods in Chapter 4.

I recognize that the researcher can never be entirely absent from the account, regardless of whether they are referred to directly (Stanley and Wise, 1993). At the same time I believe it is inevitable that, when we write of ourselves as researchers in our texts, we invariably give a partial picture. Even when researchers are in confessional mode (Van Maanen, 1988), enumerating inadequacies and describing mistakes in the field, we rarely resist the opportunity to invite sympathy, to paint a favourable portrait. Research is paved with deceits and conceits – the researcher's more than the researched. At the same time it is important to state that I was also a mother at one of the schools where I conducted the research. Both my children attended Milner and I have lived in its catchment area for over 25 years. A number of the mothers that I interviewed were and remain my friends.

I have also been a primary school teacher for 20 years and that experience has also shaped my relationship to my data and the resulting analysis. Just as I have been anxious to assert that mothers are not responsible for educational inequalities, I have been reluctant to blame teachers. As Valerie Walkerdine asserts, 'blaming teachers is like blaming mothers for failing to make the fiction of social democracy work' (Walkerdine, 1989: 208). Rather, both mothers and teachers are caught up in the workings of an educational market that is geared to produce unequal outcomes, despite the best intentions and ceaseless activities of many mothers and teachers. Power lies with policy-makers and, despite government rhetoric, neither mothers nor teachers have any great influence on educational policy in 1990s England.

This book, then, is about parental involvement with a difference or, rather, the differences which permeate parental involvement. Chapter 2 provides a brief overview of the literature on parental involvement, focusing on what normative conceptions of 'parent' miss out. It is argued that it is vital to include the issues of gender, 'race' and social class hidden by normative constructions. The importance of recognizing not only difference and diversity, but the ways in which they are rooted in inequalities, is stressed. In particular, it is argued that, despite the homogeneity reigning in the texts on parental involvement, educational professionals often adopt deficit conceptions of certain parent groups, based on assumptions relating to ethnicity, gender, marital status and social class. Juxtaposing such taken-for-granted assumptions with textual constructions which deny difference is becoming increasingly important within a contemporary context in which increased parental involvement and parental choice are invariably presented as beneficial.

Chapter 3 is concerned with developing a theoretical framework for the present study. The chapter starts with a brief examination of social-class orthodoxies regarding women and social class (Goldthorpe, 1980; 1983; Lockwood, 1986; Goldthorpe and Marshall, 1992). Against this theoretical background it is argued that mothers' involvement in children's schooling provides a different way of approaching the 'women and social class' debate; one that conceptualizes class as a process rather than as a position. Bourdieu's notions of habitus, cultural capital and field are critically reviewed and adapted in a feminist reworking which both makes a space for women and extends analyses to 'race'.

Chapter 4 describes the existing structure and organization of the two schools in the study, before giving a detailed description of the local communities in which the two schools are located. Contrasts of class and 'race' are drawn which reveal the 'white, middle-class' character of Oak Park and the multi-ethnic, working-class nature of Milner. The chapter ends by introducing the reader to the sample of 33 women whose relationships to primary schooling are documented in depth in the following chapters. In particular, their own complex, subjective understandings of their class position, and how these are intersected by ethnicity and marital status, are discussed.

In the first part of Chapter 5 the reader is invited to understand habitus as history. The ways in which women's personal histories and their educational experiences influence their involvement in their children's schooling is outlined. The extent to which women are dealing with different layers of continuity and discontinuity between their own and their children's educational experiences is elaborated and discussed. Themes of separation and connection between home and school in mothers' own educational experience are related to current patterns of involvement. The chapter explores the merging of history and geography in women's lives through an examination of the experience of women who are migrants to Britain. It is argued that their cultural capital is often in the 'wrong' currency, because the experience of attending schools in other countries undermines their capacity to engage productively in the contemporary British educational market. The chapter moves on to an exploration of the powerful impact of geography on women's contemporary options, examining the constraints and possibilities of local educational markets and how these influence the educational choices available to mothers and their children.

Within the theoretical and empirical context set by the preceding chapters, Chapters 6, 7 and 8 document and examine the extensive and diverse range of mothering work underpinning parental involvement. In Chapter 6 the many different types of mothering work are detailed. Practical maintenance, educational and emotional work are all examined. Mothers are shown to be engaged in class- and 'race'-differentiated ways of monitoring and repairing their children's education. The chapter examines how some activities generate cultural capital, while others are far less productive. In particular, activities of complementing, compensating and modifying children's educational provision produce very different outcomes. Compensating for, and modifying, state education often requires material and educational resources disproportionately located within middle-class, rather than working-class families. While working-class mothers are primarily engaged in complementing school provision, the data indicates the ways in which many of the middle-class mothers weave in and out of all three roles. The significance of 'race' is highlighted through evidence that shows that black, working-class mothers are more likely to be compensating for perceived deficits in state education than their white counterparts. In particular, insufficient attention to both black culture and racism within schools resulted in many black families sending their children to black supplementary schools.

In Chapter 7 class differences both in how mothers communicate with their children's teachers and how those communications are received are elaborated. The extent to which mothers and teachers are conducting a dialogue or just talking past each other, and the extent to which this is influenced by social class, is discussed. The considerable degree of working-class disaffection and dissatisfaction is explored through women's own conceptualizations of 'talking to a brick wall' and 'being fobbed off'. In contrast, middle-class mothers are shown to be far more likely to be asking for, and getting, what they want.

In Chapter 8 the influence of 'race' and social class are explored extensively. In particular, there is a focus on the role of socializing in the acquisition of social and educational accomplishments within middle-class families. The intricate social arrangements and busy lives of middle-class mothers and children, and the much more routine, home-based activities of working-class mothers and children, are contrasted. The crucial role of material resources in the generation of social and cultural capital is an important theme running throughout the chapter.

In Chapter 9 the ways in which fathers are absent or absent themselves from the day-to-day work of parental involvement are examined. The chapter draws on empirical data to demonstrate that fathers are far more likely to be 'helping hands' rather than equal partners in their child's education, and that in some cases they actually add to, rather than subtract from, mothers' work. There is also an examination of class differences in which middle-class fathers act as 'public personae', taking a high profile in the public sphere of home–school relations but leaving the day-to-day management to female partners, while working-class fathers are rarely involved either in school or at home.

The enormous inequalities of gender, 'race' and social class embedded in the home–school relationship are the subject of the concluding chapter –

Chapter 10. The social-reproduction debate is briefly revisited in an analysis which recognizes the centrality of women and the family to understandings of social class. Shifting understandings of social class from those rooted in location – namely, men's labour market position – to encompass understandings embedded in activity – the activities of mothers in support of children's schooling – reveal the crucial part mothers play in social-class reproduction. I argue that we need a version of mothering which recognizes the complex interplay between mothering work and the educational market. An analysis which conceptualizes mothering work as strategically located in relation to schooling systems allows for an understanding of mothering work as generative of social-class differences. Within a capitalist society in which market forces are ascendent (Hutton, 1995), 'acting in their child's best interests' inevitably means middle-class mothers are simultaneously acting against the interests of the children of other, less privileged, mothers. This is not to blame middle-class mothers but, rather, to see all mothers as caught up in an educational market which operates on the (il)logic of 'to her who has, yet more shall be given'.

The chapter finishes with a discussion of the implications for feminisms. The difficult issue for feminisms of the involvement of women in the perpetuation of social-class inequalities is raised. It is argued that, in giving a gendered account the assumptions underpinning social class, orthodoxies are destabilized, 'race' becomes central and reflexivity a paramount project. The book concludes by emphasizing that feminisms need to reclaim class and 'race' from the margins and place them centrally alongside gender in feminist thought.

Although this book is primarily about class processes, class location is the key to understanding women's narratives. In order to help the reader, I have used a simple device to identify the women's class positions throughout the text. Women who both identified themselves as middle-class and were clearly middle-class in terms of the criteria that I used to categorize women's social class (see Appendices 1 and 2 on pages 168–70), have all been given pseudonyms beginning with L. Similarly, working-class women have all been given names beginning with J. The small group of women with contradictory class locations, whom I discuss in detail in Chapter 4 (see pages 41–3) have been given pseudonyms beginning with C.

Chapter 2

Hidden from View: Mothers in Parental Involvement

> Behind the scenes created in the texts of conventional sociologies of education, women have been at work as mothers. (Dorothy E Smith, 1989a: 123)

Neither mothers' involvement in their children's education nor mothering more generally are seen as worthy, substantial or theoretical topics by academics working in the mainstream. For them – mostly men – the issues are about ungendered parents (Glatter and Woods, 1993; Macbeth, 1995). Similarly, in the British schooling system, government policy emphasizes ungendered, unclassed and 'unraced' parents as individual consumers of their children's education in the marketplace (David *et al.*, 1996). Both these trends serve to disguise the contribution that mothers make to their children's education. They are further reinforced by a tendency to view mothering as 'caring' both within and without feminist writing; a construction which I argue elides important differences of class and 'race' between women. Below I elaborate how constructions of mothering as caring have operated to deny the work women do as mothers.

Constructions of Caring

The work women do in support of their children's education is often hidden behind assumptions of mothering as a natural, easy process, far removed from what counts as 'real' work. As Uta Enders-Dragasser argues, whether an activity is viewed as work or is thought to 'be done out of love' has much more to do with the acting individual's sex than the nature of the activity (Enders-Dragasser, 1991: 554). Prevailing discourses on mothering construct it as something that comes naturally, as distinct from something that needs to be worked at. It is almost as if, once a woman has given birth, the labour involved in mothering is over.

In the 1970s and early 1980s housework and, to a lesser extent, mothering were written about by feminists in terms of work (Oakley, 1974; Fenstermaker Berk, 1985). This was part of a wider feminist project to uncover gender exploitation within the domestic sphere. I would suggest that theorizing about mothering in terms of work which reproduces class as well as gender oppression is a far less inviting project for feminist academics. It is a project which reveals their own social advantage. In contrast, to assert mothering is 'caring' rather than work can suggest that it is rooted in intrinsic qualities rather than productive activity. Unlike work, caring is an adjective as well as a verb. Such a conceptualization operates discursively to deny white, middle-class advantage. If what women do is 'love' and 'care for', then understandings of 'the social organisation of macrosocial relations such as class as the accomplishment of actual individuals, of women' (Smith, 1989a: 123), remain unexplored.

Mothering, then, is often conceived as a state of 'being' rather than doing. Patricia Hill Collins asserts that this is because understandings of motherhood are derived from the experience of white, middle-class women. Commenting on feminist theories of motherhood, Collins asserts that feminists producing such theories:

> are themselves participants in a system of privilege that rewards them for not seeing race and class privilege as important. Their theories can ignore the workings of class and race as systems of privilege because their creators often benefit from that privilege, taking it as a given and not as something to be contested. (Collins, 1994: 72)

Her own preferred term is 'motherwork' (Collins, 1994). bell hooks, too, views mothering 'as significant and valuable work which must be recognized as such' (hooks, 1984: 136). At the same time, she writes of the dangers of implying motherhood is a female vocation. Not only are such implications fundamentally sexist, but they also carry an implicit criticism of women who do not mother. Such a perspective suggests, wrongly in hook's view, that motherhood 'is more important than women's other labour and more rewarding' (hooks, 1984: 136). Recent work by white feminists has also taken up this theme of mothering as work (O'Barr *et al.*, 1990; Ross, 1995). Ellen Ross writes about 'the unending hard work' involved in the love and care of children (Ross, 1995: 398).

It is Dorothy Smith who has been at the forefront of conceptualizing maternal involvement in education as work. She writes that women's mothering work is often taken for granted both by the women themselves and the academics who write about parental involvement in education (Smith, 1988). She asserts that this is because 'our forms of thought put together a view of the world from a place women do not occupy' (Smith, 1988: 19). At various points in her writing, Smith discusses the missing work of mothering that she has personally engaged in, yet failed to find in sociological texts:

> The relations and apparatuses of ruling have certain very distinctive features, among them the social organisation of an objectified work,

virtual realities mediated by texts . . . Their objectified modes claim neutrality with respect to gender, race and class, but the subtexts are gendered, are in and of class, are structured racially. (Smith, 1991: 157)

All too often the consequences are that women are left out. When they *are* included, it is primarily the experiences of white, middle-class women that are incorporated as normative. Dorothy Smith argues that what real people do in real situations becomes hidden under layers of conceptual formulations, that ' "psychosocial processes" rather than people become the in-text protagonists' (Smith, 1991: 164). Smith advocates a specific focus on the detailed mechanics of what women actually do on a daily basis in order to uncover their labour. I have attempted to do this in my own research.

Recent work in Germany and Britain has begun to elaborate just how extensive this work can be (Enders-Dragasser, 1987; 1991; David, 1993; Standing, 1995; Walkerdine and Lucey, 1989). Uta Enders-Dragasser writes about her disquiet at uncovering the 'enormous amount of unpaid work' German mothers undertook for schools (Enders-Dragasser, 1987: 211). In Britain Kay Standing's research into lone mothers' involvement in both secondary and primary schooling theorizes maternal involvement as:

a form of unpaid household labour that breaks down the public/private divide by taking the work of the home into the school and that of the school into the home. (Standing, 1995: 2)

Pressures of marketization within the British educational field have accelerated this exportation of schooling into the home and the associated importation of mothers into the classroom, intensifying mothers' work in the process.

The Texts on Parental Involvement

When I came to research parental involvement in schooling, I found myself investigating an area of social practice where most of the activities are carried out by women. However, what I found in the textbooks on the subject was rarely a recognition of the myriad aspects of mothering work women were undertaking. In the place of any such elaboration were assumptions of gender neutrality. Most of the texts seem to be premised on an implicit and unexamined norm, namely that of the unitary, ungendered subject. While feminist and post-structuralist theory throughout the 1980s and into the 1990s has deconstructed the concept of the unitary individual (Henriques *et al.*, 1984; Barrett and Phillips, 1992; Kerfoot and Knights, 1994), the parental involvement debate has been largely immune to their influences. While post-structuralists and feminists, alike, recognize that implicit in modernist conceptions of the unitary (male) self is a denial of the social differences which produce inequalities, there is little evidence of parallel thinking within texts on parental involvement (see David, 1993; David *et al.*, 1996; 1997; Lareau, 1992 for exceptions to this general rule). The resulting omission of any clear articulation of the place of gender within home–school relationships masks a number of important issues. First, it serves to hide from the reader's view inequalities operating within parenting relationships. Secondly, it results in a privileging of 'the male' in the text. Usage of the term 'parent', without any qualification as to *which* parent, acts as an invitation; it leaves open the possibility of paternal involvement. Its consequences are the inclusion of fathers in an area which, in reality, many have left to their children's mother.

Much of the writing on parental involvement assumes that all parents share an identical experience of involvement in their children's schooling (for example, see Topping and Wolfendale, 1986; Bastiani, 1989; Wolfendale, 1989; Hughes, Wikeley and Nash, 1994). This 'genderless' parent operates discursively to deny women's work. However, this universalizing theme of the discourse not only renders invisible inequalities between the sexes but also those existing between mothers. The rarefied realm of the texts ignores materiality. Structural constraints of gender, 'race', class and marital status are missing except when they emerge reworked as 'problems to be dealt with'. As Miriam David points out in her discussion of typologies of parental involvement:

> What none of the typologies or schemes paid attention to, however, are the definitions of and changing practices with respect to the notion of *parent*. In particular, the gendered and racialised notions of parent were not acknowledged, nor was the idea that family forms have changed to such an extent that the exercise of a parental role may now be fundamentally different. (David, 1993: 99 (author's own italics))

When subjected to scrutiny, it rapidly becomes apparent that most of the texts on parental involvement are premised on the unexamined assumption that parental involvement is a shared, equal task between parents and between parents and teachers. The term 'partnership', which regularly appears in the texts, acts discursively to imply reciprocity and equality between parents and school. As Carol Vincent points out, the reliance on consensual language, such as 'partnership', 'involvement' and 'dialogue', which features strongly in the home–school literature, edit out of the relationship tension and conflict, and the inequalities underlying them (Vincent, 1996: 73). Behind assumptions of equal, harmonious relations between teachers and parents lies a second implied partnership – one between both parents in relation to their child's schooling. Even Flora Macleod's book on *Parents and Schools*, which explores extensively the influence of gender differences among children, and includes an article on 'the gender dimension of home–school relationships', makes only three references to parents as gendered (Macleod, 1989: 51), and has no analysis of the gendered division of labour operating in the home with respect to parental involvement.

Far more frequently gender is only there in the snippets of transcript when the neutral 'parent' metamorphoses into mums and dads talking about actual children in actual schools. Even more rare are the voices of children. In *At Home in School* by Viv Edwards and Angela Redfern gender is not discussed by the authors. However, children were not so reticent about which of their parents was the most involved in their schooling. In their section on 'children's voices' there are sixteen references to mothers, one to a grandmother and three to fathers (Edwards and Redfern, 1988). Their book is unusual for its inclusion of quotations from children. More frequent is the inclusion of parental perspectives. Hughes, Wikeley and Nash begin their book on *Parents and their Children's Schools* with three parental case studies; all three are of mothers. Although they refer throughout the text to parents, over 84 per cent of their interviews were conducted with mothers (Hughes, Wikeley and Nash, 1994: 47).

Often, even when the perspectives of actual parents are included, mothers' far greater involvement in their children's education is denied as, in an effort to achieve 'balance', quotations from mothers are juxtaposed with opinions voiced by fathers. In John Bastiani's *Working with Parents* 20 quotations from mothers are offset by 12 from children's fathers. Still, it is only when the texts illustrate the issues with 'the voices of real parents' (Bastiani, 1989: 37) that they begin to hint at the differential in involvement existing between mothers and fathers. As Ann Manicom points out:

> The use of the word 'parent' hides the fact that most encounters teachers have with parents are with mothers, and that when teachers talk about a meeting or discussion or telephone call with a parent, the pronoun they use most often is 'she'. (Manicom, 1984: 80)

By working with abstracted references to 'parents', most of the literature on parental involvement omits any discussion of how schooling affects the work of mothers. However, recent feminist work on the interaction of home and school reveal how extensive these influences are (New and David, 1985; Walkerdine and Lucey, 1989; Lareau, 1992; Ribbens, 1993; David, 1993; David *et al.*, 1993). Gaskell and McLaren criticize texts on parental involvement for taking mothers' work for granted. They assert:

> This traditional examination of the family–school linkage is taken from the point of view of educators. It is approached from the standpoint of those who work within the educational system, not from that of mothers. It does not ask how women's work is shaped by schools; how child rearing is related to educational pedagogy; how both

> teaching and mothering are affected by changing educational re-
> sources; or how gender affects the work of teachers and mothers.
> (Gaskell and McLaren, 1987: 27)

The discourses which construct the majority of men as 'deviant' and 'deficient' because of their minimal involvement in childcare are yet to be developed. Implicit norms operating in society position women as the parent responsible for 'parenting work'. However, they do not inform the texts on parental involvement. Instead these are informed by a subtle deceit, a sleight of terminology, which propels men from the wings to centre stage, nudging women out of the way in the process. As the evidence in this book indicates, beneath the texts it is mothering work, not fathering work, which is primarily being carried out in support of children's education.

The literature on parental involvement is made up of a number of half-told stories. It leaves out not only difference and diversity, but the ways in which differences are rooted in inequalities. Mothers are no more an homogeneous group than the fictional, undifferentiated parents of many of the texts. This study of women's involvement in their children's primary schooling is concerned centrally with issues of difference; differences between women and men and differences existing among women.

Prevailing Discourses of Mothering and 'the Good Parent'

Alison Griffith and Dorothy Smith (1987) raise the problem of being trapped inside 'the discourse of mothering'. It seems likely that the parameters of the discourse preclude access to non-judgemental perspectives and lead to a pathologizing of individual mothers, rather than a problematizing of the role. They assert that the educational role of mothers is coordinated through a discourse of mothering that holds the absent mother responsible for her child's behaviour in the classroom. The same discourse sets up an ideal that the reality of most women's lives makes impossible for them to achieve. Griffith and Smith assert that this discourse, in attempting to establish 'norms' for maternal practices in relation to children's schooling:

> articulates to a class structure. Its recommendations do not recognize
> what mothers do as work, hence do not attend to the material and
> social conditions of that work. (Griffith and Smith, 1987: 97)

I recognize a need to 'work both from outside and inside the discourse to reshape it' (Griffith and Smith, 1987: 100); quite how to achieve such plural positionings is another matter. More recent writing by Dorothy Smith and Alison Griffith has included a critique of their empirical work for failing to centre the experience of working-class women (Griffith, 1992; Smith, 1993). I share with Griffith and Smith a belief that the problem lies not with mothers themselves, but in an inherent bias of the discourse, which articulates with middle-class, not working-class, resources (see also Walkerdine and Lucey, 1989 for a similar exposition). It is a relatively easy step to see the need to reshape the discourse so that those subjugated within it have a voice. It is a much more difficult venture to accomplish such a reshaping.

What is clear is that the prevailing discursive *status quo* results in heavy costs for all those mothers operating outside the parameters of what constitutes 'the good parent'. Despite the homogeneity running through both government policy and parental involvement texts, educational professionals often adopt deficit conceptions of certain parent groups based on assumptions relating to ethnicity, sexuality, gender, marital status and social class. Carol Vincent found that inequitable power relationships between teachers and parents were 'maintained by teachers' adherence to the ideal of the "good parent" – a non-negotiated view of "appropriate" parental behaviour imposed upon an unsuspecting parent body' (Vincent, 1996: 112). The 'good parent', surprisingly ungendered in view of teachers' frequent reference to, and contact with, 'mothers', was in reality also a classed and 'raced' entity. Rather, the image that the 'good parent' conjured up was of a white, middle-class, heterosexual married mother. Lone mothers, lesbian mothers, mothers surviving on benefit and those trying to make ends meet on income support and, from inside and outside those groups, black women, are all operating within contexts permeated by such taken-for-granted assumptions.

Although the main focus of this book are the activities that comprised maternal work in support of children's schooling, the backdrop to mothering work is the attitudes and assumptions that teachers and the mothers themselves brought to their understandings of their involvement. Josie, one of the mothers in the sample and a friend, told me two years after the fieldwork had been completed:

> I just can't understand how I manage to get everything wrong. I have made all the wrong choices, really messed up Leigh's chances. I just don't understand when I've put so much time and energy into his education how I've managed to make so many mistakes. I must be really stupid. I just feel so bad about it every choice I've made has been wrong. Now they are closing his secondary school down because it failed its inspection what chance has he got and I feel it's down to me – that I've made the wrong choices. Put that in your book – that our kids are 'the lost children'. (Josie, November 1996)

Motherhood is subject to evaluations and judgements which are very different from those of fatherhood. Despite the lack of attention to questions of gender, as well as class, 'race' or sexualities in public policy discourses, it is often mothers who hold themselves, and are held, responsible for children's educational performance. However, as David *et al.* point out, the reality is more complex:

> Behind the rhetorical nature of public policy discourses hides a range
> of policy intentions which serve in the maintenance of inequalities in
> access to and benefit from schooling. (David *et al.*, 1997)

Social class has always played a crucial role in educational opportunity. Traditional studies of inequalities in education have stressed the work of selection and differentiation carried out by schools and teachers, as if social class, racial and gender injustices are concentrated in classrooms and playgrounds. Although I recognize the inequalities that permeate relationships in schools (Reay, 1995a; 1995b), this book looks beyond the classroom to examine the complex processes through which mothering work is positioned in the 1990s educational marketplace to produce social class inequalities.

Chapter 3

Women and Social Class: A Different Version

Social Class Orthodoxies

> The treatment of women in classifications of social class has become
> something of a scandal. (Britten and Heath, 1983: 46)

Perhaps a more apposite term would be 'women's lack of treatment'. The
conventional sociological view of women's social class position is that it is
mediated through their relationship with men (Goldthorpe, 1980; 1983;
Lockwood, 1986; Goldthorpe and Marshall, 1992), while men's social class is
deemed to be independent, unaffected by the women they live with. However,
this theoretical position has been increasingly contested. Some feminist ana-
lysts have developed an 'individualistic' solution based on the class position
of individuals, irrespective of that of other family members (Acker, 1973;
Stanworth, 1984), while theorists such as Britten and Heath (1983) and
Leiulfsrud and Woodward (1987; 1988) espouse a joint approach which draws
on both partners' positions in the labour market. Walby (1986; 1990) has
developed a theory according to which women are viewed as having two social
class locations, one as paid worker, the other as housewife. In spite of these
theoretical developments, the prevailing view is still that of Goldthorpe, who
argues that the focus for class theory is the inequalities arising out of the
labour market. Because of women's domestic responsibilities, combined with
the part-time, intermittent nature of their employment, they are deemed to be
peripheral to the labour market. In the conventional approach the family is
adopted as the relevant unit of analysis, and its class position is seen to be
determined by its male 'Head'. As a result:

> The characteristics of married, or even single women for that matter,
> are considered to be irrelevant to class formation, class fate and even
> the class action of family members. (Hayes and Jones, 1992: 464)

This male focus has lead to the invisibility of women in other areas of research.
The absence of women in theory translates into a practice of excluding women
from empirical studies. Within the more specific sphere of the sociology of
education, studies of social class and education over the past two decades have

been overwhelmingly about men. The Coxon and Jones study (1978 and 1979), the Oxford mobility study (Halsey *et al.*, 1980), the Cambridge study (Stewart *et al.*, 1980), Hopper, 1981 and the Scottish mobility study (Payne, 1987) all have male-only samples. Women have no status in these surveys, either as respondents or as independent contributors to the social-class allocation of their sons. Their absence is all the more puzzling when set alongside two bodies of evidence. First, a number of studies over the past 25 years have stressed the importance of the role of mothers in educational attainment, and, concomitantly, social mobility (Jackson and Marsden, 1966; Baker and Stevenson, 1986; Stevenson and Baker, 1987; Walkerdine and Lucey, 1989). Secondly, more recent empirical research emphasizes the complex, and at times, contradictory ways in which gender, 'race' and class interact (Mirza, 1992; Edwards, 1993; Mac an Ghaill, 1994; Griffin, 1996).

When women are made visible in classificatory systems such as Goldthorpe's, it becomes apparent that the relative stability of men's social class status is being achieved at the cost of a hidden, female, social-class instability. With current rates of one divorce for every two marriages (HMSO, 1995), Stanworth's assertion that the Goldthorpe model leads to ever-increasing rates of family mobility as 'women assumed an independent class position on divorce and subsequently relinquished that position through remarriage' (Stanworth, 1984: 165) seems justified. However, this is just one example of contemporary changes which conventional theory fails to account for. As well as single parent families, current high levels of unemployment and female involvement in the labour market are subjects not incorporated into Goldthorpe's stratification system (Reid, 1986).

The work of Marshall *et al.* (1988) has gone some way towards revealing a role for women in accounts of class formation and social mobility. Women are visible in their analysis, albeit in a minor capacity. The authors found that the strongest observed association was between a wife's class and her own qualifications, rather than with her partner's class, and conclude that:

> These results are quite inconsistent with Goldthorpe's arguments that the social class positions of most wives are indirectly determined and, as it were, 'derived' from the male 'family Head'. (Marshall *et al.*, 1988: 72)

Instead, they state that the appropriate unit for analysis is not the family but the individual, thus endorsing Stanworth's model and suggesting that Stanworth's theory of the articulation of sex with class structure seems to be just as credible as Goldthorpe's thesis of women's dependence on men within families. One of their main criticisms of Goldthorpe is his assumption that class processes are independent of the social division of labour and, as such, do not have to be accounted for in analyses of class formation. Their belief is that:

the manner in which the class structure is (at least in part) constituted through relations between the sexes is . . . intrinsic to class analysis. (Marshall *et al.*, 1988: 84)

They develop a view of the labour market which is characterized as much by its gender divisions as by its class segmentation:

Whether one looks at mobility trajectories or conditions of employ-ment, women tend to be generally disadvantaged when compared with men. They are no less divided by class differences, but tend to have inferior market situations and work situations to those of class comparable men, and to receive proportionately fewer rewards for their educational achievements. (Marshall *et al.*, 1988: 272)

However, although Marshall and his colleagues raise some of the inherent complexities of class in discussion, their empirical work reflects a more con-ventional approach. They point out that unemployed men and women are omitted throughout their data analysis. At the same time they issue a dis-claimer that 'this is not to argue that unemployed men and women are somehow outside the class structure' (Marshall *et al.*, 1988: 85). In effect, they are empirically regulating the unemployed, male and female, and full-time carers to a position where they do not count. Marshall *et al.* state that they are keen to include any factors which might explain the sexually-segregated social division of labour 'if for no other reason than that the class experience of men is largely unintelligible without reference to those of women' (Marshall *et al.*, 1988: 266). Clearly any focus on women is subordinate to the primary focus on men.

Broadening the Base: Extending Class to the Domestic Sphere

Regardless of whether the social class debate is being conducted by men taking the 'conventional' stance, other men seeking to modify that stance, or feminists contesting the *status quo*, the focus is still on the labour market position. Even contemporary research which argues for the inclusion of women in classifications of social class works exclusively with women as employees in the labour market (Lampard, 1995; Evans, 1996). As Helen Roberts' review of the debates surrounding social class over the last two decades makes clear, the focus is firmly rooted in a view of social class as one of location; an issue of where you are situated, rather than the processes that got you there (Roberts, 1993). This labour-market focus neglects the key role of women in class formation. Holton and Turner point out that the continuing emphasis on occupational measurement neglects wider dimensions of social action and economic power, including any discussion of the contribution of gender to economic inequality (Holton and Turner, 1994: 804). Similar criticisms are made by Breen and Rottman who argue that current debates over the relationship between class and gender challenge some of the fundamental premises through which mainstream class analysis is conducted (Breen and Rottman, 1995a; 1995b).

On the evidence of critics of the conventional approach it appears that, over and above the technical problems endemic in conventional classificatory systems, simple categorization based on male, labour-market participation overlooks the complexity inherent in the relationship between gender and social class. A growing number of studies which look at women's relationship to class and gender inequalities (Cavendish, 1982; Porter, 1983; Coyle, 1984; Westwood, 1984; Webb, 1985; McRae, 1986; Abbott and Sapsford, 1987; Toomey, 1989; Delamont, 1989; Walkerdine and Lucey, 1989; Mahony and Zmroczek, 1997; Skeggs, 1997) highlight the need to review an oversimplistic model which marginalizes women's relationship to class. One example, Holland and Skouras' research into girls' occupational aspirations, found that fathers' occupational status was inadequate to explain girls' future plans and needed to be complemented with information about mothers' work, if simplistic conclusions were to be avoided (Holland and Skouras, 1977; 1979). In addition, more recent research (Charles, 1990; Griffith and Smith, 1990; Devine, 1992) reveals a diversity of perspectives which enhance our understanding of women's relationship to social class.

In Charles' study of 200 women (1990), although the occupational class of partners was significant for women's personal class allocation, their own occupational status was crucial to their wider relationship with, and understanding of, social class. Furthermore, Charles found that women for whom occupational factors were of prime importance in their assignment of social class cited their parents and their own occupational status almost as often as that of their partners. For one group of women, those with a strong sense of their own class identity, the occupation of parents was of greater significance than that of their partner. A further group of women associated class with level of income, citing consumption patterns and housing tenure as determinants of social class. Their understanding of social class could be encapsulated in the view that 'the more you had, the more you were able to buy and the higher up the social scale you were' (Charles, 1990: 84). A final group of women in the study described class as the need, or lack of need, to work. However, for the women quoted by Charles this need to work was gendered as in 'my mum always worked', and, 'mum goes out to work'. Whether their mothers, or the women themselves, had to work or not was taken as a sign of a household's class position.

Charles concludes that her research demonstrates:

> the importance of women's occupational and educational back-
> grounds to the ways in which they understand class and suggests that
> using partners' occupation only to define the class of married and
> cohabiting women is likely to cloud rather than clarify the processes

which lead to class identity and class consciousness. (Charles, 1990: 85)

For Charles, women have a complex relationship not only with their partner's occupational status, but with their own and that of their parents. In addition, women are influenced by a range of factors which include housing tenure and educational qualifications, all of which are constitutive of class identity. Abbott and Sapsford assert that:

> Both American and British studies suggest that educational factors are more important for women than for men in determining their occupational class irrespective of how long they have been in the labour market. (Abbott and Sapsford, 1987: 85)

Fiona Devine's research indicates that, in order to obtain a composite picture of how both men and women experience social inequalities, an understanding of their subjective relationship to class is needed to complement more objective aspects (Devine, 1992). Abbott and Sapsford write of a sea of change with occupation ebbing as the major characteristic of class for women:

> Occupation is not seen as a major determinant of class by the women in this sample, despite the high correlation they display between objective occupational class and subjective class assignment. They are more concerned with status factors as a whole (among which occupation is only one) and with subjective factors, which might tend perhaps to suggest that the majority see society in terms of a continuous hierarchy rather than in terms of bounded classes. (Abbott and Sapsford, 1987: 137)

Janeen Baxter, in her research on social class identity in Australia, found that educational levels and total housework hours were the most significant predictors of social class identity for women working full-time in the labour market. Baxter discovered that the more time women spent on housework the more strongly they defined themselves as working-class. At the same time, she asserts that there is virtually no relationship between class position and women's housework hours. She goes on to state that her findings:

> ... provide initial support for the argument that women define domestic labour as 'real' work, and as work that is highly exploitative, and low in status and rewards. (Baxter, 1991: 217)

She concludes by emphasizing the influence that factors which are extra-local to the labour market have on women's class identity.

The need for a gendered view of class is supported, therefore, by the growing amount of data on gender differences in relationships to class.

In addition to the relatively greater importance for women of education as an influence on social class allocation (Ritter and Hargens, 1975; Abbott and Sapsford, 1986; 1987), there is some evidence that women are more willing to assign themselves to the middle-class than male respondents (Townsend, 1979; Jackman and Jackman, 1983; Britten, 1984; Abbott and Sapsford, 1987). Both attitudes and identity are the key to an understanding of the class allocation of women (Abbott, 1987; Crompton, 1989). There is also research which suggests that it is middle-class, more than working-class women, who hold a conception of themselves as belonging to a class that is distinct from, and has different interests from, other classes (Abbott and Sapsford, 1987; Frazer, 1988; Phoenix and Tizard, 1996). It was Frazer's upper middle-class girls attending private schools who spontaneously raised class as an issue, and went on to reveal clear perceptions of class structure and class conflict. In contrast, her working-class comprehensive school girls had a far less clearly defined sense of class identity and lacked any clear information about social class (Frazer, 1988).

Mothers' Involvement in Children's Schooling: A Different Way of Looking at Women's Relationship to Social Class

As can be seen from the growing amount of feminist literature on women and social class cited above, there is a range of ways in which social class can be understood. Dorothy Smith asserts that empirical work can link the social organization of macrosocial relations such as class to the accomplishment of actual individuals, namely women (Smith, 1989b). This study attempts just that; exploring the complexities of women's relationship to class through an investigation of the reciprocal influences of children's schooling and mothers' lives. Class enters into all spheres of life, not just the economic:

> Relationships between adults and children, relationships between men and women, domestic life, cultural practice, sexual practices, are all essential parts of the picture of class. (Connell, 1983: 168)

If the complex and complicated interweavings of gender and class are to be unravelled, it is the processes of their interaction, at home as well as in the economy, that need to be explicated, rather than women's socio-economic location:

> There must be some understanding of the processes by which women actually establish and maintain their social position. (Sanderson, 1989: 27)

Mainstream debates are slowly shifting towards an analysis which includes issues of gender. Marshall *et al.*'s critique of Goldthorpe, for instance, recognizes the vital role of gender in class formation. They take up the point made by Britten and Heath (1983) that women make a difference, and state that that difference has efficacy in the sphere of class formation:

> People are distributed to places through time according to processes
> that are powerfully shaped by gender. (Marshall *et al.*, 1988: 84)

However, their continuing focus on position in the labour market precludes a perspective which encompasses the private as well as the public. All too often, it is only when women are engaged in paid employment outside the home that they are deemed important enough to be included in class analysis.

Recent feminist work has begun to focus on how women's social networks inform our understanding of women's complex relationship to social class (Oakley and Rajan, 1991; Bell and Ribbens, 1994). Broadening such explorations to include a focus on the processes operating within the family, in addition to those at work in the labour market, is vital in order to capture the complexities of social class reproduction. As Pamela Abbott asserts:

> Research is needed that attempts to provide an understanding of
> women's experiences in the private and public spheres, and how in
> making sense of these a woman's class orientation is formed and
> translated into action. (Abbott, 1987: 101)

Her views are echoed by Janeen Baxter:

> Ultimately what is required is a substantial rethinking of class theory,
> which will allow women's dual experience as both unpaid house-
> wives, and members of the labour force, to be incorporated into class
> analysis. (Baxter, 1988: 121)

By focusing on class as process not position, class can be seen as determined not simply by men's occupational status, but also produced by women in their work as mothers. This perspective with its focus on women's actions reveals both the constraints and the possibilities maternal practices are subject to:

> Mothering is produced and regulated – correct and incorrect, normal
> and abnormal. (Walkerdine and Lucey, 1989: 30)

Walkerdine and Lucey argue that it is the actual organization of mothering through child rearing, housework and 'the meanings through which they are produced and understood' which result in key class differences (Walkerdine and Lucey, 1989: 72). Mothering and, concomitantly, women are central to their theory of class production. They assert that to become middle-class two things are necessary – 'the right brains and the right mothers' (Walkerdine and Lucey, 1989: 178).

Griffith and Smith (1990) develop a similar thesis in which they assert that an examination of the work mothers undertake in response to their children's schooling establishes how that work is embedded in the social relations of class. For Smith, the family and forms of family work and living are 'integral to the active process of constructing and reconstructing class relations' (Smith, 1983: 7). An essential part of this process is achieved through the work mothers do to support their children's schooling (Griffith and Smith, 1990; Smith and Griffith, 1990), with the home becoming an essential component 'in organising the abstracted modes of ruling in the context . . . of the local and the particular' (Smith, 1983: 16). Smith writes of a process in which mothers' work in the home is subordinated to the educational system. For Griffith and Smith, as for Walkerdine and Lucey, the work of mothers in relation to the school has become a vital mediating process in the production and reproduction of class relationships between the middle- and working-classes. In *The Everyday World as Problematic* Dorothy Smith defines social class as 'a complex of social relations coordinating the activities of our everyday worlds with those of others with whom we are not directly connected. Such relations exist only as active practices' (Smith, 1988: 135). Using Griffith and Smith's thesis, therefore, a case can be made that a social organization of production, generating important class differences, inheres in women's work in support of their children's education just as much as it does in men's productive activity in the workplace. Class and its actual character can be discovered as 'a routine daily accomplishment' (Smith, 1988: 135).

The work of Griffith and Smith, Walkerdine and Lucey, and also that of Lareau (1992) reveals a relationship between home and school that is both classed and gendered. Their research points to the achievement of social class through complex, sometimes contradictory processes; processes in which the impact of gender, and I would add 'race' (Reay, 1991), can have both predictable and surprising effects. The impact of 'race' on social class is far less debated than that of gender, although recent research indicates that it has a significant effect on class-consciousness and the extent to which women espouse a class identity. A number of mature, black, female students in Edwards' sample felt class categories were largely irrelevant to their self-identity. Instead this was based on 'race' and gender, rather than social class (Edwards, 1993). Similarly, Phoenix and Tizard (1996) found that 41 per cent of the young black people that they interviewed said that they did not know what was meant by social class. However, Bhachu, in her study of British Sikh women, found that the way in which they defined themselves was the product of their experience 'in different class and regional cultures' (Bhachu, 1991: 408). Gender, 'race' and class can clash, coincide, or to quote Connell *et al.* 'amplify, twist, negate, deepen and complicate each other' (Connell *et al.*, 1982: 182).

It is not, as Pahl asserts, that social class has ceased to be a useful concept (Pahl, 1989); rather that an exploration of social class through the mechanism of a rigid theoretical framework grounded in occupational categorization has ceased to tell more than a fraction of the story of social class. Avtar Brah asserts that processes of inequalities and exploitation can no longer be 'addressed purely as class issues without reference to other modalities of differentiation' (Brah, 1994: 812). Important contemporary feminist writing defines class as socially-organized courses of action, ones in which women have a vital role to play (Griffith and Smith, 1990; Smith and Griffith, 1990; Walkerdine and Lucey, 1989; Lareau, 1992). A focus on the work-processes of both women and men, in the private as well as the public sphere, is far more revelatory of how social class is achieved and the ways in which class organizes social relations. Individuals do not occupy a location, they act in situations. As a consequence, the questions which would appear to be the most useful in any exploration of women and social class are not ones about the class location of women, but ones which elicit the class relations into which they enter, and allow us to uncover how far these relations are being formed by women's activities (Ashendon *et al.*, 1987; Bell and Ribbens, 1994; David *et al.*, 1997).

Pierre Bourdieu and Social Class: Making a Space for Women

> Sociological language cannot be either 'neutral' or 'clear'. The word 'class' will never be a neutral word as long as there are classes: The question of the existence or non-existence of classes is a stake in struggle between the classes. (Bourdieu, 1993a: 21)

Within 'malestream' sociology, it is predominantly the work of Pierre Bourdieu which has contributed to a refocusing of current theorizing on social class. Bourdieu's own work rarely has a gender focus, and when it does, as in his study of the Kabylia in Algeria, it emphasizes the collusion of women with male oppressiveness (Bourdieu, 1990c). According to Bourdieu, women in Kabyle society act out in their behaviour the negative, inferior identity that has been socially imposed on them, and in doing so confirm such an identity as natural (Bourdieu, 1990c: 10). However, despite a tendency to position women as responsible for their own oppression, his writing on male domination throws into relief continuing inequalities of power in relation to gender as well as social class, and thus lends itself to feminist adaptation. Furthermore, through his continual insistence that classes only exist 'on paper' (Bourdieu, 1990b), and that they have to be maintained continually through individuals' efforts, he invites a focus on what women are doing. His attempts to deploy the concept of habitus to overcome the dualism between agency and structure, and his development of cultural capital as a device for linking class to culture, constitute an important advance in thinking about social class (Savage, 1994). Later I outline Bourdieu's theoretical framework, in particular his concepts of cultural capital, field and habitus. However, in this section I wish to concentrate on what Bourdieu adds more generally to the continuing debates on social class.

What Bourdieu does first and foremost is move social class theorization beyond simple attempts at categorization:

> My work consists in saying that people are located in social space, that they aren't just anywhere, in other words, interchangeable, as these people claim who deny the existence of 'social classes', and that according to the position they occupy in this highly complex space, you can understand the logic of their practices and determine, inter alia, how they will classify themselves and others and, should the case arise, think of themselves as members of a 'class'. (Bourdieu, 1990b: 50)

Bourdieu is as interested in the qualitative divisions of social class – art, culture, taste, education, lifestyle, cuisine – as he is in the quantitative division of occupational categorization. Although he draws on the work of both Marx and Weber, he attempts to move beyond understandings of class that are based solely on either economics or social status. For Bourdieu, class lies neither in agency nor in structure, but in their interaction. Loic Wacquant claims Bourdieu's work exemplifies:

> The shift from abstract theorisations of 'objective' class boundaries flowing from economic structures to a focus on the structural formulation or self-production of class collectivities through struggles that simultaneously involve relationships between and within classes and determine the actual demarcation of their frontiers. (Wacquant, 1991: 52)

Bourdieu describes the boundary between social classes as 'a flame whose edges are in constant movement, oscillating around a line or surface' (Bourdieu, 1987: 13). Linear representations of class are displaced in Bourdieu's theoretical framework. In place of class as structure he has developed a theory of social space into which class maps or scattergrams of class groupings fit far more readily than vertical continuums. Bourdieu's social space reveals a multidimensional distribution of power in the form of different types of capital (cultural, economic, symbolic and social), underlying social positions (Wacquant, 1991).

Society for Bourdieu, is a space of social relationships, similar to geographical space, in which effort and time expended are productive of movement:

> Moving up means raising oneself, climbing and acquiring the marks, the stigmata, of this effort. (Bourdieu, 1985b: 725–6)

In Bourdieu's social space there is transverse movement, as well as movement up and down, as changing historical circumstances result in groups, at danger from eroding social distinction, struggling to maintain their position. Because Bourdieu shifts the conceptual space in which class is defined from the arena of production to that of social relations generally, within his theoretical framework:

> Class divisions are defined not by differing relations to the means of production, but by differing conditions of existence, differing systems of dispositions produced by differential conditioning, and differing endowments of power or capital. (Brubaker, 1985: 761)

At the same time Bourdieu's interweaving of individual with class trajectory invites complex analyses, which recognize differences within social class groupings as well as between them. Bourdieu's analysis of social practices as including forms of social choice in everyday life can be utilized to focus on women's activities both inside and outside the labour market. In particular middle-class women, in their work in support of children's schooling, can be seen to be 'manifesting all the signs of being both conscious of material interests and capable of protecting them' (Crompton, 1994: 198).

Class analysis through the lens of Bourdieu's theoretical framework can be seen to be concerned with a far wider set of issues than occupational class schemas (Crompton, 1994; Savage, 1994). In broadening the scope of class analysis, he offers the prospect of a space for women. Bourdieu's theory of the relationship between women and social class cannot be fully understood without examining his concepts of cultural capital, field and habitus. His conceptual framework proffers exciting, new perspectives. However, it also includes theoretical closures, and the ambiguities, gaps and allusions that Lamont and Lareau document (see Lamont and Lareau, 1988).

Theoretical Starting Points: Cultural Capital, Habitus and Field

Annette Lareau has utilized Bourdieu's concept of cultural capital to explain the social processes underpinning home–school relationships (Lareau, 1989). Her project has been to clarify the empirical practices through which initial dispositions (which Bourdieu terms habitus) translate into educational profits or cultural capital (Lareau, 1989: 178). However, before examining the work of Lareau, it is important to define more clearly what Bourdieu means by cultural capital and his related concepts of habitus and field.

Cultural Capital

> The notion of cultural capital initially presented itself to me, in the course of research, as a theoretical hypothesis which made it possible to explain the unequal scholastic achievement of children originating

from different social classes by relating academic success, i.e., the specific profits which children from the different classes and class fractions can obtain in the academic market, to the distribution of cultural capital between the classes and class fractions. (Bourdieu, 1986: 243)

Cultural capital encompasses a broad array of linguistic competencies, manners, preferences and orientations, which Bourdieu terms 'subtle modalities in the relationship to culture and language' (Bourdieu, 1977a: 82). Bourdieu identifies *three* variants of cultural capital: first, in the embodied state incorporated in mind and body; second, in the institutionalized state – that is, existing in institutionalized forms such as educational qualifications; and third, in the objectified state, simply existing as cultural goods such as books, artifacts, dictionaries and paintings (Bourdieu, 1986).

Cultural capital is not the only capital accruing to individuals. It is primarily a relational concept and exists in conjunction with other forms of capital. Therefore, it cannot be understood in isolation either from the habitus that generates it or the other forms of capital that alongside cultural capital constitute advantage and disadvantage in society. As well as cultural capital, these include economic, symbolic and social capital. Social capital is generated through social processes between the family and wider society, and is made up of social networks. Economic capital is wealth either inherited or generated from interactions between the individual and the economy, while symbolic capital is manifested in individual prestige and personal qualities, such as authority and charisma (Bourdieu, 1985b: 733). Richard Jenkins states that cultural capital is seen by Bourdieu:

as acquiring its significance only in the context of a complex of social life encompassing social capital (class position and social network) and economic capital as well. (Jenkins, 1982: 276)

In addition to their interconnection, Bourdieu envisages a process in which one form of capital can be transformed into another. For example, economic capital can be converted into cultural capital, while cultural capital can be readily translated into social capital.

The overall capital of different fractions of the social classes is composed of differing proportions of the various kinds of capital (Bourdieu, 1993a). It is mainly in relation to the middle- and upper-classes that Bourdieu elaborates this variation in volume and composition of the four types of capital. For example, individuals can be adjacent to each other in social space yet have very different ratios of economic to cultural capital. These differences are a consequence of complex relationships between individual and class trajectories. Moreover, the value attached to the different forms of capital are stakes in the struggle between different class fractions. Bourdieu uses the analogy of a game of roulette to describe how some individuals might 'play':

those with lots of red tokens and a few yellow tokens, that is lots of economic capital and a little cultural capital will not play in the same way as those who have many yellow tokens and a few red ones . . . the more yellow tokens (cultural capital) they have, the more they will stake on the yellow squares (the educational system). (Bourdieu, 1993a: 34)

Habitus

Bourdieu describes his development of the concept of habitus as an attempt to overcome the latent determinism in structuralist theory (Bourdieu, 1985a). Instead of working with what he considers to be a flawed conceptualization, that of the 'active subject confronting society as if that society were an object constituted externally' (Bourdieu, 1990b: 190), Bourdieu has developed the concept of habitus to demonstrate not only the ways in which the body is in the social world, but also the ways in which the social world is in the body (Bourdieu, 1981):

> The habitus as the feel for the game is the social game embodied and turned into a second nature. (Bourdieu, 1990b: 63)

For Bourdieu, then, key aspects of culture are embodied. This is a repeated theme in his work. He describes the dispositions, the tendencies to think, feel and behave in particular ways, that make up habitus as 'meaning-made-body' (Bourdieu, 1990a: 43). While for Bourdieu there is an implicit tendency to behave in ways that are expected of 'people like us', there are no explicit rules or principles which dictate behaviour, rather 'the habitus goes hand in glove with vagueness and indeterminacy' (Bourdieu's own italics, 1990b: 77). The practical logic which defines habitus is not one of the predictable regularity of modes of behaviour, but instead 'that of vagueness, of the more-or-less, which defines one's ordinary relation to the world' (Bourdieu, 1990b: 78).

Habitus, perhaps more than cultural capital, provides a conceptual tool for recognizing difference and diversity between members of the same cultural group. Habitus, within as well as between social groups, differs to the extent that the details of individuals' social trajectories diverge from one another:

> The singular habitus of the members of the same class are united in a relationship of homology, that is, of diversity within homogeneity reflecting the diversity within homogeneity characteristic of their social conditions of production. Each individual system of dispositions is a structural variant of the others, expressing the singularity of its position within the class and its trajectory. (Bourdieu, 1990a: 60)

At the same time Bourdieu seems to be suggesting a degree of uniformity:

> The practices of the members of the same group or, in a differenti-
> ated society, the same class, are always more and better harmonised
> than the agents know or wish, because, as Leibniz again says, 'follow-
> ing only (his) own laws', each 'nonetheless agrees with the other'.
> (Bourdieu, 1990a: 59)

It is difficult to come to any conclusion about the relative weight that Bourdieu
attributes to individual as opposed to collective trajectories. Certainly he sees
a propensity for the habitus of individuals in the same group to converge. A
person's individual history is constitutive of habitus, but so also is the whole
collective history of family and class of which the individual is a member. Thus
for Bourdieu 'the subject is not the instantaneous ego of a sort of singular
cogito, but the individual trace of an entire collective history' (Bourdieu,
1990b: 91). Bourdieu attempts to justify his collective definition of habitus. In
reference to class habitus he asserts that:

> interpersonal relations are never, except in appearance, individual-
> to-individual relationships and that the truth of the interaction is
> never entirely contained in the interaction. (Bourdieu, 1990b: 81)

A collective understanding of habitus is necessary, according to Bourdieu, in
order to recognize that individuals contain within themselves their past and
present position in the social structure 'at all times and in all places, in the
forms of dispositions which are so many marks of social position' (Bourdieu,
1990b: 82).

It is important to recognize how enmeshed habitus and cultural capital
are. Scott Lash perceives 'the habitus as made up of cultural capital' (Lash,
1993: 197). However, most writers, including Bourdieu, view the two concepts
as slightly more separated out. Bourdieu is very explicit about the relationship
between the two. In *Distinction* he maps out a formula which elaborates their
interconnection, '(Habitus × Capital) + Field = Practice' (Bourdieu, 1984:
101). My understanding of this interconnection is one in which habitus lies
beneath cultural capital, generating its myriad manifestations.

Field

Field for Bourdieu is the context in which practices take place. It can be
understood as a site of struggle and dialectic. Bourdieu defines field as a
configuration of objective relations between positions and writes that:

> As a space of potential and active forces, the field is also a field of
> struggles aimed at presenting or transforming the configuration of
> these forces. (Bourdieu and Wacquant, 1992: 101)

The concept of field, therefore, adds to the possibilities of Bourdieu's conceptual framework and gives habitus a dynamic quality:

> The relation between habitus and field operates in two ways. On one side, it is a relation of conditioning: the field structures the habitus, which is the product of the embodiment of the immanent necessity of the field (or of a hierarchy of intersecting fields). On the one side, it is a relation of knowledge or cognitive construction: habitus contributes to constituting the field as a meaningful world, a world endowed with sense or with value, in which it is worth investing one's energy. (Bourdieu in Wacquant, 1989: 44)

As Stephen Ball and his colleagues point out 'a field implies both common ground and a composite of apparently contradictory environments' (Ball *et al.*, 1994: 1). Utilizing the concept of field, parents can be understood to be variously positioned in relation to the 'specific profits that are at stake' in the educational field (Wacquant, 1989: 29).

Cultural Capital and Maternal Involvement in Schooling: The Work of Annette Lareau

Lareau's empirical study has demonstrated that cultural capital is not just about the relationship of different social groupings to the educational system, but also about the centrality of the family to any understanding of cultural reproduction (Lareau, 1989). Bourdieu, in his article co-authored with Boltanski, states:

> the educational system depends less directly on the demands of the production system than on the demands of reproducing the family group. (Bourdieu and Boltanski, 1981: 142–3)

Annette Lareau's study attempts to realize the potential within Bourdieu's theoretical framework (Lareau, 1989). Lareau's research is primarily a study of the linkages between home and school in two socially-contrasting elementary schools in America. She focused on 12 families over the course of their children's first two years of schooling, and concluded that home–school relationships are characterized by separateness for working-class families and by interconnectedness for middle-class families. Her findings suggest that all parents, irrespective of class, valued educational success, and that teachers used similar, at times identical, steps to involve parents, regardless of parental social class. Her thesis is that differences in parental involvement are shaped by familial cultural capital. She identifies a gap in Bourdieu's theorization of cultural capital, asserting that he does not develop any elaboration of the processes through which dispositions become activated into capital and function to realize a social profit (Lareau, 1989: 178). For Lareau cultural resources do not automatically generate social advantage as is implicit in Bourdieu's own work. Rather, they need to be activated. Accordingly, she claims to modify the passivity in Bourdieu's thesis through her insistence that activity underpins cultural capital (Lareau, 1989: 145).

In particular Annette Lareau challenges assertions of working-class devaluation of schooling and acceptance of failure (Lareau, 1989). However, while the working-class parents in Lareau's study were far from inactive, they lacked confidence, both in helping their children educationally, and in questioning teachers' professional judgments. Because of their belief that they lacked the resources to help their children improve educationally, they were far more dependent on the teacher than were the middle-class parents. Lareau also discusses the contributory influence of social capital. Her working-class sample had no social access to teachers or professional educators:

> There was a separation between home and school which was linked to cultural and social capital, particularly parents' educational knowledge, their disposition to defer to teachers, and their social networks. (Lareau, 1992: 220)

In contrast, the middle-class parents had both cultural and social capital which they utilized on their children's behalf. It is in relation to middle-class parents that Lareau elaborates Bourdieu's original thesis. She describes a process in which middle-class families' cultural capital is activated in interaction with external organizations, such as the school. In developing the concept of cultural capital to embrace the dynamic function of generating social profits, Lareau extends Bourdieu's theory to cover the meaningful practice of social actors in their cultural context. However, her research only refers to effective middle-class agency. In her analysis, the working-class parents' ill-informed and unconfident activity on their children's behalf was invariably unprofitable.

For feminists like myself one crucial shortcoming in Lareau's theory is that she works unquestioningly with a male model of social class. Because she starts with an understanding of class which is premised on men's relationship to work, she develops a thesis in which home–school relations are seen to be influenced by the nature of the fathers' employment in the labour market. She describes middle-class parents as having a pattern of interconnectedness between work and home, while the working-class parents have a pattern of separation between the two spheres (Lareau, 1989: 172) and asserts that this mirrors their work–family connections. Later, she goes on to comment on the greater freedom for working-class parents in their time at home (Lareau, 1989: 185). Such an analysis denies the centrality of women to the understanding of home–school relationships, as well as the importance of the work they undertake. Paradoxically, because it is particularly for working-class women that the home is a site of work in as much as they lack middle-class possibilities of

employing domestic labour, Lareau identifies the working-class home as operating with a separation of home and work as discrete spheres. In contrast, she
argues that the middle-classes have a vision of work as a diffuse, round-the-
clock experience, taking place at home and at the work place (Lareau, 1989:
172). According to Lareau, this social-class pattern shapes parental involvement in education. The result is a thesis of separation versus interconnectedness which is based on a dichotomy between the classes, drawn from
Lareau's understanding of the experience of male employment.

Although in her later work 'Gender Differences in Parent Involvement in
Schooling' (Lareau, 1992) Lareau does not modify this underpinning tenet of
her theory, she does develop her analysis to explore the role mothers play in
cultural capital reproduction. Her starting-point is the neglect of gender within
research into parents' efforts to transmit privilege (Lareau, 1992: 208). She
suggests that it is predominantly mothers who are managing their children's
school careers, and writes that it appears that there are two types of parent–
school relationships: 'his and hers' (Lareau, 1992: 210). This is because it is
women who are not only undertaking the work of parental involvement, but
also organizing and coordinating any involvement of the fathers. She stresses
that it is middle-class mothers' investment of familial cultural capital, rather
than that of parents *per se*, which leads to substantial educational profits for
their children. Based on her findings of the gender disparities I have outlined
above, Lareau concludes that improving models of the reproduction of social-
class inequality with more developed notions of gender roles, as well as the
understanding of the intersection between social structure and biography,
remains one of the most pressing problems facing social scientists (Lareau,
1992: 222). However, her research still generates homogeneous notions of
'middle' and 'working' class. In order to develop understandings of class which
recognize difference within as well as between classes, I have utilized
Bourdieu's concepts of habitus and field alongside the notion of cultural
capital that Lareau employs. Below I outline the ways in which I have
attempted to use these three concepts empirically.

Using Bourdieu's Concepts Empirically

Bourdieu describes his ideas as 'open concepts designed to guide empirical
work' (Bourdieu, 1990b: 107). In an interview with Beate Krais, Bourdieu
suggests that the chief strength of concepts such as habitus and cultural capital
lies in their empirical relevance:

> Ideas like those of habitus, practice, and so on, were intended, among
> other things, to point out that there is a practical knowledge that has
> its own logic, which cannot be reduced to that of theoretical knowl-
> edge; that in a sense, agents know the social world better than the
> theoreticians. And at the same time, I was also saying that, of course,

they do not really know it and the scientist's work consists in making explicit this practical knowledge, in accordance with its own articulations. (Bourdieu *et al.*, 1991: 252)

I have attempted to operationalize cultural capital, field and habitus in my research but recognize that:

they do not lend themselves to precise definition or close empirical assessment, in part, because of their very interconnection. (Collins, 1993: 123)

I have tried to ensure that my utilization of cultural capital, field and habitus has been a process of adaptation rather than adoption. I prefer to work with Bourdieu's later conceptualization of his concepts as constituting 'a research method' (Bourdieu, 1985, quoted in Mahar, 1990: 36) and have attempted to use the concepts as mechanisms for understanding social processes within the home, in the classroom, and between home and school. As such, their role is that of conceptual tools rather than an overarching framework. My aim throughout has been to generate theory which grows out of 'context-embedded data'. As well as utilizing existing theoretical concepts, I have worked with a grounded approach to the data in order to harness *a priori* theory in a process which both avoids theoretical imposition and 'keeps preconceptions from distorting the logic of evidence' (Lather, 1991: 62).

Using cultural capital ensures a focus on particular types of resources women can draw on in their attempts to support children's schooling. It suggests questions which explore the differences between women, but at the same time emphasize the inequalities which permeate those differences. While recognizing the importance of material resources, cultural capital provides a means of developing a more complex analysis which incorporates psychological aspects of women's involvement in schooling. These include confidence, ambivalence or a sense of inadequacy about providing support, the amount of expertize women feel in the educational field, and the extent to which entitlement, assertiveness, aggression or timidity characterize women's approaches to teaching staff. It is these and other subjective aspects of cultural capital which I have tried to elicit in my interviews with women, as well as more straightforward aspects, such as educational qualifications and income level.

Habitus, perhaps more than cultural capital, is a concept which is difficult to demonstrate empirically. I have used it as a way of looking at what women are doing; a way that conceptualizes the present in terms of the influences of the past, stresses the differences as well as the commonalities among social groups, and, in connection with the related notion of field, emphasizes the impact of the wider social context. I have attempted to adapt habitus so that it allows a focus on individual psychologies as well as social positionings. Habitus demands a complex analysis which both recognizes diversity within social groupings and highlights the crucial importance of the context in which actions take place.

Habitus is primarily a method of analyzing the dominance of dominant groups in society and the subordination of subordinate groups. Katherine McClelland asserts that:

> it can easily be applied to the analysis of gender (or racial and ethnic) disadvantage as well. (McClelland, 1990: 105)

Habitus can be used to focus on the ways in which the socially advantaged and disadvantaged play out the attitudes of cultural superiority and inferiority ingrained in their habitus in daily interactions. As McClelland stresses, such dispositions are influenced by gender and 'race' as well as by social class. While Bourdieu has written about gendered habitus (Bourdieu, 1977c; 1990c), 'gender as an analytic category almost never appears in the construction of concepts' (McCall, 1992: 851).

Similarly, in more recent empirical work Bourdieu mentions, but does not elaborate on, the ways in which habitus is differentiated by 'race' (Bourdieu, 1993c). However, it is possible from his extensive writing on the concept to develop an understanding of habitus as shaped by 'race'. For example, I would suggest that taking whiteness for granted is integral to self-evident understandings of the social world embedded in the habitus of white people. In 'Social Space and the Genesis of Groups' Bourdieu touches on the importance of 'race' to understandings of habitus:

> The social world ... may be practically perceived, uttered, constructed, according to different principles of vision and division – for example, ethnic divisions. (Bourdieu, 1985b: 726)

Bourdieu goes on to assert that class differences mediate ethnicity, resulting in ethnic groups being arranged hierarchically in social space. However, by turning his argument around, it could equally be argued that 'race' differences mediate social class, with the result that black and white individuals belonging to the same class grouping are allocated differentially in social space according to their 'race'.

Bourdieu describes habitus as 'a system of dispositions common to all products of the same conditionings' (Bourdieu, 1990a: 59), and, as such, it can just as readily be understood in terms of 'race' and gender as of social class. I have developed understandings of habitus, field and cultural capital that attempt, first, to extend the concepts to encompass aspects of gender and 'race' and, secondly, to address the issue of working-class agency. Habitus, field and cultural capital reveal a blend of possibilities, promises and problems as conceptual tools for examining mothers' involvement in schooling. When habitus is viewed from a gender perspective, excavating the institutionalized domination mothers face in the family and the school becomes an empirical possibility. This raises the issue of lone mothers' relationship to institutional domination and the extent to which it overlaps with, and extends beyond, that of mothers in two-parent families. Furthermore, habitus permits an analysis of social inequality which is not dependent on fixed notions of economic and social location. At the centre of the concept are the social practices which are the outcomes of an interaction between a habitus and a field. The focus is as much on process as on position. In terms of my own research project this focus on process allows me to conceptualize mothers' practices in support of their children's education as generative of social class.

Bourdieu provides a conceptual framework that offers the prospect of developing a theory of class formation to suggest other possibilities than those inherent in the conventional stance (i.e., Goldthorpe, 1980, 1983; Erikson and Goldthorpe, 1992; Goldthorpe and Marshall, 1992). Bourdieu conceptualizes social class as social relations in general, rather than specifically in terms of relations of production (Brubaker, 1985). As a result, his work would seem to suggest that social class is just as readily captured by empirical studies of the family as by those of the marketplace. For Bourdieu the family is the primary site of social reproduction. He claims that for over 20 years his work has been directed at understanding the specific logic which groups, especially families, use to produce and reproduce themselves (Bourdieu, 1990b: 74). He emphasizes the crucial role which the family plays in the maintenance of the social order through social reproduction, citing it as 'the main "subject" of reproduction strategies' (Bourdieu, 1996: 23). Within this focus on the family, emerging understandings of habitus as gendered (Krais, 1993), the importance of parental time devoted to children's education (Brubaker, 1985), and the extension of cultural capital theory to include new aspects, such as emotional capital (Nowotny, 1981; Allatt, 1993), all point to the centrality of the mother.

Bourdieu's theoretical framework with its organizing concepts of cultural capital, field and habitus provides a mechanism for understanding the way in which social structure interweaves with human activity. Bourdieu's concepts locate structure as 'embodied', i.e., expressed through people's activities and dispositions (Bourdieu, 1984; 1990a). They also provide a means of responding to criticisms of conventional ethnography, which claim that it fails to study the constraints operating on research subjects (Hammersley, 1992). Because of the possibilities which cultural capital, field and habitus offer for 'reading off' structure from people's actions and, concomitantly, their ability to integrate macro and micro processes, they facilitate a broad focus on the macro relations between education and inequality, while simultaneously allowing for close attention to the micro details of mothering practices. In the ways that I have outlined earlier all three concepts invite an exploration of difference and diversity among mothers. I try to illuminate some of these differences both within, and between, social classes in the following chapters.

Chapter 4

Mothers and their Children's Schools

The Two Schools: The Geography of Parental Involvement

Milner

Milner School is situated in a densely-populated, predominantly working-class, inner-city area of London. The school is boxed inside a small triangle bounded by three busy main roads. The traffic noise is always audible and sometimes makes it difficult to hear children's contributions to class discussion sessions. The immediate area is a clutter of retail outlets and leisure facilities. The municipal sports centre is just round the corner. There is a swimming pool across the road in one direction, while Sainsbury's is across the road in the other. Lowcost, Waitrose, Marks and Spencer are within three or four minutes walk. Burger King, Macdonalds and Pizza Hut are all in close proximity. In addition, the school's catchment area includes an area of multi-occupied Victorian terraces, in what used to be a housing action area, two, large, inter-war council estates, a high-density, modern council development, a homeless families hostel, and a number of short-life properties also used for homeless families. The area has a mobile population with many migrants from other parts of the British Isles and overseas – Asia, Africa, the West Indies and Cyprus. Twenty-three different languages are represented among the 310 pupils in the school.

The social and economic circumstances of the pupils' families are equally diverse. The school was designated an Educational Priority school in the 1970s. Currently 45 per cent of the pupils receive free school meals. The 1992 census figures for the local ward, in which the school is situated, gave an unemployment level of 15 per cent, but local Labour party statistics give an unofficial figure of 24 per cent. Most of the parents who are in work are employed in skilled, semi-skilled or unskilled manual work. In the two Year 5 classes in which I conducted my research over 90 per cent of the children going on a school journey required local education authority grants because their parents could not afford to pay the full cost. At the same time there is a sizeable minority of middle-class pupils (12–15 per cent). For example, three of the teaching staff have children attending the school. Recently there has been a noticeable increase in the admission of children from refugee families, and those in homeless accommodation now represent 14 per cent of the roll. Over a third of the children come from lone mother families. In the school year 1993–4 the school raised £2 100 through the Parent–Teacher Association.

The school is housed in a traditional, three-storey, Victorian building. Each floor has an identical plan; a central hall accessed by two stone staircases and six rooms, most of which are used as classrooms. The classrooms are large and spacious, but with very high walls ending in windows that are too high for the children to see out of. The school has a tarmac playground, with space for ball games and fixed climbing apparatus. Three years ago the school obtained funding to convert part of the playground into a landscaped garden and quiet area.

The majority of the 16 full-time teaching staff are white. However, a sizable minority come from other ethnic groups. There are three black British teachers as well as one Asian and one Turkish member of staff. The length of teachers' time in the school varies from 1 to 20 years. The Headteacher, Maggie, a white woman, has been in post for 8 years.

My observation in Milner was carried out in both the Year 5 classrooms with 9- and 10-year-olds. Mandy and Maxine's classrooms are on the second floor, adjacent to each other. There is an interconnecting door but it is rarely used. Mandy is white and in her late thirties. She has been teaching in Milner for the past 10 years. Her background is in literacy; she did a degree in English before a Postgraduate Certificate in Education. She has a reputation among the parents for being 'a good teacher'. A number of the mothers said that she was 'firm but fair' and she describes herself as 'a no-nonsense teacher'. She is single with a partner she does not live with, and has no children. Her classroom always hums with children's activity, apart from the few occasions when the children 'aren't listening' or are not 'working sensibly'. Then all the children fall silent while Mandy tells them off. Maxine is black and in her mid-twenties. She did her teaching practice in Milner while on a 4-year Bachelor of Education course and has worked there ever since. I was the advisory teacher responsible for supporting her through her first year of teaching. She was one of a handful of excellent teachers out of the 120 that I supervised. Her classroom is always quiet and productive. While the school has many positive black images on display, they are especially prominent in her classroom. There are posters of famous black scientists on the walls.

The school brochure states that parents are always welcome in the school to talk to, or to work alongside, staff. The school had a full inspection in 1991 and the inspection report notes that parents were observed in the school, supporting teachers and hearing children read. There is a home school-reading programme operating in the school, which is introduced in the reception classes and continues on throughout the school. When children start in the reception class parents are invited to a meeting where the reading programme is explained to them and they are told they will be expected to hear their children read three or four times a week. All pupils are invited to take books home. Each pupil has a reading folder with a leaflet explaining the scheme. The leaflets are available in a range of different languages.

The parents interviewed by the inspectors commented that the school had developed clear lines of communication including formal parents evenings, informal discussions between teachers and parents, and the exchange of views via a parent support group. Two to three years after the inspection when I was doing fieldwork in the school, all three forms of communication were still in evidence. The deputy Head was acting as the teacher representative on the parent support group and was responsible for reporting issues and concerns back to the rest of the staff. The school also had a parent and toddler group organized by an education worker. A mobile classroom sited in the playground was used by this group four mornings a week. An average of 12–15 mothers attended regularly. Bengali mothers had their own separate session on another morning.

Oak Park

Oak Park is located in one of metropolitan London's most affluent areas. The neighbourhood, although adjoining a busy main road, is primarily quiet, self-sufficient and residential, with wide streets of large, elegant, semi-detached houses, criss-crossed with roads of smaller terraced cottages. One of the most prestigious roads in north London lies within the catchment area. It has a broad sweep of detached mansions set in their own grounds with values ranging from half to thirty million pounds. However, although nearly all the mothers I interviewed mentioned the road, none actually lived on it. The nearest shopping centre, five minutes walk from the school, contains a delicatessen, a coffee shop, a greengrocers and a couple of expensive boutiques.

Oak Park is set in its own spacious grounds and has a roll of just over 400 pupils. The school sits in the middle of two acres of grass, surrounded by oak trees which screen the school from the main road. A driveway sweeps up from the impressive wrought-iron gate entrance round the grassed area to the school, which is perched on the rim of the hill. The school was built in 1952. It is a sprawling, one-storey building with three wings, housing classrooms, which all branch off from the central auditorium. The school has its own swimming pool in a corner of the grounds.

The teaching staff at Oak Park are all white. There are 18 full-time members of staff. Their duration at the school ranges from 1–26 years with over half of the teachers having worked there for at least 10 years. The Headteacher, Miss Richards, has been in post since 1979.

Mrs Symmonds, the Year 5 teacher in whose class I carried out participant observation, is married but has no children. She is in her late thirties and has worked in Oak Park for the last 5 years. Prior to that she worked in an inner-city primary school, but has also held part-time posts in sixth-form colleges and university. Her background, unusually for a female primary school teacher, is in Science; she has a chemistry degree. Her classroom is a vibrant hub of activity. Unlike her colleagues, she organizes a lot of collaborative group work in the classroom. Consequently, her classroom is often noisier than the adjacent rooms, where most of the work is tackled individually by pupils.

The parents at Oak Park are predominantly middle-class professionals. The Headteacher told me on my initial visit that 'the average father is a lawyer, an accountant or high up in business and most of our mothers work. They can afford nannies and cleaners. We have some very rich families here'. The relative affluence of the parental population is reflected in the school's fundraising total. In the year 1993–4 Oak Park raised £19500 through its Parent–Teacher Association. Slighty less than 8 per cent of the pupils qualify for free school dinners, while just over 8 per cent of the pupils are deemed to be working-class. Two of the children in 5S were from working-class backgrounds. The pupils are also predominantly white. Fifteen per cent of the pupils are Asian, the ethnic group with the largest representation. However, 25–30 per cent of children in the school are Jewish. Three of the 13 mothers that I interviewed were Jewish.

As Connell *et al.* point out 'every school is to some extent a class mixture' (Connell *et al.*, 1982: 171). However, Milner has a very different class mixture from Oak Park. On one level the two schools represent both ends of the class spectrum of London state schooling. At the same time, both, but in particular Milner, are characterized by heterogeneity rather than homogeneity, not just in terms of ethnicity and family type, but also in terms of social class. While the sample of mothers comprises mainly women whose social trajectories are defined by stability and continuity over time, it also includes women whose experiences are of upward mobility, and a few who have experienced downward mobility. The result is a complicated concoction of change and stability which I explore later in this chapter.

Making Contact

From February 1993 until July 1994 I spent an average of two days a week conducting fieldwork in Milner and Oak Park. During my time at the schools I worked in the Year 5 classrooms, attended staff meetings and, in Milner, attached myself to the mother and toddler group which met in the school premises four mornings a week. My history as a parent at Milner meant that I already had a network of informal contacts with other mothers, and access was straightforward. None of the mothers I approached in the playground or locality said no to my request for an interview. I rapidly built up a sample of 20 mothers whom, in addition to being formally interviewed from one to three times over the course of the fieldwork, I also met informally on a regular basis.

Although sometimes this informal contact was purely coincidental – a consequence of living in the locality – often it was not. 'I loitered in the school playground, spent a lot of time circling aisles in the cut price supermarket, and started to drop in to the local Burger King on a regular basis' (Reay, 1995c: 206). The result was that, in addition to more formal arranged interviews, I also built up a data bank of numerous informal conversations with mothers about children's schooling.

At Oak Park, making contact was far less easy. Virtually all the children were dropped off and collected by car at the school gate. Making face-to-face contact with parents was extremely difficult. After I had been working in a Year 5 classroom for three weeks, I sent a letter home to parents of all the children in Year 5. After two weeks, however, I only had three response slips, so I embarked on the strategy that had worked so well in the Milner context. In the process I learnt a great deal about different urban geographies. In Milner the school was a focal point of the local community and somewhere that mothers congregated at the beginning and the end of the school day, whereas children attending Oak Park travelled from much farther afield. Loitering around the locality was a fairly solitary activity. Often, apart from individuals walking their dogs, I was the only pedestrian in the vicinity. Especially on winter evenings, hanging around waiting for parents in cars to collect children from after-school clubs, I had a distinct feeling of unease never experienced loitering around inner-city Milner.

When I finally came face-to-face with mothers with a child in Year 5 they often prevaricated about finding time to be interviewed. For example, it took three approaches before I persuaded Liliana to agree to be interviewed. Even then she was still protesting that she had no time (see Reay, 1995c: 210). Eventually, partly through a determined process of attrition, wearing down mothers who popped in to talk to the teacher, and partly by using children as intermediaries, I achieved a sample of 13 mothers. However, informal contact with Oak Park mothers was rarely possible. Apart from chats with Lavinia and Louise who helped out in classrooms on a voluntary basis, the only informal conversations were at the Christmas Fair and the school pantomime. Also, unlike the Milner sample where I achieved equal numbers of mothers with daughters and sons, my sample in Oak Park had a strong gender imbalance. The reason for this lies in Oak Park's relationship to the private schooling sector. Many of the boys who attended Oak Park transferred into the private sector in Year 3. As a result, there was a ratio of two girls to every boy in Year 5. This was reflected in my sample of mothers, nine of whom had daughters and only four of whom had sons.

The Women

I want to draw out demographic differences and commonalities among my sample of 33 women (see Appendices 1 and 2). I interviewed 20 women whose children went to Milner and 13 whose children attended Oak Park. As I explain above, while in Milner I managed to obtain a gender balance; 10 of the mothers had sons and 10 had daughters, in Oak Park nine of my respondents had daughters and four had sons. In Milner there were equal numbers of women who were lone mothers and women living with partners. However, in Oak Park all the mothers that I interviewed were married, apart from Lucy, who was one of only two lone mothers in 5S. As I have stated earlier all the women who both identified as middle-class and were middle-class in terms of more objective criteria have been given a pseudonym beginning with L. Working-class women have been given a pseudonym beginning with J, while those women who occupy contradictory class locations have been given pseudonyms beginning with C.

The ethnic mix of the women interviewed reflected that of the schools' catchment areas. In Milner four of the mothers were of black, one African and three Afro-Caribbean. In addition, two mothers, Jane and Joyce, were of mixed race and two were Asian. In Oak Park where there was a much smaller percentage of ethnic-minority pupils, one mother was black African and two were Asian. However, mothers' 'race' did not tell the whole story. In Milner, Carol, who was white, had a son who was of mixed race, while both Jenny and Julie had children whose fathers were Greek Cypriot.

When demographic factors, such as owner occupation, income level and educational level, are examined, a complex picture emerges of differences between the two groups of women moderated by varying degrees of overlap (see Appendices 1 and 2 on pages 168–70). In Oak Park all the families, apart from Jean's, were owner occupiers. In Milner, three women, Lelia, Linda and Christine, owned their own homes. All the other women were living in accommodation rented from either the council or a local housing association. Six of the Milner lone mothers lived on state benefits, while Julie and Claire received income support. Only the three women mentioned earlier lived in households with incomes over £20000 a year. In contrast, income levels were much higher in Oak Park, except in the two instances where the recession had intervened. Lavinia and Lisa's situations had changed recently from being in two-income families to managing on one income. Even so, both families earned marginally more than £20000 a year. It was Lucy, also suffering from redundancy, who as the only lone mother was in the most insecure situation. On losing her job she had become self-employed and had in her own words 'a wildly fluctuating income'. In Oak Park the norm was to earn in excess of £40000 a year.

Only two of the Milner mothers (10 per cent), Cassie and Carla, had been to university, although Carmel was halfway through a degree course. Four women had obtained professional qualifications, Linda as a teacher, Lelia as a social worker, Cathy as a nurse and Christine as a beauty therapist. Claire had an art diploma she had never utilized in the labour market. In Oak Park eight of the women (over 60 per cent) were university educated; two had been to teacher training college, one to art college and one to a college of further education to do a computing course. All the Oak Park women, apart from Jean, therefore, had been involved in full-time education after the age of 18. In Milner the figure was eight out of 20. Of these eight, four defined their background as middle-class and four as working-class. The other 12 had left school at the age of 16 or, in three cases, even earlier. When the focus is on male partners' educational qualifications, the overall picture changes very little. Eleven of the 13 fathers at Oak Park had been to university. In Milner Lelia and Linda's partners were university educated, Claire's husband had completed teacher training and Jane's partner was in the first year of a part-time degree course. The other six male partners had left school at the age of 16 and were currently employed in a range of skilled and semi-skilled manual jobs, including tyre fitter, plumber, train guard and lorry driver.

Giving Women a Social Class?

Although in Chapter 3 I have argued for a view of social class as process, in this section I explore briefly where the women position themselves in the social space of class relations. I do not want the reader to think my focus on class as process is a ploy for avoiding any examination of their social-class location. Rather, I hope my focus in later chapters on the processes of maternal activities will demonstrate a different way of envisaging social class – one that allows for a much deeper, more complex analysis which vividly colours in the rich, yet subtle, shadings that a monochromatic map of social class position leaves out.

Bourdieu talks of the boundaries between social classes as 'flames whose edges are in constant movement' (Bourdieu, 1987: 13). All the Oak Park mothers, apart from Jean who told me without hesitation that she was working-class, came from middle-class backgrounds and saw their current status as middle-class. Conventional approaches to socio-economic categorization would endorse their view of themselves. However, in the Milner sample there was lots of flickering around the edges. The black mothers of the teenage girls that Heidi Mirza interviewed had occupations such as social worker, nurse and teacher, but would be categorized as working-class because their male partners were employed in skilled and semi-skilled manual work. However, as Mirza points out, the reality is more complex (Mirza, 1992). In Milner, Lelia, Jalil, Linda, Carla and Cassie all came from middle-class backgrounds. However, for Carla, Jalil and Cassie issues around 'race', geography, immigrant status and current impoverishment lead them to question the relevance of middle-class labels in understanding their present situation. In fact Jalil was adamant that she was working-class in spite of her parents' middle-class status prior to emigrating to Britain. As a lone mother with no academic qualifications surviving on income benefit and living in council housing, she was very clear that there was no way she could call herself anything other than working-class and that is how I have categorized her.

The other 15 mothers in Milner all came from working-class backgrounds. However, five of these women expressed ambivalence about their social class location. While they shared similar class backgrounds to the other 10 women, their habitus had subsequently been shaped by different educational trajectories from that of the others, ones which had been affected by a degree of educational success. For Cathy, a black woman with a nursing qualification, her current occupational status gave rise to feelings of ambiguity about her social class. She talked in terms of coming from a working-class background but 'not really being working-class now'.

Dealing with Uncertainty: Women on the Edge of Social Class Boundaries

There were seven women, therefore, whose relationship to social class was characterized by ambivalences and ambiguities – the consequences of habitus having to deal with very different circumstances to the one in which it had originated (Reay, 1997b). Two were coping with the difficulty of reconciling a middle-class background with current impoverishment, while the other five, including Cathy, were dealing with a changing sense of self-resulting from educational and/or career success and how that interacted with the influences of a working-class background. The ambiguities of Cassie's social status are captured in her words:

> I suppose I am middle-class, but middle-class living in a council flat on a working-class income.

Christine told me:

> I don't like to think in terms of class. I mean we're all much the same now. I prefer to think of myself as classless.

and Carla commented:

> I'm poor. I think that's the most important thing. I may have a middle-class background but at the moment I'm poor and that's the most important thing about my life.

Claire, who shares my coal mining background, laughed:

> I don't know really. We are certainly not well off. Like we were saying it's difficult for a coal miner's daughter to call herself middle-class.

These women, together with Carmel, Carol and Cathy, seemed to inhabit 'the oscillating borderland between classes' (Bourdieu, 1987: 13). However, this was not the position in which most Milner mothers found themselves. Lelia and Linda were very clear that they were middle-class, while the rest saw their current status as working-class. Despite their expressed ambivalences, Carmel, Cathy, Christine, Carol and Claire seemed to be closer in social space to the working-class than to the middle-class women. Carmel, Cathy, Christine and Carol all used the rhetoric of 'people like us', which set up a contrasting, more privileged 'other' in their narratives to explain why they may be denied the academic success they desired for their children. While Cassie and Carla entered into a discourse of 'middle-class but . . .', these five women resisted class labels because they recognized the uncertain, shifting territory they occupied – a class landscape of 'maybe' and 'perhaps' where personal history shaped current consciousness and where there were none of the certainties of conventional middle-class horizons.

For Carmel, Christine, Carol, Claire and Cathy the interaction of educational and/or career success with working-class background had resulted in a sense of not fitting into either the middle- or the working-classes. Social mobility had resulted in transferring out of their original class status, but none of the women felt they had achieved middle-class status as a consequence. The aspirations of all five women lacked the certainty of the middle-class women's aspirations for their children. Subjective class identity – for three of the women, as classless, for the other two as 'not really working-class' – did not bridge the gap between their high aspirations and an expectation that they would fail to secure their children's educational success.

'Stuck with Being a Mother'

These words were spoken by Jalil but were echoed by many of the other mothers, particularly those bringing up children without the support of a partner. Mothers, regardless of 'race' and social class, all talked in terms of constraints when discussing the effects of children's schooling on their lives (see also David *et al.*, 1996; 1997). These effects are powerfully mediated by marital status and labour market participation.

The effect of children's schooling is elaborated most poignantly in the accounts of lone mothers. Most of the lone mothers were vividly explicit in linking having school-age children to being in an economic strait-jacket:

It makes it absolutely impossible to do anything else. (Carla, Milner)

You're limited to getting a job between 9 and 3.30. (Jenny, Milner)

You could say it affects my life to the extent that I can't do anything else. (Josie, Milner)

The constraints on labour market participation are central to lone mothers' accounts:

> I can't work because of the hours. I just can't afford to pay for her to be looked after before and after school and you tell me what job I can get that starts half an hour after school starts and ends half an hour before it ends and lets you take 6 weeks holiday in the summer. I'm stuck with being a mother. You know if I get a job, right then Diane I need to make sure that I'm coming home with at least £150 a week in my hand, after tax and insurance because otherwise it just isn't worth it. Otherwise after I've paid for someone to take Chantelle to school, pick her up, look after her in the holidays I'll be getting less than I get on social security. (Jalil, Milner)

June commented wryly that she had given up looking for paid employment:

> Look, who is going to take me when there are masses of people who are much better qualified? I'd only get shit work and for that you get shit pay. I mean the dole's bad enough but I'd be getting even less money in the kinds of jobs I could get. (June, Milner)

Valerie Polakow charts the prohibitive effects of child-care costs for lone mothers in America (Polakow, 1993). Mothers like Jalil, Carla and June were similarly trapped, with no possibility of earning enough to cover child-care and living costs. Paid employment was not an option currently available to them.

Prospective low levels of pay were not the only hurdle lone mothers faced. Jenny told me more than once that if she did not get a job soon she would go mad. However, as she explained in detail, the logistics of her child-care arrangements meant that she could 'only really cope with a job in a school. I'd have to try and get a job as a helper or a mid-day meals supervisor'. One of the four lone mothers who had a job talked in terms of how difficult it was to manage full-time employment with her child's schooling:

> Well, today the school was closed, we were only given 24 hours notice so I had to take the day off. It doesn't make you look very professional does it? (Jill, Milner)

The responsibilty for managing their children's schooling had led a number of the mothers with partners to make a deliberate decision to work part-time because they felt the cost of the child-care, required to enable them to work full-time, was prohibitive:

> I was forced into working part-time really because it would have been prohibitive to pay for full-time child care. (Lelia, Milner)

Both Linsey and Lucinda had opted for part-time employment because of their child-care responsibilities. The women's accounts raise issues about whether women with school-age children choose part-time work or rather that their situation of having young children dictates part-time rather than full-time involvement in the labour market. Although Liliana protests when I ask her about the effects of Sergei's schooling on her life:

> I'm not a good person to ask. I don't think I'm a good example because for me it makes my life very difficult. I can't get a proper job.

In actual fact, her account is replicated time and time again in what the other women say. It is only the professional women, on salaries of £20000 plus, in relationship with high earning partners, who do not talk in terms of restrictions on their work opportunities.

The Structuring of Women's Time

Karen Davies has written about the way in which women's time within their families is shaped by the time requirements of the daily lives and needs of partners and children (Davies, 1990). All the women, regardless of their employment status and income levels, spoke of their children's schooling influencing their daily agenda. All the women talked about engaging in work specifically directed at supporting their children's schooling. For many of the women in full-time employment this time spent with children was even more pressurized because it had to be concentrated into smaller amounts of contact time with their child. As Liz comments:

> Well, having primary aged children does not stop me going to 5 o'clock meetings but it does mean I have to do lots of organizing before I can. It also means I can't just come home and concentrate on cooking the meal. I have to find time to sit down with Martin and help him with his homework. I also have to find out what he needs in terms of books because although we've got lots of books I can't just produce one on the Stuarts at the drop of a hat, so there's a lot of running around before I even get to the point of sitting down. (Liz, Oak Park)

However, the school day had a differential power to structure women's time. For women like Jackie, who worked full-time in the home, it dictated their weekday routine:

> It affects everything because you're always watching the clock like say three o'clock I'll think it won't be long before she comes home now. It's bound to affect your day isn't it. (Jackie, Milner)

Even women with some part-time employment talked in terms of working around the school day:

> Well it takes up all my day really. It's a question of fitting my cleaning jobs in. On Tuesdays and Thursdays I won't call in at the shops I'll go straight to Orchard Road to clean. The rest of the week though, by the time I've popped into the supermarket I find I don't get back until eleven. Then I've got to leave again just before three. There's not a lot of hours in the day left for me to get things done. (Josie, Milner)

All the women were organizing and planning around the school day. However, particularly for those women who worked full-time in the home, the school time-table had the power to dictate daily routines.

Conclusion

In this chapter I have described the two schools I studied and the mothers who comprized the research sample. I have drawn out demographic differences and commonalities among the 33 women, in particular, exploring how the complexities of social class as they impact on women's lives make socio-economic categorization problematic in relation to a sizeable minority of the sample. The chapter also argues that marital status, women's labour market participation, or lack of participation, powerfully influence the home/school relationship. In the next chapter I utilize Bourdieu's concepts of habitus, field and cultural capital to examine the ways in which women's own educational histories and the workings of local and wider educational markets shape their involvement in their children's schooling.

Chapter 5

Lessons from Life: The Influence of History and Geography

Habitus as History: Mothers' Own Educational Experiences

The amount of cultural capital mothers are able to draw on in the present is not simply a consequence of their current situation. Women's personal history and their educational experiences have an effect on their propensity for some types of action over others. There is a need to investigate women's experience of education in the past in order to understand maternal activities in the present. In place of a narrow focus on where people are located currently, habitus emphasizes the importance of the social location people have come from, as well as highlighting the social space they have moved through, in order to reach their current position.

Continuity in Women's Accounts of Schooling

Four of the mothers in Milner, Janice, Cathy, Jenny and Carmel, had actually attended the school themselves, while Jill and Christine had both attended a primary school less than a mile away. In addition, Jackie, Carol, Josie and June had all been pupils at schools in the immediate locality. In contrast, none of the middle-class mothers whose children went to Oak Park had themselves attended Oak Park. However, sending one's own child to the primary school the mother had herself attended was not coterminous with 'doing what seemed natural'. It did not indicate an unthinking process. Rather, mothers operated with different agendas of choice, which were influenced not only by social class, but also by 'race'.

Working-class women, both black and white, were actively engaged in choosing their child's primary school, but they were making that choice within a framework of constraints that did not operate in relation to middle-class women's decision-making. One paradoxical outcome of such constraints was that there was a strong continuity spanning the educational experience of many working-class mothers and their children. Half of the Milner sample were sending their children either to the primary school they had attended or one down the road from it. This was primarily due to wider economic factors. First, they were dependent on the local authority for housing, and therefore geographical mobility was not a feature of their lives in the way it was in middle-class women's, three of whom had purchased a house in the Oak Park catchment area solely so that their child could attend the school. Secondly, while all the Oak Park mothers, apart from Jean, had access to family cars, 9 of these 10 Milner mothers had no transport of their own.

Unlike the middle-class mothers, working-class women rarely had the option of either moving home or travelling any distance in order to attend primary schools with good reputations. In fact a number, Jalil, Jenny, Claire and Cathy, talked about the travelling problems which had led them to reject schooling in far-flung areas of Northton. However, within these geographical constraints, black and white working-class mothers had very different agendas of choice. These differences lay in the narratives around 'race', racism and equal opportunities that both black mothers and white mothers of 'mixed race' children used to explain their choices and which were absent in both the accounts of the Oak Park women and those of white mothers with white children at Milner. Carol, whose son is mixed race, told me 'the good thing about Milner is that it has a happy multi-racial atmosphere, that's another reason I liked it'. Joyce drew on her own experience of racism as a schoolchild to explain her rationale for choosing a primary school: 'I wasn't going to send her anywhere where she'd be called "half-caste". I had enough names called me. I don't want her to have to go through it'. There was a strong sense in the black women's accounts of a disjuncture between an educational field and a habitus – nothing can be 'taken-for-granted'. June explaining her rationale for choosing said:

> There are some schools over here I wouldn't let Rosetta go to be-cause they're racist. I don't want her to ever go to a school where she's called racist names. So I'd have to go to the school first to check it's not racist. I'd have to find someone who's got a kid at that school and who isn't white. It's no good asking a white person about racism. It's a waste of time going up to a white mother or a white child and saying 'How does your child get treated?' 'How do you get treated at school?' because they won't know what you're talking about. (June, Milner)

While Carol, herself mixed race with a black son, commented:

> I deliberately didn't choose the nearest school, it had a lot of racial problems. Milner seemed to be a more inter-racial school, much more integrated and that was important for us. (Carol, Milner)

For black mothers and white mothers with mixed race children there were additional constraints around primary school choice linked to 'race' and rac-ism. However, it can be argued that, even while white women are taking their white privilege for granted, their lives are just as shaped by 'social geographies of race' as those of the black women (Frankenberg, 1993).

'Remembering the Bad Bits'

The above quote is taken from Jean's interview. She told me it was 'much easier remembering the bad bits', but the same tendency is reflected in other mothers' memories of schooling. Vivid detailed accounts of schooling were generally coterminous with negative experiences and were articulated primarily by working-class mothers. A majority of middle-class women spoke nostalgically of their schooling. For all except three, education had been an arena where they had distinguished themselves (Bratlinger *et al.*, 1996):

> I just sailed through school coming top in everything. (Lesley, white, middle-class mother)

> I was a normal clever hardworking little girl. I did really well at school. (Lucinda, white, middle-class mother)

It was middle-class mothers like Linda and Lisa, who summed up their schooling as 'generally happy', who had the greatest difficulty recollecting their school-days:

> I don't think I can remember anything much about it. I can remember seeing some production on the stage that I can't remember much about but I can't really remember anything else. (Linda, Milner)

> I haven't really got any memories of primary school, it was all fairly bland. Nothing much stands out. I was happy there. (Lisa, Oak Park)

Even when I attempted to probe further, these mothers still had difficulty remembering anything substantial about their primary school experience. When they did recall their school experiences, most of the middle-class mothers were generally positive, if short on detail. Lucinda said of her primary schooling:

> I remember going to this brand new spanking school and the beauty of it all and I had the most wonderful years there.

while Liz told me:

> I loved school. I really adored it.

In contrast, mothers who had had negative experiences rarely needed prompting and their memories were far more vivid and detailed:

There was one teacher I was petrified of her. She used to make me shake with fear. If she picked on you had to stand up and chant your times tables and heaven help you if you got it wrong. Even now I can feel her hitting me with that ruler. I learnt my times tables out of sheer fear. I was terrified, I was. I was petrified of her. (Jean, Oak Park)

and:

I think with Maths there were public tests with the whole class and if you got one wrong you had to stand on your chair. It was all about making you feel bad about yourself. If you were really bad at Maths you stood up all on your own. It was all about humiliation. My nerves alone would stop me getting it right. If I get put on the spot my brain seizes up. My brain just refuses to work so I spent a lot of time standing on my chair. (Claire, Milner)

Memories like Jean's and Claire's were predominantly articulated by women from working-class backgrounds, although both Lelia and Lavinia had parallel tales to tell from a middle-class perspective:

I lived in a village in Surrey and the first school I went to was private and quite small. I lasted about six months and I think they said I wasn't responding and my memory was basically of being very frightened, not understanding what was going on around me and I remember being told I was never going to read. At five you can imagine it was horrible. Then they sent me to the village school which was actually quite big for a village school but it seemed enormous through the eyes of a small child. It was the classic set up, desks in a row with the teacher standing at the front and I was just lost, totally lost. I stayed until I was six and a half and I don't think I learnt anything at all. I certainly couldn't read or write and they actually told my parents I was ineducable. Yes, I know it's amazing. I haven't got any pleasant memories of that school at all. I have this vision of being very, very tiny, everything going on above my Head and not understanding a thing. Amazing, it was all rote learning, no personal contact so my parents took me out and found a private school through contacts. (Lelia, Milner)

The differences between Lelia's account and that of the working-class women is that Lelia's affords other possibilities. Jenny, like Jean, talks vividly of how terrified she felt in primary school. At the same time she accepts that parental intercession was not a realistic possibility:

> You could have done with your mother coming in to protect you
> because I was frightened you know, petrified, but my mum would
> have said it was a lot worse when I was at school and it probably was.
> (Jenny, Milner)

Fear was a recurring theme in working-class women's accounts, often
underpinned by a feeling that parents were unable or unwilling to protect
them. In Jill's interview she struggles to make sense of her mother's seeming
failure to respond to her unhappiness at primary school and her insistence
that Jill comply with the demands of schooling, regardless of her intense
misery:

> I really hated school right from the beginning. I didn't start until
> I was five and that first day I went and stood in a corner all day
> and cried and I did that for most of the first year. I really, really
> hated it. I don't know why. I was a very nervous child. I can't
> think back to explain to you how I felt, just that I hated it. I never,
> ever wanted to go. I used to do my utmost to be ill every day. Of
> course my mother made me go. It's very odd because I was talking
> to a friend the other night and saying that I don't know about
> the rights and wrongs of it, but in those days people didn't think
> like now that if you chastise a child you should sit down after-
> wards and go through the rights and wrongs of it. No one thought
> should I have done that, can I look at it from my point of view or
> do I have to take the child's point of view as well. Years ago
> parents didn't. They told the child what they should do and that
> was right. I can never ever remember my mother sitting there and
> saying 'Well, perhaps I'm being unreasonable, perhaps I need to
> talk this through with Jill.' She never ever questioned the teachers
> and that it might have something to do with what they were
> doing.

Cultural capital weaves its way through women's accounts of their own schooling just as much as it does in their tales about their children's. Familial
resources enabled Lelia to be rescued from her negative school experience.
There was no similar reprieve for Jenny, Jackie, Jean, Jill, Josie, Jasbir, Jalil
and Josie.

Class differences were very evident in the language mothers used to
describe their educational experiences. Words such as 'horror', 'humiliating',
'horrible', 'like a nightmare', 'terrible time', 'petrified', and 'terrified' suffuse
working-class women's accounts. The response of some of these women in
the face of feeling that they could say nothing right was to say nothing at all.
Jean describes graphically her reaction to what she perceived to be a hostile
secondary school experience:

I went to a really horrible school. I hated it. They thought I was no good from the start. I didn't get on with anyone, teachers, children, no one. None of my friends went with me so I didn't talk to anyone. I didn't talk to anyone for three or four months. Even after that I didn't talk much.

This theme of silencing in working-class women's accounts has strong resonances with the work of other feminist academics writing about working-class girls and education. In particular, Valerie Walkerdine has explored the regulation of speaking and silence within primary schooling (Walkerdine, 1985), while in the USA, both Wendy Luttrell and Michelle Fine have developed similar theses (Fine, 1987; 1991; Luttrell, 1992; 1993).

The experience of being silenced as a schoolgirl resulted in a sense of not being able to speak the language of middle-class institutions. The most graphic example of misunderstanding and incomprehension is to be found in Josie's account of the worst day among many unhappy days she spent in primary school:

There was one day where I'd been asking about a subject and the teacher was telling me and I kept on asking because I still didn't understand and on the third occasion she made me leave the classroom and I had to stand outside the door. I stood there and after half an hour a girl came out and said 'The teacher says you can come in if you apologize'. Then she shut the door. I stood there thinking what does apologize mean. I didn't know what the teacher wanted me to say so I didn't know what to do. If she had said, you know 'sorry', but I didn't know what apologize meant. The teacher came out half an hour later and said 'You can come in if you apologize' and shut the door, didn't give me time to ask her. She left me there all day. In the end she came out, she was furious with me and she shook me, 'How dare you not come in and apologize'. I just burst into tears. I felt so awful. She went 'Uhm'. I said 'I don't know what apologize means' so she said 'Oh, it means sorry' I said 'Well, I am sorry'. As if, you know, if I'd have known what it meant . . . I was just too embarrassed to go in. I was only seven and it was a class of 35 children and she'd be standing there saying 'Come on, apologize' and me not knowing what apologize meant. I daren't go in. So it was a whole lot of misunderstanding.

Class and ethnicity combine in Josie's case to locate her outside the implicit values and standards of the educational system. Her sense of not belonging is starkly reinforced by being placed outside the classroom for the whole day. Other working-class women recounted similar experiences of being positioned outside the learning context. June, Carmel, Julie and Jenny talked about being made to stand either outside the classroom door or in a corner.

As is clear from Josie's account, it was not only social class that had a bearing on the extent to which mothers perceived their own schooling as positive or negative. Cassie describes in great detail her experience of coming to England at the age of 15 to attend a private girls' school. She does not talk in terms of being silenced. She does, however, describe an educational experience in which others felt entitled to speak on her behalf:

> I had to cope with the whole thing of middle-class racism. It was hell on earth, really hell. In hindsight the girls were very protective towards me, a kind of really suffocating, patronizing kind of kindness. If I had to open a bank account I had to be escorted. There had to be two or three hand holders to show me what to do.

Two of the working-class women I talked with, one black, one white, had been expelled from school. Jill was a persistent truant from the age of 12. She often had panic attacks when she did manage to make it through the school gate and could only cope with her sense of fear by running out of school:

> I hated every minute of it. I was frightened as well, some of the boys were really wild. I just hated it right up until I was told to leave. I never liked it. I never ever felt that I fitted in. It was atrocious. Boys fighting, throwing chairs across the room at each other. Would you want to go? I honestly felt that school had nothing to give me.

She was finally expelled when she was fourteen and a half. June lasted slightly longer. She spoke about her initial feelings of terror on starting at her mixed sex comprehensive. Within 2 years she was truanting regularly:

> I started to skip off school. I couldn't be bothered with it all, the uniform, the rules, all that. I turned out to be a rebel. My mother practically disowned me. I became a real rebel. I said 'I can't see what school's doing for me'.

She was expelled when she was 15, just before she was due to sit her CSEs. However, unlike Lelia, who places the responsibility for her negative school experience firmly with the school and its staff, both Jill and June blame themselves. June tells me she 'must have had a lot of problems to get into all that mess', while Jill believes 'it must be something to do with me, you can't blame the school'. It is impossible to unravel the complex and convoluted influences such experiences exert on mothers' current feelings of efficacy in relation to their children's education, but it seems unlikely that the damage inflicted on these women by their own educational experiences will make it an easy task to remedy any damage they may perceive in their own children's schooling.

Experience of Separation in the Past

One recurring theme in the mothers' accounts of their own school-days was of separation between home and school. However, the nature of that separation was differentiated by social class:

> There was a much clearer distinction in those days. You learnt at school, not at home. There was a clear distinction. (Claire, Milner)

While Lesley, speaking of her own primary schooling, comments 'It was in the days before they discovered parental involvement'. For Lesley the 'discovery' of parental involvement had definitely been a change for the worse. She also talks of a clear distinction between home and school in her own schooling experience, but one that is shaped by a middle-class upbringing. She differentiates between her schooling which was the site of 'repetitious learning' and the home, which was where children had fun: 'All the creativity went on at home, unlike these days'. It is extremely unlikely that the 'clear distinction' Claire speaks of was premised on a similar dichotomy. She speaks of parents, who were 'particularly hard-up' and relays an occasion where she was given a packet of coloured pencils to take home in order to complete a piece of homework:

> I don't know if we were so hard up my parents couldn't afford them but the school had these pencils for children to take home to do work with. I do remember bringing this packet of pencils, these Venus pencils and I was worried because I might lose them because I had to take them back to school.

The art work Lesley describes doing at home, both painting and sketching, were highly unlikely to figure in Claire's recollections when even coloured pencils had to be supplied by the school.

Separation in the dual sense of parents not undertaking educational work in the home, either on their own initiative or in response to school demands, was a common feature in the working-class mothers' descriptions of their schooling:

> I don't think my parents were involved at all. There was probably a parents' association but I don't think my mum ever went. She had nothing to do with school at all. (Jean, Oak Park)

There are similar absences in the descriptions of school-days by other women from working-class backgrounds. Only Carol talked about an involved mother. Jasbir, Jenny, Claire, Cathy, Jackie, Josie, Janice, Jill and Carmel all responded that their parents were uninvolved. This theme of separation is analogous to Lareau's outline of separation between working-class parents and schooling in the 1980s (Lareau, 1989). However, unlike Lareau's working-class sample's limited involvement, the working-class mothers I interviewed all talked in terms of regular involvement in their children's education which spanned curricular as well as social issues.

Despite Lesley's assertion that her primary schooling was in the days prior to parental involvement, the story was different for most of the middle-class mothers at primary school in the late 1940s and the 1950s and 1960s. Rather, there was a submerged text of historical continuity in middle-class women's accounts, because in general they had had mothers who had been involved in their schooling. In spite of the greater separation between home and school over those decades, Laura, Linsey, Lucinda and Leena had all had parents who had been involved in either the school's PTA or the governing body. A number of Oak Park mothers and Linda at Milner mentioned regular informal contact between their parents and teachers. In addition, out of the 12 middle-class women, who attended state schools, Lucy, Linda, Lucinda, Linsey, Lola, Lisa, Liz, Leena, Laura and Liliana referred to being taught at home by their mothers. Of the four women who attended private schooling, Cassie, detailed the instruction she received from her maternal grandfather, and Lavinia and Lelia talked about completing homework under their mothers' supervision. In all, over two-thirds of the middle-class mothers had been taught at home by their own mothers.

Schools may not have been making educational demands of mothers but that did not mean many middle-class mothers were not independently undertaking educational work with their children in the home. This class difference is related to differences in cultural capital. It was facilitated by home circumstances and the much greater availability of mothers in middle-class homes. While the vast majority of women from working-class backgrounds had mothers who were working full-time outside the home (15 out of 17), more than half of the women from middle-class backgrounds had mothers who had been full-time housewives while their children were growing up. The situation of relative affluence, which most of the Oak Park mothers grew up in, provided material and social conditions under which cultural capital could be generated. Dorothy Smith outlines a similar historical process in which middle-class mothers' time and attention produces educational profits (Smith, 1989a; Walkerdine and Lucey, 1989).

The Influence of Women's Educational Experiences on
Involvement in Their Children's Schooling

Mothers' own educational experiences impact on their involvement in their children's schooling in a powerful process which infuses all aspects of their mothering work. One consequence of being taught by one's mother, as was the case for 12 of the middle-class women, is that teaching one's own child becomes a process of doing 'what comes naturally' (Bourdieu, 1984). It is already ingrained in the habitus that a majority of the middle-class women bring to the contemporary educational field. When mothers worked full-time in the labour market, as most of the middle-class women did, the belief that children needed to be taught in the home did not dissipate. Rather the situation became one in which mothers employed educational specialists to undertake the educational work that they did not have the time to carry out themselves.

By contrast, for Jenny, a white working-class mother, who regularly teaches her son, Andreas, her contemporary mothering practice represents a disjuncture, a break with the past, a deliberate, conscious effort to be different from her own mother. Jenny is an example in which awareness of the negative impact of her own schooling has resulted in a determination to have a very different relationship with her son's education. Throughout Jenny's account runs a very clear theme of repairing the damage of one's own education in interaction with that of one's child. Jenny's own negative educational experiences have consequences that are played out in the present:

> My mother was never ever there for me. She was too busy working. At my school if you were off for any time they would have chased up. You had to take in a note for a day off or whatever, had to take a note in. I can remember hassling my mum like mad for this note while she was rushing to get ready for work cos we went to school by ourselves and I was saying 'mum write a note please cos I can't go into school without a note', and if she didn't have time to write the note I'd be too frightened to go to school. So it was frightening at primary school.

Jenny has very deliberately decided to be actively involved in Andreas's education on a regular basis, to protect him and act as his advocate in dealings with the school because of the consequences of her mother not assuming this role in her own schooling: 'I wasn't going to let what happened to me happen to my kids'. Jenny's account illustrates the powerful push for change that mothers' own educational experience can exert on their involvement in their child's schooling. She is attempting to generate profits of cultural capital, but in a situation of little prior investment. Rather than replicating habitus, which was the process most of the middle-class women were involved in, she was attempting 'the transformation of the habitus' (Bourdieu, 1993a: 87).

As Jenny's case illustrates, women's own experience of education sheds fresh light on their current experience of their children's schooling. The influences of the former weave through the latter in myriad ways (Rubin, 1978; Connell *et al.*, 1982; David *et al.*, 1994). Lelia's passionate espousal of progressive education needs the backdrop of her labelling as 'ineducable' in a very formal educational system to illuminate it. It is difficult to assess the repercussions for involvement in children's education of an education which many of the working-class mothers experienced as 'like being in a horror movie' (Jill, Milner). It may have contributed to the importance these mothers placed on their children's happiness in school (see also Walkerdine and Lucey, 1989). However, working-class women's own negative experiences were always there in the background, constraining mothers' potential with relation to their children's schooling. Habitus continues to work long after the objective conditions of its emergence have been dislodged (McNay, 1996). As Jill stated passionately:

> God knows, I'm nobody to make those sort of demands on my own daughter.

while June told me:

> I was no good at school, a total failure, didn't get anywhere. Who am I to tell Rosetta what she should do with her life.

Such working-class accounts raise questions of the degree to which psychological resources, including an individuals' sense of their own social worth, influence patterns of school involvement (Reay and Ball, 1997).

Similarly, some working-class women's silence in the face of teachers' expertize needs to be understood in the light of their versions of how school silenced them. Mrs Symmonds told me on the morning following parents' evening that 'all the parents had a lot to say for themselves'. Then she qualified her statement with 'except for Jean. She didn't really say anything at all, just listened to me. That makes a change'. However, Jean's silence is unsurprising when it is placed in the context of her extremely negative educational history. Experiences of learning to be silent in educational contexts have already been assimilated by Jean's habitus. The result is 'a linguistic sense of place' which Bourdieu asserts:

> governs the degree of constraint which a given field will bring to bear on the production of discourse, imposing silence or a hyper-controlled language on some people. (Bourdieu, 1992: 82)

Jean's earlier experiences of schooling have taught her that the safest course of action is to say nothing.

Women were dealing with different layers of continuity and discontinuity between their own and their children's educational experience. The continuity experienced by many of the middle-class mothers was undercut by the discontinuity produced by changing social values. Historical change is the key to understanding the current attitudes and actions of these mothers, the majority of whose own primary school experience was in the late 1950s and the 1960s. Often the tension and lack of fit between a habitus, developing in a period when family and school were largely designated as separate spheres, and a contemporary educational field where parental involvement is expected, resulted in high levels of resentment among both sets of mothers.

Nonetheless, as I have tried to indicate, this commonality across social class was undercut by important differences. Middle-class women, who had frequently been taught by mothers who worked full-time in the home, now had to contend with the demands of the labour market and the consequent erosion of sufficient time to teach their own child. The situation for working-class women was different. Some, particularly lone mothers living on benefit, had time on their hands, but no personal experience of home as a site for maternal involvement in educational learning. Others, while sharing with the middle-class women the experience of juggling paid employment with mothering work, did not share the benefits of a personal history of being taught themselves in the home.

For most of the middle-class mothers, parental involvement was much more an issue of continuity with the past, than disjuncture. It was a question of doing more of what one's mother did rather than, as it was for most of the working-class mothers, doing something different. What working-class mothers did share with middle-class women was the high value placed on education. The importance attached to education by working-class mothers was often in spite of their own negative experiences and current misgivings about the particular version of education on offer (Connell *et al.*, 1982). It is important to point out that working-class women like Jill, June and Jenny did negotiate the psychological barriers constructed through their own experience of schooling. This process of negotiating and trying to overcome residual negativity illustrates how the work they were undertaking in support of their children's education was of a different scale and level of difficulty to that carried out by most of the middle-class women. Parental involvement neither came naturally nor could be taken for granted. It had to be worked for extremely hard.

The middle-class mothers far less frequently found such powerful barriers impeding their involvement. A reasonable experience of schooling and the availability, and resulting involvement, of their own mothers, seemed to bequeath to a number of middle-class mothers a legacy of certainty. Educational problems, when they did arise, were due to deficits in schooling, rather than something located either in themselves or their child. Leena's, Lucy's, Laura's and Liz's accounts rested on an unquestioned assumption – that the school was to blame. By contrast, many of the working-class women had learnt from their own experience of schooling that educational difficulties were due to failings in the individual, rather than the system. Although many of them now questioned that message, it continued to influence the present. Working-class women's criticism of contemporary schooling was a complex issue, riven with inconsistencies and doubts. Their cultural capital lacked the certainty and sense of entitlement of their middle-class counterparts. The working-class mothers were far more likely than middle-class women to qualify any criticisms they made of their children's schooling. A strong sense that 'teachers are the experts therefore they must know best' permeated their transcripts, undermining a conflicting feeling that their children were being treated unfairly. As Josie pointed out:

> You have this feeling they should be doing something about your child not doing well. But then you're made to feel that you don't know best and that they are the ones who know best and that you, you really don't know. I've felt that way that, you know, they're the teachers, they must know.

The Migrant Experience

Class alone, however, does not tell the whole story of the influences women's educational experiences have on their involvement in their children's schooling. For women educated in countries other than Britain the resulting strangeness of their child's educational experiences undermines the efficacy of their cultural capital. It seems likely that it will be more difficult to accrue benefits of cultural capital which can impact on your child's education when as Lavinia states 'your educational experience relates to a completely different cultural experience'. According to recent research, irrespective of social class, recent immigrants to Britain have a cultural capital which is in the wrong currency (Gewirtz *et al.*, 1994a; 1994b). Nine of the mothers that I interviewed had been born in countries other than Britain – five from Milner and four from Oak Park. Most talked of the resulting erosion of expert status:

> I have a disadvantage in not knowing the English system. I feel I'm a stranger looking in from the outside rather than having gone through it myself and then comparing it with my daughter's. It's a very different system. (Carla, Milner)

> You see I don't know the system here. (Jalil, Milner)

Yao has also written about how the migrant experience can result in parental insecurity and confusion regarding their children's education (Yao, 1993). However, not all of the mothers viewed dealing with a new culture negatively. Lavinia can see advantages as well as disadvantages:

> You see I find myself coming from a different culture and have a completely . . . it is worlds apart you see the education I had and the education she is experiencing. The curriculum is so different. I don't know what they teach at school so I have to find out from the teacher what exactly are the things I need to teach her, what books I need to

buy . . . Take History at the moment they are doing Tudors. I don't know anything about Tudors. We learnt Indian history. I didn't even know who the Tudors were. Riva brought home work on the Mary Rose. I said 'Who is she?' and Riva said to me 'Mummy she's not a queen, she's a ship'. To me it's an education as well. I'm learning new things. I'm constantly having to go to the library to find out. I'm learning alongside Riva and I say to her 'Mummy doesn't have all the answers'. She knows it's a situation where sometimes she is the one with the answers, not me. I think that's excellent.

However, submerged rather than articulated in Lavinia's account is the vast amount of mothering work necessitated by keeping up with her daughter's unfamiliar curriculum. This undercurrent of extra mothering work is taken up and elaborated in other women's narratives. Liliana tells me:

I end up doing Sergei's work twice because I need to find out about it first before I can help him.

This extra work involved in understanding and acclimatizing to an educational system you have had no prior experience of surfaces in what Cassie says about the impact Akin's schooling has on her life:

Akin's education has an enormous effect on my life because I am not used to the system of education here, the nursery rhymes, the fairy stories I have not grown up with. They are not part of my culture. It is fascinating for me to sit here and read with him things I have never heard of. Parents, who are born here, automatically fit into the English system whereas for me it's a whole new dimension. I am not automatically able to fit into it. I have to read it up and find out about it with him.

Sharon Gewirtz *et al.* discuss the impact of parents attending schools in other countries on their capacity for engaging productively in the contemporary educational market, irrespective of social class (Gewirtz *et al.*, 1994a). While Leena's and Laura's middle-class status seems to have been a resource in counteracting their lack of familiarity with the English system, Liliana has enormous problems:

I don't know about the schools here. It is very difficult for me to find out. The other mothers are, how do you say it, cliquey. They do not really talk to me so it is hard for me to find out.

Being a recent migrant, plus lack of sufficient language skills, seems to have disadvantaged Liliana in relation to other middle-class mothers. However, geography has a wider impact on home–school relations beyond the influences of migration. Below I examine the powerful impact of school locality on mothers' involvement in schooling.

The Local and the Particular: The Impact of Local Educational Markets

Over half of the mothers at Milner referred to local secondary schools as an overriding constraint on their educational choices:

> I'd love him to go to University, that's why I've taken out the saving plan I was telling you about. But there isn't a decent secondary school in the borough. I can see that standing in his way. (Carol, Milner)

Her concerns were reiterated time and time again:

> Of course I'd like them to get as far as they can educationally but it's not that easy. The only decent school is in the next borough and will they take my kids. No they've got enough white, well off, kids wanting to go there as it is. (Carmel, Milner)

and:

> It was like I was saying about getting your child into a decent secondary school, that's the first stage if you want your child to do well and what are the schools like around here – rubbish. (Cathy, Milner)

Again and again Milner mothers said they wanted their children to go to 'a good secondary school'. The irony of this desire was not lost on a number of them. Cassie told me, 'I want Akin to go to a secondary school where there is a social mix, not one that is a working-class or black ghetto'. However, the middle-class mothers in Oak Park did want their children to attend 'educational ghettos'. They were seeking a match between the habitus of the home and the habitus of the school. Mothers of daughters unanimously wanted them to attend Margaret MacMillan, where selection was by entrance exam and parental interview. Although a third of the pupils are bilingual in Margaret MacMillan, girls are overwhelmingly from middle-class backgrounds. As will be demonstrated later in other aspects of mothers' involvement in their children's education, among the constraints working-class mothers have to struggle against are the repercussions of middle-class women's actions and desires:

> Lisa: 'Melinda couldn't possibly go to Weedon. It is typically, well it's not typically for handicapped children but it does take a lot of low ability children.'
> Diane: 'You mean children with special educational needs?'
> Lisa: 'I suppose I mean inner-city children, children who have got a lot of discipline problems. The discipline there is terrible.'

Sharon Gewirtz and her colleagues found that, although parents they interviewed were generally reluctant to cite class or 'race' as factors influencing secondary school choice the subtext in transcripts were the 'class related messages/signs to be read off from the school setting, the demeanour of students and the attitude of staff and that parents may be said to be seeking a match between family habitus and school habitus' (Gewirtz *et al.*, 1994b: 10). They also found that racism was a covert factor influencing the school choice of white working-class parents. While 'race' was not raised as a contributory factor to the 'good secondary school' white mothers wanted for their children, in this study, as can be seen by the comments of Carmel and Cassie above, black women did refer to the racist preferences of white middle-class parents and teachers. In a conflictual reversal, which must have had repercussions for their own self-esteem, two of the white working-class mothers said the best schools, and the ones they desired for their child, were those that had few children like their own, but which drew instead from 'well-off homes'. When the dilemmas of this position are explored with the possible costs ensuing for both child and mother, it becomes increasingly understandable why working-class parents' desires for their children to attend élite, high-standard, secondary schools are infused with doubts and ambivalences and often discarded (Reay and Ball, 1997; David *et al.*, 1996):

> Well I suppose if I had a choice I'd want her to go Trent Girls. I know it's got very high standards but I suppose there's always the worry the other girls would look down on her, you know not see her as clever enough to be there. (Jackie, Milner)

As Loic Wacquant found in his survey of primary schooling in New Caledonia, class segregation seems to be a feature of urban schooling:

> Inequality in . . . education appears to be rooted in the very structure of the school space. (Wacquant, 1989a: 212)

The Difference Three Miles Makes

Geography exerted a powerful influence on the options available to mothers. In order to account for differences in cultural capital between different social groups, Bourdieu asserts that 'one would have to take account of their distribution in *a socially ranked geographical space'* (Bourdieu, 1984: 124, authors' own italics). Access to scarce resources is a combination of position in social space and 'the relationship between distribution in geographical space and the distribution of the scarce assets in that space' (Bourdieu, 1984: 124). Three miles distance between Oak Park and Milner made an enormous difference:

> The educational fate of individual kids is affected by the way their school is working, its general educational relationships and social dynamics; these in turn are profoundly affected by the social composition of the school's 'catchment' and by the history of the relations that catchment has with the state, with academic knowledge, and with the teaching trade. (Connell *et al.*, 1982: 105)

I have discussed how Milner mothers felt their choices were seriously constrained by the local educational market within which they had to operate. These constrictions, and the greater choice of Oak Park mothers, can be understood in terms of the differing educational status of the two schools. In their research into elementary schooling in the Netherlands Rupp and de Lange develop the concept of educational status (Rupp and de Lange, 1989). This is determined by the level of secondary schooling for which the school prepares children. When the focus is on Milner and Oak Park, it becomes apparent that the two schools have widely differing educational status. Over the 10 years from 1984 until 1994 no Year 6 child in Milner has taken a selective school examination. However, the Headteacher of Oak Park told me that the norm was for 50 per cent of Year 6 children to sit selective state secondary and private school examinations. The Governors' report from summer 1995 indicates that, while only 25 per cent of the boys successfully passed examinations for selective secondary schooling, 70 per cent of the girls did. Of this 70 per cent, half (12) went to Margaret MacMillan while the other half went on to private schools. The differing educational status of Oak Park was reflected in the secondary school status outcome, especially for girls.

The Influence of Institutional Habitus on Mothers' Efforts to Generate Cultural Capital for their Children

Patricia McDonough describes institutional habitus as the impact of a cultural group or social class on an individual's behaviour as it is mediated through an intermediate organization (McDonough, 1996). The concept of institutional habitus shows how the organizational cultures of Milner and Oak Park are linked to wider socio-economic cultures through processes in which schools and their catchments mutually shape and reshape each other. While the educational status of a school constitutes an important part of institutional habitus, there are other interlinked elements; curriculum offer, expectations and teaching practices, all of which I discuss below.

At Milner a lot of the mothers expressed a desire for a more formal curriculum but met with little success in their interactions with teachers. Some mothers – for example, June and Christine – agonized in their interview with me about their child's unmet needs for a more challenging curriculum. In Oak Park the curriculum was far more formal than in Milner. Even so, one of the main criticisms made of Mrs Symmonds by parents was that 'she is not formal enough'. There did seem to be in Oak Park a reciprocity which stemmed from the power of the parental group in the sense that teachers responded to the expectations of the parents as much as parents responded to the expectations of the staff. In my field notes there are regular examples of Mrs Symmonds deliberately modifying the curriculum offer in order 'to keep the parents happy'. On one occasion she inserted a computational maths session from text books, on another she set the children a timed composition to write. Both times she commented to me that she needed to do these things from time to time because that was what the parents expected. At Milner the same pressure on teachers from parents did not exist. Dissatisfaction permeated the playground, but far less frequently managed to get through the school doors. This difference raises the spectre of social power – parents in Oak Park were far more feared than in Milner. Mrs Symmonds told me she was dreading parents' evening. In contrast, at Milner mothers were conceptualized in terms of their 'nuisance factor', not as a threat. Maxine the Year 5 teacher in Milner told me that parents evening the previous night had

> been fine apart from Leigh's mother, who just went on and on, poor woman.

While there are multiple references to 'pushy parents' in both mothers' and teachers' accounts at Oak Park, there is not even one use of the term in relation to Milner parents.

Differences in School Practices

Schools made a difference over and above the influence of mothers' activities. Connell *et al.*, 1982, similarly found in their study of secondary schools in Australia that schools were active and influential producers of educational outcomes. There are complex issues involved which require an analysis that conceptualizes the home and the school as dynamically interactive spheres which both influence, and are influenced by the other. It seems that schools can generate profits of cultural capital for children over and above the actions and resources of the home. Miss Richards commented:

Just occasionally we get a bright girl from a poor background into Margaret MacMillan. That's always very gratifying.

The Oak Park ethos had a powerful influence on the home-based behaviour of Susan, the one working-class girl in 5S. Jean, her mother, told me:

> I mentioned to her teacher that she gets such a lot of homework and she said 'Well I only expect her to spend half to three-quarters of an hour on it'. But you can't tell Susan that. She's setting herself very high standards, she seems to do an awful lot and I can't say anything. She'll sit up until 11 o'clock tapping away on her typewriter saying 'I've got to get this done, I've got to get this done' and if she makes a mistake she'll start all over again.

Annette Lareau writes in terms of homogeneous school practice in relation to parental involvement in her two socially-contrasting schools. Her conclusion about the two elementary schools, one working-class, the other middle-class, is that:

> In summary, the schools were very similar in their relations with parents. No pattern of institutional activity emerged that could account for the differences in parents' family–school interactions. (Lareau, 1989: 106)

Perhaps this homogeneity is more characteristic of earlier stages of schooling. Certainly I found little commonality across the two schools in which I conducted my research. Not only does Lareau write that the evidence she collected supports the view that teachers behave impartially with middle- and working-class parents, but she refers to the paradoxical situation of teachers wanting more parental involvement from working-class parents, while staving off often unwelcome intervention from middle-class parents, as an endorsement of her position. However a different reading could be made of 'the missionary zeal' of teachers in 'working-class Colton' (Lareau, 1989: 106) as they stressed the importance of reading at home to children. Such zeal is not simply indicative of teachers' active commitment to partnership with working-class parents. As the terminology suggests, it could also be informed by deficit models of working-class mothering. Lareau does not attempt to relate her findings to existing research that indicates differences between schools serving middle-class and working-class catchment areas (King, 1978; 1989; Anyon, 1980; 1981; Connell *et al.*, 1982). Consequently there is no elaboration of the differences in school standards and teachers' practices between the two schools. In my own research I have explored school differences that contribute to the production of very different institutional habituses, because it is evident from the data that schools as well as homes make a difference.

Parents had access to far more educational information at Oak Park than they did in Milner. Oak Park seemed to have more in common with the private primary school described by the upper-middle-class girls in Roker's study of private schooling, than it had with Milner, both in terms of early focus on large amounts of homework and frequent testing (Roker, 1993: 126). Conscientiously responding to the demands of the two schools has widely differing implications for mothers' work. There was also evidence of differing standards. In Oak Park children with a reading age which matched their chronological age were deemed to need regular reading support both in school and from parents. The same provision was not available in Milner where such children were regarded as good readers who had passed the stage of needing regular support. As a consequence, the messages communicated to the home about the reading needs of Fola in Milner and Robert in Oak Park, who both have reading ages of 10.0 years, were very different. None of the Oak Park mothers could have commented as one of the Milner mothers, Carol, did:

> I think with the standards the school expects of children it's not important that they do homework. (Carol, Milner)

Mothers at Milner had to create their own programme of educational work for their child, because the school had a no-homework policy. Although parents were asked to hear their children read and spellings and time tables were sent home on a regular basis, there was no systematic procedure, as there was in Oak Park, of sending work home for children to do. This created difficulties for mothers on two counts: first, it made monitoring the school curriculum difficult; and, secondly, in cases where mothers felt they lacked educational expertize, it made undertaking academic work with children in the home doubly fraught. Not only did such work lack the sanction of the school, but also many mothers were very vague about the level of the work they should be giving their child and, concomitantly, the standards they should be applying. As a consequence, some working-class mothers only undertook educational work in the home when their child volunteered to do it, while others, like Julie and Josie, found themselves caught up in a stressful, conflictual interaction with children who were clearly aware of their mother's ambivalence and lack of confidence about the whole process. Even mothers like Cassie, who felt reasonably confident about assuming a teacher role in relation to her son, found the uncertainty and lack of validation hard to deal with:

> I go and buy books for him, work books for him to do at home. At the same time I worry that I'm overloading him. I worry that it doesn't fit in with what he's doing at school and I don't want to jeopardize the relationship. I'd rather be doing something that fitted in with the school programme then I'd feel a lot happier about taking it on. I really don't know (long silence). I really don't know if I'm doing the right thing. (Cassie, Milner)

In contrast, regular set homework was an integral part of the learning experience in Oak Park and played a vital part in ensuring that the curriculum was covered.

A further difference which caused concern to a number of the mothers in Milner was the school's lack of any testing regime. Jenny, Carla, Julie and Cathy all talked about insufficient preparation for secondary school both in relation to homework and in terms of testing:

> In one sense it's like a muscle, it's like the difference between a gymnast who's used to exercizing all the time and someone, who never exercizes at all, both being asked to go through the same exercize sequence. The last person freaks out, you have a bit of adrenalin because you are nervous but it doesn't get you over the bar. You need to get gradually used to it. Lilly's school does not give her that sort of practice, not at all. (Carla, Milner)

From the evidence of these two primary schools schooling is no unitary, homogeneous product. Educational provision appears to be shaped by a combination of the perceived needs of different pupil intakes and the power of the demands made by their parents. In particular, inner-city, working-class primary schooling seems to be caught in a conundrum. In attempts to banish the humiliation and labelling of working-class children so endemic in their mothers' educational experiences, contemporary primary schooling seems to have jettisoned one betrayal of working-class potential for another. Contemporary inner-city, working-class schooling could be seen to be characterized by the happiness rather than the humiliation that pervaded many of the women's own experience of education. A majority of children in both schools were happy in school. The difference was that in Oak Park the institutional habitus – a complex mix of curriculum offer, teaching practices and what children bring with them to the classroom – made it possible for happiness to go hand-in-hand with high achievement. In Milner, the same ingredients resulted in markedly lower standards. Jeannie Oakes writes that:

> In our search for a solution to the problems of educational inequality, our focus was almost exclusively on the characteristics of the children themselves. We looked for sources of educational failure in their homes, their neighbourhoods, their language, their cultures, even in their genes. In all our searching we almost entirely overlooked the possibility that what happens within schools might contribute to unequal educational opportunities and outcomes. (Oakes, 1985: xiv)

To veer from a version of events which makes parents accountable for children's educational performance to one which makes teachers accountable is to replace one fiction with another. It is important to remember that contemporary home–school relationships are being forged out of a history of nearly 20 years of New Right government policies which have reinforced rather than eroded traditional class and 'race' hierarchies within the educational system (Gewirtz *et al.*, 1995; Vincent, 1996; Bagley, 1996). A better representation of reality emerges out of a focus on the complexities of interaction. It is in the cocktail of teachers' expectations of children, parental expectations of school, differential relationships of power between parents, teachers, children, local government and the state, as well as the intricate layering of discourses informing both parents' and teachers' understandings of the relationship between culture and educational achievement that a more complete picture is revealed. The school effectiveness literature has simplistically asserted that what schools, or more specifically, what teachers do makes a difference (Reynolds and Cuttance, 1992; Scheerens, 1992). There has been little attempt to investigate the effects of the social composition of school catchment areas. As Lawrence Angus asserts:

> Family background, social class, any notion of context, are typically regarded as 'noise' – as 'outside' background factors which must be controlled for and then stripped away so that the researcher can concentrate on the important domain of school factors. (Angus, 1993: 341)

By contrast, this research stresses the relational aspects of mothers' and teachers' work. I argue that curricula differences between schools, such as Milner and Oak Park, are the result of an interactive process emerging out of the relationships between and among parents, pupils and teachers.

Beyond the social dynamics of the catchment area lie the more general, but still powerful, influences of local and national educational markets and central government policies. Both mothers' and teachers' actions take place within the context of an English educational market, which rewards particular class and racial forms of cultural capital but not others. Mothers' activities in support of children's schooling need to be viewed against the backdrop of inequitable government policies in relation to choice and selection which consistently privilege white, middle-class cultural capital. It is out of this complex tangle of social relations within, and stretching beyond, school catchment areas that social class and 'race' inequalities are generated. The interaction of habitus with very different educational fields translates into widely-differing possibilities and options available to mothers in the two schools.

As this chapter has demonstrated, history and geography have a powerful impact on mothers' potential for generating cultural capital. A complex interlacing of time and place infuse habitus and compound, complicate or clash with influences of gender, 'race' and class. The result is an intricate and very complex patterning of cultural capital reproduction. Nevertheless, what stands out from all of the many positions the observer may take is the overpowering theme of inequality criss-crossing the weave of mothers' activities. In the next four chapters I discuss the myriad aspects of mothering work women are undertaking in relation to their children's schooling. However, the backdrop to these activities is the powerful influence of history and geography which permeates maternal practices and shapes mothers' responses to the contemporary educational field.

Chapter 6

'A Labour of Love'

In this chapter I explore the many different types of work mothers undertake in support of their children's education. In doing so I employ cultural capital, and habitus as conceptual tools for examining how those activities, despite apparent similarities, add up to significant class differences. It was evident that there was little difference across the sample in either the importance attached to education or the mental energy women devoted to their children's schooling. However, underlying the similarities were the ways in which working-class women's support of their children's education did not count to the same extent that middle-class women's did: first, it was not invested with the certainty of the middle-class women's interventions; secondly, it was not underpinned by financial resources; and thirdly, it was conducted in a process uninformed by knowledge of just how uneven the playing field actually was.

Looking at Women's Work

For some of the mothers, work was something that happened outside in the labour market as in 'I'm lucky I can fit my work around the children's day. I'm lucky a lot of people don't have that' (Cathy, Milner). However, not all the mothers differentiated between work and child-care. A number of black and white working-class women were explicit about the work involved in mothering:

> I hear her read everything, Diane honestly I do, but It's not my job. It's hard enough work bringing up a child on your own without having to do the teacher's job as well. (Jalil)

and:

> He's hard work I can tell you that for free. (Jenny)

One key difference between the groups of mothers was that the working-class women, and women like Cathy and Carmel who came from working-class backgrounds, nearly always focused on the domestic work they needed to do in the evenings, while middle-class women rarely mentioned domestic work. In part this could have been due to the employment of domestic help in middle-class homes. I knew, not from the mothers' own accounts but from disclosures by their children in the classroom, that at least half of the middle-class women had cleaners, au pairs or both.

Working-class women, in contrast, sounded hard-pressed:

> When I get in I get them both something to eat, then do whatever needs to be done in the house and that includes getting their clothes ready for school so by the time everything done I find I never have a minute to sit down until half eight or nine. Then she'll come and sit with me and read and that's every night. (Jill, Milner)

and:

> When I get in in the evening the first thing I need to do is cook them something, get them to eat, a little bit of schoolwork or whatever, you see by the time I pick them up about half five or six o clock it hardly leaves you any time to do the schoolwork. You are kind of thinking about getting them ready for school the next day, you know, making sure they've got clean underwear, something ironed, sorting out anything they may need to take into school. So it's not a relaxed atmosphere. Straight away I need to start thinking about what needs to be done, meals, washing up, cleaning, ironing and on top of that the spellings and the reading – it's hectic. I can't sit down and relax with the children. (Cathy, Milner)

Josie, Julie, Carmel and Jean all talked about the competing demands of domestic tasks and educational support for children.

It was only working-class women who spelt out the details of their domestic labour. Middle-class women's accounts all, seemed to stop short of doing the dishes. For example:

> Generally after school is all about ferrying one here, picking another one up there, making sure they've done their homework. (Louise, Oak Park)

Their busyness all seemed to be expended in pursuit of their children's academic excellence.

Only one middle-class women, Louise, mentioned the shopping. By contrast, tales of shopping on the way home were a regular feature of Milner mothers' accounts:

> Well we often go into Sainsbury's on the way home and he'll want this and she'll want that. I'm better off shopping on my own.

Anything sweet – chocolate, ice cream, they're trying to put it in my basket. Last time he did show off. I said 'No' and he was down on the floor in the supermarket. But they'll be wanting things we can't afford. He'll go 'Can we buy this?' and I'll say 'no Dane' and he'll go 'Why?' and I'll say 'Money, Dane, it costs too much money'. (June, Milner)

I suggest there are clues in June's account which shed some light on possible reasons for this class difference. For the working-class women shopping was much more of an obstacle race, littered with things they could not afford. This may well have contributed to shopping looming much larger in their lives. Also to shop once a week like Louise does you need a car, an asset the majority of mothers at Milner did not possess.

A paradoxical reversal seems to be operating. Working-class women reveal their mothering as unambiguously located within the sphere of work, while stressing their children's entitlement to play. On the other hand white, middle-class women hide their maternal labour, while clearly delineating what their children do out of school as work. Linsey told me:

I feel I have to balance the social side of their lives. I know I expect an awful lot of them so we have this thing that summer holidays are for leisure. They don't have any lessons in the holidays they are allowed to take the six weeks off. We have this time because we have very high expectations of them in term time. Then we do set clear rules about how much work they need to do in their time out of school.

Lucy, Lavinia, Lola and Leena all stressed that their child needed to work hard at educational tasks outside school as well as in the classroom, if they were to succeed academically.

However, while there were class differences in the extent to which mothers stressed the work involved in supporting children's schooling, the transcripts showed that what the women shared was their participation in a range of maternal tasks. Women were involved in practical maintenance, emotional and educational work in support of their children's schooling on a daily basis.

Practical Maintenance Work

It is in their descriptions of early morning routines that recurring evidence of women undertaking the manual work of parental involvement is to be found;

Cathy: (laughing) 'Well I have to drag her out of bed.'

Laura: (laughing) 'Well sometimes I have to drag him out of
bed.'
June: 'I'm dragging them out the door, saying "Quick, we'll be late
for school".'
Joyce: 'Well it means I have to get them up at the same time every
week day and drag them into school.'

If women are not dragging children out of bed, then they are to be found
chasing them out of the bedroom:

Jalil: 'I actually have to chase her into the bathroom. I mean it, I
actually do.'

Although the language used, as in the above examples, is often redolent of
hard, physical work, on occasions, detailed descriptions were pre-empted by
middle-class women with a denial of the labour involved. Linda responded to
my query about how she supported her son's education with 'Not a lot, not
really at all, he's not a child who particularly wants help', while Louise told me
'In the morning I'd say I don't have to do much'.

When I later asked Linda to describe in detail the previous school week,
she gave a graphic description of the physical and emotional labour involved
each morning in getting her son to school, which was in sharp contrast to her
earlier response:

Well he is very, very dependent on me for getting to school at
all because getting him out of bed is absolute hell, it's a
nightmare ... It's an absolute nightmare getting him out of bed,
dressed, washed, getting him to eat his breakfast, getting him out the
door with the right things at the right time, actually getting him there,
the fact that he's so laid back. Mark does not rush about, no way. It's
a real problem. I have to literally wake him up and almost drag him
out of bed and say 'For God's sake get on with your breakfast' and
'Haven't you got your shoes on yet?', everything. Getting him out of
the house is murder so it's always off to school with moans and
groans.

This account is from a woman who claims to not really do much to support her
child's schooling.

Louise's account produced a similar version of hard work and emotional
strain that contradicts her claim to 'not do much':

The first thing I have to do is yell 'Get out of bed'. Now she's
motivated to read at night I'm loath to say 'Lights out' but I pay for
it in the morning because of course she can't get up. So there's a

process of me trying to get her up and nagging her, for instance, to brush her hair 'Don't you know where your hairbrush is?'. Then of course she's incredibly grumpy when she hasn't had enough sleep. It's awful and then she takes it out on her brother. That's the bit I can't stand, drives me to distraction, the way when she's tired he'll say something and she'll just bite his Head off. I do feel that I'm doing more of all this than is necessary, that she should be remembering her own things to take into school instead of relying on me. She will ask me to check she's got her homework, lots of things like that . . . In fact this morning I said 'I think I am actually just going to allow you to be late' but I never have. I just can't bear it. I just cave in and rush around but it does make me very cross. She's not the sort of child who is champing at the bit for independence. I am actually having to kick her out the door.

Many middle-class women seem to be working with a text of mothering as 'non-work' which is only revealed as illusory when they begin to engage with the micro-details of their practice. There are parallels here with Valerie Walkerdine and Helen Lucey's findings that, while working-class women made the labour involved in their mothering visible, middle-class mothers were far more likely to be involved in a process of simultaneously concealing and transforming their mothering work:

> generally, domestic tasks are rendered invisible in middle-class homes. They are spoken about far less and often the only indication that these women indeed do any housework is in the fieldnotes made by the observer. Housework thus goes underground with the effect that it is presented as far less pressing for most middle-class women than for their working-class counterparts. (Walkerdine and Lucey, 1989: 72)

Embedded in these accounts of getting children ready for school are strong threads of stress, conflict and coercion. Early mornings rarely seemed to approximate to quality time for either mothers or their children. Far more frequent were tales of tension and temporizing:

> Well, she's not easy to get up, not any more, it's classic. I even had a letter from school reminding us about the time she should get to school because she's got progressively more dozy in the mornings. I find myself negotiating with her over when's a reasonable time to get up. I'll say she needs to be up at quarter to eight. She says 'quarter past eight', then it's five to. No, she's really dozy in the mornings. She seems to do everything in slow motion, not just getting out of bed. I find it terribly hard to keep my temper because it has repercussions for all of us. You have to keep on encouraging her to get on with the

process and at the same time there's a need to encourage her to take responsibility for getting herself up and ready. She is starting to do that, it's just that it takes so long from getting her up to getting her out the door you want to scream. (Lelia, Milner)

As I discuss in Chapter 9, men are noticeable by their absence in women's accounts of early morning routines. Women's focus is on unshared pressures, both on their time and their emotional energy:

If he's got spelling that day I'll go over them with him at breakfast, then again in the car, but it's hard to squeeze in. You see my children learn instruments by the Suzuki method in the morning. They have to listen to their tape and all that so at breakfast I put the cello tape on. I have three of them doing it so three of them have to hear their tape at some stage in the day so the cello tape goes on at breakfast. (Laura, Oak Park)

Almost half of the mothers across the sample talked in terms of cajoling, pleading and persuading children in order to get them to school on time. There were no accounts of leisurely, relaxed breakfasts.

Time was always an issue even when mothers saw themselves as either extremely organized, having an effective system for getting children ready, or, less often, having a child who could do the job themselves. However, all too often the backdrop to children's declared independence was a web of maternal organization:

He's very independent about getting himself to school, but I suppose behind all that I've organized everything. It all has to be organized for him so for instance his clothes are always laid out in the same place ready for him to put on. I've got a list in the kitchen of the things he needs for school and what day he needs to take what in. (Jane, Milner)

She's very good at getting herself up and ready now, so there's not really much for me to do. Of course I do help her with organizing what she needs. I do say 'Don't forget your homework'. (Lucinda, Oak Park)

Sometimes, mornings became occasions for open conflict between mother and child:

Liliana: 'He's hopeless, absolutely hopeless, he doesn't even want to get out of bed in the morning so it's "Get up" all the time.'
Diane: 'So you have to persuade him to get up?'

> Liliana: 'Not persuade, force. I have to shout, it's awful. He can't do anything. He is still tired and I try and force him to eat his breakfast because he does not eat properly at school.'

and:

> Getting him up is hell. We have even got to the stage where I have poured a cup of water over him to get him up. It's awful on a school day. He's dreadful, just dreadful, it's something about first thing in the morning. I used to physically manhandle him out of bed but I can't now because he's in the top bunk. I just throw things at him and shout at him to get him up. (Carol, Milner)

Mornings for mothers across the sample are very similar experiences in which women, whether they acknowledge it or not, have to work hard at producing a presentable, adequately fed and properly resourced child for the classroom.

Emotional Work

Recent research which has explored the area of emotional relationships within families found that the majority of women perceived themselves to be making 'the emotional running in persuading men to father their children, but with the unforeseen result that some men had then abrogated physical and emotional responsibility, treating their children as belonging to their wives alone'. (Duncombe and Marsden, 1993: 226). It is difficult to separate emotional work from the other aspects of mothering work. Often emotional work is directed at smoothing out the transmission of educational knowledge – for example, helping children work on barriers to learning, such as lack of confidence. Although I have attempted to separate the different types of mothering work, at the same time I wish to acknowledge the ways in which they interlace, tying together maternal support of children's schooling. Nicky James writes that:

> Women's emotional labour involves preparing children for their environment and circumstances, shielding them and defending them as they age and preparing them for work. (James, 1989: 24)

Emotional support was a daily part of what mothers did. A crucial component of mothers' work was to ease their child's school passage, to intervene when their child felt unhappy, unconfident, or when they felt they had been unfairly treated. Most interventions only went as far as talking with the child:

> He complains, yes, he complains a lot. He does get a bit upset and he talks to me about it. He used to be a bit frightened of his teacher, but

I'd tell him she was strict not because she didn't like him but because she wanted him to learn. (Jenny, Milner)

However, as I elaborate later in Chapter 7, many of the mothers also recounted tales of trips into school to put their child's case. Also, to call what mothers did simply talking to children glosses over the hard work that went into this aspect of their mothering. The bulk of Lesley's involvement in Simon's education was directed towards providing emotional support:

> I've spent a lot of time talking things through with Simon. There was a stage when he was being bullied and we discussed it at length how he could use humour and wit to diffuse this child's power and it did work eventually. Also he gets terribly undermined about not being as clever as the other children so I do need to spend a lot of time building up his confidence. He's had a lot of problems relating to teachers, as well as children, so I spend a lot of time building him up so that his time in school is reasonably happy. I do much more of that sort of thing than helping him with his homework.

Although few mothers were as explicit as Lesley, examples of emotional bolstering of children weave themselves through most of the women's accounts. In response to my question 'what do you see as your part in Nicholas' education?' Claire said 'to be there for him to talk to if he has any worries'. She went on to tell me that Nicholas has always got 'terribly nervous':

> Claire: 'He always gets terribly anxious about things. He is good at talking about it if he is worried about anything. He does let you know in little ways.'
> Diane: 'What sort of things does he worry about?'
> Claire: 'Well he's been having a bad time in the playground, that's caused real anxiety, but he's even been worried about the Spellathon. He got very nervous about getting it right. Then he was very worried about swimming at one stage. Then we had to have a very long discussion about death, there's a boy in his class with leukemia, who is very ill and Nicholas got very upset about it. So there's been quite a lot of things he's wanted to talk through with me.'

The emotional wear and tear on mothers of providing emotional support is evident in the data I have collected. Part of the weight of this support, I would suggest, is due to its unshared nature. Stevi Jackson writes that women are the emotionally literate sex, while men are unable to construct 'wider discourses of emotion' (Jackson, 1993: 216). In this emotional division of labour we can see the influence of gendered habitus affecting both mothers' and fathers' behaviour. Mothers see themselves as having the responsibility for their children's emotional needs, while the fathers feel they have a licence for leaving women with the responsibility for emotional support. The result is that women are often left doing the emotional work for the family. Jean Duncombe and Dennis Marsden found that most of their female respondents felt 'their male partners were lacking in what might be called "emotional participation" in their relationships – a lack which women who were mothers feared was also a feature of men's relationships with their children' (Duncombe and Marsden, 1993: 225). Although Annette Lareau's research stresses the costs to children when mothers are over-involved emotionally (Lareau, 1989), my research identifies parallel costs to mothers from being the adult responsible for providing emotional support:

> It's particularly awful at the beginning of term, very often then we get tears and Melinda can't sleep. Life is just awful, a tragedy because somebody is not speaking to her. Melinda is absolutely desolate if her group aren't friends, very unhappy. (Lisa, Oak Park)

and:

> Lilly's nervousness about school is a constant worry for me, a small anxiety that never goes away but rarely gets so bad that I do anything about it. (Carla, Milner)

Pat Petrie points out that undertaking school-related child-care tasks makes different demands on families, according to the social grouping they belong to, and that concomitantly 'the stress involved in them may be greater for some groups than for others' (Petrie, 1991: 530). All the mothers, without exception, undertook educational work in the home with their child. However, often the working-class women's support was characterized by lack of knowledge of appropriate educational standards, and uncertainty and self-doubt about their competence as educators. As Josie's comment illustrates, bringing a habitus shaped by extremely negative experiences of schooling to the competitive field of contemporary education makes parental involvement a very stressful affair:

> I find it really difficult helping Leigh with his work ... I'm the wrong person for it because I'm already angry in myself because of my education and how that sort of progressed, and all the problems I had to go through, all the embarrassment and humiliation. (Josie, Milner)

Working with children on educational tasks was often accompanied by extremely ambivalent feelings for the working-class mothers, as well as psychological barriers the middle-class women rarely had to negotiate (Reay, 1998).

Josie's was far from the only case of mothers finding involvement stress-ful. Teaching staff, male partners and the mothers, themselves, invariably perceived the mother as the parent who was accountable for the child's behaviour (Van Galen, 1987). As a consequence, many of the women often found it extremely difficult to disentangle themselves emotionally from their child's school performance. When I asked Jill to describe how the past week had differed from an average school term week, she said:

> I don't think I can bear to talk about last week. There were problems with Lucy's older sister's schoolwork and the school sent me a letter asking me to make sure she did her homework. I had a really bad week emotionally with her. It was terrible. It was a really bad week last week.

Her experience of policing Gemma's homework and the conflict which it caused had negative reverberations that coloured Jill's attitude to all aspects of the previous week. Liliana told me that she had had to stop going into school regularly to liaise with teachers because 'the only thing I hear is the criticisms. His teacher said that he only enjoys doing the things that he wants to do and I thought actually that is my nature'. The qualities that make Sergei's adjust-ment to schooling difficult are not simply Liliana's responsibility, they are her own qualities also, so she is doubly implicated in his 'wilful behaviour'. She went on 'I must accept some responsibility for making him more childish. He started a new life in a new country when he was five and I protected him as if he was a baby'. Within her construction of events she is clearly to blame, which only increases the intensity of her emotional involvement. In addition to Liliana and Josie, Julie, Carla and Christine all mentioned worrying about their child's education more than five times over the course of the interview. Carla, Christine and Julie cried during the interview, so great was the emo-tional intensity of their feelings.

Although most of the mothers did not have to face the hurdles Josie, a migrant to Britain, had to confront in her efforts to support Leigh's education, tales of the powerful feelings evoked in supporting children emotionally were commonplace:

> It's been an awful cause of concern. The worst year was last year. They all go on a school trip. Well for my Amy, this was like torture. The rest of the class were in raptures and my Amy was tearing her hair out. She'd never slept away from home before so for four weeks every night I had 'Mummy I don't want to go' I had to sit down and explain why she had to. It was a horrible experience. She did go and she just did not fit in with the group that was going. She wasn't old enough to say 'I'm just not going to let it bother me' and make the best of it. It was terrible when she got back. Someone asked if she had enjoyed herself. She is always very polite with people outside

the family so she said 'Yes' If only they knew. We really struggled with it. (Louise, Oak Park)

Even mothers who initially expressed a great deal of certainty and confidence about undertaking educational work with their child went on to reveal the emotional tensions of assuming a teaching role. Although middle-class mothers like Leena clearly do not have to deal with the pain and anxieties evinced by Josie, their involvement is not free of emotional costs. Leena's recounting of a conversation she has had with Negar spells out very clearly the costs to herself, to Negar, and to their relationship:

> I hate having to be the educator, in that sort of role. 'Mummy the teacher says I am very bright so why do I have to do all this?' I had to sit her down and say to her. 'Negar, the thing is I have a real problem with your secondary school. I have to try and get you into a good girls' school. It is very important and there are hardly any girls' schools in this area. I'd love you to go to Ferndale but the chances are very slight. It means I might have to get you into a private girls' school but unfortunately that means exams. I hate you having to do exams. I'd love to find you a school where they didn't have to do exams, where you would be seen as an asset to the school, where just by chatting to you, they'd see you as wonderful for the school but because they have so many applicants we have to do this work every night'. She has kind of accepted it now. I think we have got past the fussing and bothering about doing it. It used to be 'Can we do something interesting?' but I think now she understands how important it is.

In Leena's account both mother and child are engaging in a daily interaction neither of them enjoys. Leena's words encapsulate a frequent theme in middle-class mothers' accounts; the prioritizing of future prospects over interaction in the present.

Across the sample mothers were involved on a daily basis in emotional support of children; support often necessitated by the children's experiences at school. This emotional support, rarely shared with the child's father, could be accompanied by maternal stress, especially if mothers became intensely involved in their child's schooling. However, emotional costs for both mother and child could also be a direct result of mothers assuming a teaching role.

Competing Demands

A number of mothers stressed the negative consequences for their child's schooling of being emotionally preoccupied with other aspects of their lives. Their words highlight the delicate balance mothers have to hold between keeping their child's needs in view and addressing problems in other areas of their life. Carla had tried to deal with her ex-partner's acute depression, becoming very involved in trying to support him through his psychiatric problems. It was only in retrospect that she realized that Lilly had become withdrawn and uncommunicative about school. Only by refocusing and deliberately trying to make up lost attention did she discover that Lilly was regularly being bullied in the playground. Lucinda talked at length about a prolonged period of unhappiness Jessica had experienced earlier on in her school career, identifying it as the period when she had been trying to combine paid employment with doing a part-time MA.

However, it is Cassie's account which brings most sharply into focus the competing demands on mothers lives and the consequences of taking your finger off the pulse – consequences which could result in mothers needing to redouble their efforts in support of children's schooling:

> Earlier in the year Akin was having a crisis at school and it was a very difficult situation. He saw this other boy as being racist but his teacher felt he was the one provoking the situation. It all happened at a very difficult time for Akin because I had a refugee from Africa staying and therefore I was not very attentive to him. This situation made Akin very pent up with anger and frustration over the course of the week. By Friday evening he just exploded. He yelled 'The bastard' and ran up to his room and really was in a rage, crying with anger. For a long while I left him, thinking, you know, 'Oh, my God'. Then I went up and said 'What happened?' and he was being blamed by a teacher for something and the teacher did not believe he hadn't instigated it and Akin was really hurt. It really did hurt him. Also he thought the other children were ignoring him but really he was being over-sensitive. It was just one boy in particular, who was picking on him. I spent a long, long time talking it through with him. It was complex because it was something to do with race as well. In the end he was very pleased that I understood his side.

Cassie's example demonstrates that emotional work requires regular weekly, if not daily, input. It is not intermittent and episodic in nature:

> There are times when she comes home and says 'Mummy, I don't think I'm liked at school,' and when we sit down and analyze it it is perhaps one child, who has said something and Riva thinks that means she is not liked at school. She is generalizing from just one comment and I try and point out what healthy relationships she has with nearly all her classmates. (Lavinia, Oak Park)

and:

> He has problems with his peer group. There are little problems which I feel are used against him. It is part of being little and having a funny,

squeaky voice. The problem is once he gets home from school he doesn't want to talk about it. It comes out in drips and drabs later on. If he's had a miserable time it usually comes out the next morning. I get up very early around half five and he will come down with me and talk. (Lesley, Oak Park)

Sometimes it was the commonplace that made it difficult for mothers to make emotional space for their children. The daily exigencies of living in poverty made it hard, especially for lone mothers living on state benefit, to clear away their own pressing concerns and worries and focus unreservedly on what was going on for their child in the schooling context. Jalil told me:

I'm better on a Monday, by Thursday all I'm thinking about is where the next ten pence is coming from.

Women's Emotional Work: Generating Emotional Capital?

In his book, *The Year 2000*, Raymond Williams writes that:

It is in what it dismisses as 'emotional' – a direct and intransigent concern with actual people – that the old consciousness most clearly shows its bankruptcy. Emotions, it is true, do not produce commodities. Emotions don't make the accounts add up differently. Emotions don't alter the hard relations of power. But where people actually live, what is specialised as 'emotional' has an absolute and primary significance. (Williams, 1983: 266)

It is only during the last decade that the view that emotions are somehow beneath the remit of sociologists has begun to be challenged (Hochschild, 1983; Jackson, 1993; Duncombe and Marsden, 1993). Even Bourdieu, writing recently about the family, refers to the constant maintenance work on the feelings that 'falls more particularly to the women, who are responsible for maintaining relationships' (Bourdieu, 1996: 22). However, it was over 15 years ago that Helga Nowotny, drawing on Bourdieu's conceptual framework, developed the concept of emotional capital. She saw emotional capital as a variant of social capital, but characteristic of the private, rather than the public sphere (Nowotny, 1981). The use of emotional capital is generally confined within the bounds of affective relationships of family and friends. According to Nowotny, emotional capital constitutes:

knowledge, contacts and relations as well as access to emotionally valued skills and assets, which hold within any social network characterised at least partly by affective ties. (Nowotny, 1981: 148)

Unlike the other forms of capital – cultural, economic, linguistic and symbolic which are invariably theorized in ungendered ways, Nowotny saw emotional capital as a resource women had in greater abundance than men.

Patricia Allatt has drawn on Nowotny's work in her own research into families using the private school sector. Her research demonstrates the ways in which all the capitals are interwoven in the transfer of privilege – economic capital augmenting social capital; emotional capital compounding cultural capital, etc. She defines emotional capital as 'emotionally valued assets and skills, love and affection, expenditure of time, attention, care and concern'. She found that all these aspects of emotional capital:

> were evident in these families, particularly in the way mothers devoted their skills gained from their formal education to the advancement of their children. (Allatt, 1993: 143)

So again Allatt is conceptualizing emotional capital as gendered.

I also utilize the concept of emotional capital in my research into mothers' involvement in their children's primary schooling. Across my sample, one of the few constants was mothers' emotional involvement in their children's education. Within Nowotny's conceptualization it is only positive emotions that generate profits for families. However, women experience a whole gamut of emotions in relation to their children's schooling. Guilt, anxiety and frustration, as well as empathy and encouragement were the primary motifs of mothers' involvement, while children displayed recalcitrance just as often as enthusiasm. Despite substantial areas of overlap, emotional involvement is not coterminous with emotional capital.

In my own research I found myself constantly engaged in a process of separating out emotional involvement from emotional capital. It became very clear that emotional involvement did not necessarily generate emotional capital and that there was no simple correlation between positive emotions and emotional capital. Many of the emotions that mothers felt and communicated to children in the course of supporting their education could have both positive and negative efficacy. Anger could communicate to children that the mother had clear expectations about educational performance which she would back up with sanctions. But it could result in resistance, non-compliance and the breakdown of communication. Similarly, anxiety could produce an intense involvement in children's schooling which generated educational progress. At the same time, it could result in the child becoming anxious along with the mother. So, the data showed that negative emotions were not necessarily counterproductive. As Lucy told me:

> I sat Sophie down and told her I had had enough. I was thoroughly fed up with her. I said she'd better buck her ideas up or she'll never get through any entrance exam. She'd got far too complacent, you know just coasting along, anyway it seemed to do the trick.

My research also indicated a very thin dividing line between understanding and empathy, and over-identification. Many mothers talked very poignantly of their concern at their children's distress. However, while it was natural for mothers to share in children's feelings of anxiety and unhappiness, as Josie's account demonstrates, if they became too heavily involved in children's distressed feelings, they often found themselves unable to provide appropriate support and having to deal with a welter of negative feelings. In the rest of the chapter I examine the many different aspects of mothers' involvement. However, all those different aspects need to be understood in terms of the emotions, both positive and negative, that infuse mothers' activities.

Mothers' Educational Work: The Monitoring–Repair Sequence

Dorothy Smith and Alison Griffith in their ethnographic study of mothers and schooling describe a practice they have termed the monitoring–repair sequence (Smith, 1988; Griffith and Smith, 1990). It is a two-stage process; first, the mother identifies a problem in her child's educational work; she then takes action in order to rectify it by involving the child in additional educational work in the home (Griffith and Smith, 1990: 11). Smith defines the monitoring–repair sequence as a process:

> starting with a mother deciding that work the child has brought home from school is not up to standard in some way, and proceeding to initiate some course of action with the child to remedy it. (Smith 1988: 191)

Within my own research I have utilized the concept of the monitoring–repair sequence and broadened its application to maternal intervention in the school site as well as in the home (see Chapter 7). It appears from my research that at the repair stage mothers are faced with two options: they can either attempt to rectify their child's educational difficulties in the home in the range of different ways that Griffith and Smith elaborate; or, they can try and get the school to modify their child's curriculum offer and so tackle their child's learning at a school-site level. However, in both variants what underpins the monitoring–repair sequence is mothers taking the initiative.

All the mothers I interviewed were involved in monitoring their child's educational performance.There is evidence of enormous amounts of maternal monitoring of children's educational performance, particularly in Oak Park, but of varying degrees of success in the repair sequence. This seems to be related to cultural capital. Success depended on how confident and competent mothers felt in attempting the repair process. However, a further influence is the mothers' conceptualizations of where the responsibility lies. If they see responsibility as lying with the school, then there is huge variability in whether they can get school personnel to meet their child's educational needs. If they accept responsibility themselves, there seems to be a greater likelihood of success. Leena in Oak Park decided she would not expend time and energy trying to persuade school personnel to modify her daughter's curriculum offer. Instead she focused her time and energy on teaching Negar every evening after school. However, Lelia in Milner successfully used an amalgam of the two, getting her child into an advanced writing group at school and employing a maths tutor at home.

Monitoring through Children's Accounts

Mothers had to work hard to obtain information about school work from their children. Most children did not spontaneously volunteer information about their school day. Dauber and Epstein report similar findings when they interviewed parents whose children attended inner-city middle schools in Baltimore. Of those interviewed, 55 per cent of parents felt that their children did not really enjoy discussions about what they did in school (Dauber and Epstein, 1993). A focus on the language mothers used indicates that monitoring is no straightforward, effortless process, but one that requires both time and labour. Both Leena and Lisa talk in terms of 'worming' information out of their children. Carol has to drag information about school out of Stuart, while Lucy tells me 'I have to extract information from her'. Even on the occasions when children do volunteer information it is not necessarily what mothers want to hear:

> When they tell me what's happened I don't always know whether it's the truth or what they think I want to hear. Lani will say 'I've done loads of maths work and I got them all right' and I don't necessarily know that she has and Shula will say 'Oh I didn't do anything'. So between the two of them I'm often totally confused about what's going on. (Cathy, Milner)

One glaring example of the way in which cultural capital permeates even this process can be read in one middle-class mother's description of collecting her children from school:

> I try and make sure that at least twice a week I take my children out to tea somewhere relaxed and leisurely where we can all chat about our day. I've always worked on the principle of taking my children somewhere nice for tea, for socializing since they were little, that's always been the way I have made space for them to tell me about what's happening to them. (Linsey, Oak Park)

Monitoring for Linsey is a process which involves, time, money and emotional energy. Although other mothers did not talk in terms of monitoring in a context which involved financial expenditure, they too were working hard at finding out about their child's school day:

> I want to find out what he has actually done in the class. It's generally more to do with his friends what he talks about, but this year it's been easier. He's actually had quite an interesting curriculum and he's been very willing to talk about the work he's been doing, Shakespeare, poetry, things like that. He has been really fascinated by the poetry, very keen to talk about it. I suppose that's new. Usually I have to drag it out of him what he's been doing in the classroom. (Linda, Milner)

Ethical issues around respecting a child's right for autonomy and personal space were raised in some mothers' accounts. Jill, Joyce and Carla all stressed children's entitlement to privacy, underlining the way in which it conflicts with mothers' desire to know about the school day:

> It's very difficult getting a balance between letting them have their own separate space and making sure you know enough to be sure they are alright. You need to have your finger on the pulse just in case there is a problem. But then I get this feeling from Lilly 'Keep away' and I think oh, it's none of my business. (Carla, Milner)

Maintaining a balance between needing to know in case there was a problem and respecting some children's designation of school as a sphere separate from the home became a difficult juggling act for a number of mothers. Mothers such as Leena, Laura, Lisa, Carol, Lucy and Lavinia all employed a degree of coercion, as is evident in their use of language, setting up situations of potential conflict between themselves and their child by insisting they provide information about the school day whether the child wanted to or not. However, it seems unlikely that information extracted from an unwilling child will be very reliable:

> Her school life is her school life. They are very separate. We have never got information from her. Even today you have to drag it out of her. I mean you have to ask and ask, then ask again to get her to tell you, to get her to answer a question you have asked. It is a very separate experience that she has. She has always kept it very separate. (Lavinia, Oak Park)

Monitoring through children's accounts clearly has the potential for generating tensions and stresses in the mother/child relationship and activating resistance in the child. Laura discussed Robert's resentment at what he considered to be an unwarranted intrusion, and the resulting reluctance with which he disclosed information:

He goes into go-slow mode, you know, it takes him five minutes to say five words. (Laura, Oak Park)

Linsey was the one mother who claimed monitoring was an easy, pleasurable process. However her formula, which involved converting her monitoring work into fun for the family by pretending she was not really monitoring at all, was costly in terms of her time, finances and emotional energy.

Other Ways of Monitoring

Dependence on what the child was prepared to tell you was not a feature of all the mothers' accounts. Jenny, who displayed a lot of confidence in relation to schooling, ensured she had regular feedback from the teacher on Andreas' progress:

I'll try and talk to his teacher regularly and look at his work. If I'm not happy I'll ask a question. I'll make sure I do it, not every day but at least once a week.

She also monitored through Andreas' self-initiated activities in the home:

I do try and check up at home. This weekend he was doing some writing and needed some words and I said to him 'Go and get the dictionary, see if you can find the word and then show it to me'. I help him a lot with his writing at home so I know he's a good writer but he doesn't really know how to use a dictionary. He had no idea until I showed him. (Jenny, Milner)

Other mothers also made evaluations of their children's learning, which were independent of school, either drawing on their own educational experiences or using older siblings as a standard to monitor against:

I've noticed when I'm having a conversation with Leigh about something he's watched on television that he doesn't understand as well as Terry so I'll have to explain a little bit more to him. He needs to be made more aware than Terry did. I don't think it's a mental block, it's just that he needs a bit more explaining than Terry did because when he's trying to explain something to me he goes all round the houses. I'll be listening to him and I'll think it took him half an hour to tell me this and I could have said it in five minutes. (Josie, Milner)

A further way of monitoring, used by a number of mothers, particularly in Oak Park, was by comparison with other children in the peer group.

Sometimes mothers were reassured:

> Carly lives next door and sometimes they'll read together and I know from that that Carly isn't as good a reader as Fola is, so she can't be that bad. (Carmel, Milner)

But usually, the process is anxiety-inducing. Mothers seem to recall far more occasions when their child is not doing as well as other children.

Josie spent a long time in the interview trying to make sense of why Liam, the son of a friend, was doing better than her own child when his mother 'had not made any effort':

> We are talking two single parents on the dole, Tilly's not exactly put herself out. Then I think of all the effort I've put in and my two haven't exactly turned out bright.

Most of the mothers of daughters whom I interviewed in Oak Park made invidious comparisons between their own child and a close-knit group of clever girls in 5S called 'the gang of 4':

> In terms of her class Sophia is not in the top half because I see what the other children take home and plus Sophia is very sociable with the other children so there's a lot of stopping over. When she was in Year 3, her teacher said she could be up with those girls, I think they are called the gang. The very bright ones, who sit near the front. She could easily be absorbed into the gang and push herself academically, but she hasn't. She's been quite happy to be just behind them. (Linsey, Oak Park)

Linsey's words do not highlight the problematic aspects of making comparisons within the peer group, but Lavinia's do:

> I know I mustn't compare, but we often take Oliver home and when it comes to his reading and writing ability he's much much better than Riva. We took him on holiday with us and he came with all these books in his bags – history books. He was reading them in the car, so perhaps on a daily level, unconsciously, I'm making these comparisons. I look at the way he writes and the way he reads. You see consciously I'm saying I mustn't compare but it comes out. I need to remember she's got her own strengths and weaknesses.

The pressure to excel in Oak Park meant both mothers and their children sought to find out not only the child's attainment level, but how it compared with the rest of the peer group.

All the mothers were involved in monitoring their children's educational performance. Information was obtained either through children's own accounts, comparison with the peer group or older siblings, obtaining feed-back from classteachers or by assessing children's educational activities in the home. Monitoring was rarely a straightforward, easy process, often inducing anxiety and sometimes conflict between mother and child.

Monitoring in the Classroom

In the next chapter I discuss how helping out in the classroom provided those mothers who volunteered with the opportunities for drawing on teachers' expertize and the extent to which they seized these opportunities. In the following section I explore more generally how mothers used time in the classroom to monitor in a variety of ways. Janice, Lavinia and Louise were all volunteering in the classroom over the course of my fieldwork, while Lucy came to help at three of the computer club sessions held at Oak Park. In addition, Jenny, who had worked as a helper in Milner, discussed how her job had provided her with valuable information about how teaching and learning is organized in the school:

> I couldn't see the sense of all that lining up at the teacher's desk. It was wasting the children's time. I told Andreas he should give his work to the teacher at the end of the lesson, that it's best to get on with something else rather than lining up.

Volunteering was responded to very differently in the two schools.

In Oak Park Liz told me that the Headteacher frowned on parents working in the classroom. However, Miss Richards, the Head, gave a slightly different version. She said that parents 'could be very competitive and preoccupied with their own children's academic performance'. This meant arrangements were usually made for them to work in a classroom other than their own child's. Consequently Lavinia was working with a different year group to her daughter's, and Louise was helping out with the parallel Year 5 class. In Milner, where parents were not viewed as such a threat, volunteering was dealt with differently. Janice helped out in both her children's classrooms. She told me:

> I've been really lucky because I've had the opportunity to go into school and observe how they are teaching. I've been able to get involved and learn by watching how they teach. I think it's helped with the children. They seem to tell me more because they feel I know what they're talking about.

Imbuing Janice's words are a sense of herself as the novice and the teacher as expert. Maxine, the class teacher, said 'It's great having Janice in the classroom, she's really helpful, never any bother'.

I discuss later how teachers have the power to reduce mothers to the status of children. From both Maxine and Janice's accounts, Janice's presence in the classroom has far more in common with that of 'the good helpful female pupil' than the equal of the teacher. It seems unlikely that the majority of middle-class mothers at Oak Park would accept such a construction of themselves. During the time I spent there I regularly helped out at computer club. For the first few sessions Lucy came along to help as well. At the second session, after working for a prolonged period with her own daughter and another girl on Logo, she went across the room to talk to Mrs Symmonds:

> Do you think they understand the geometric concepts underlying the work they're doing? I would have thought it was really important to ensure they do a lot of back-up geometry in the classroom.

While Janice assumes an apprenticeship role in the classroom, Lucy is much more directive. She seems to be involved in a process not only of monitoring Sophie's competence in computing but also of monitoring Mrs Symmond's competence as a teacher.

Annette Lareau describes how some middle-class mothers used their time in the classroom to examine their child's work and that of their classmates to see how they compared (Lareau, 1989: 179). However, Louise and Lavinia were not given the opportunity at Oak Park, and Janice at Milner clearly had not considered such a course of action. When, after she had described her times in the classroom, I asked her if she ever got to see Gemma's work, she looked nonplussed and told me:

> Oh, I'm not there when they do their Maths and writing. I help with reading time and then the children do art and craft activities so I don't see Gemma's work as such because I'm not there when they do their English and Maths work.

While Lucy adopts a powerful, surveillant role in relation to the teacher, Janice neither presents a challenge to the teacher nor attempts to influence the learning in the classroom.

Repairing Children's Educational Gaps

Mothers differed widely in respect of the strategies they utilized to make good any learning deficits they found. Repairing was common practice in Oak Park. While women's time was a scarce commodity for many of the mothers due to paid work, money was less so. Most mothers could afford to substitute paid tutoring for their own labour. Middle-class mothers in both schools were far more likely to talk in terms of a range of possibilities of which trying to get the school curriculum modified was only one. By contrast, if monitoring was hard work for the working-class mothers, repairing was doubly so. For many of them the monitoring–repair sequence broke down at the repair stage for a variety of reasons. The most vividly articulated reason lay in mothers' explanations of why they felt they lacked the educational competence to undertake academic work with their child. For mothers like Josie and Jalil, who both moved from their country of origin to England as children, the monitoring–repair sequence is fraught with the pitfalls, dangers and misunderstandings they encountered in their own education. As Gewirtz *et al.* point out, their cultural capital is in the wrong currency (Gewirtz *et al.*, 1994a):

> I have ended up screaming and shouting and we've had bad rows about it. I'd have put him off altogether so I've had to back off and let the school take it on. I'm the wrong person to teach him because of the emotional state I get into. (Josie, Milner)

Working-class mothers who feel ill-equipped to engage in repair work in the home and lack financial resources are reliant on the school to get the job done. I discuss in detail in Chapter 7 how cultural capital is implicated in maternal practices which involved attempting to get the school to modify the child's curriculum offer. However, it is important to point out that such practices signified very differently for mothers like Josie and Jalil and for middle-class mothers, even those who were also immigrants to Britain. Here we see the influence of working-class habitus. For Josie, in particular, the school had come to be perceived as 'the last and only resort'. Her personal history of immigration, working-class background and academic failure resulted in a sense that there were no other options:

> When I went to see his teacher I was pretty upset about Leigh not reading and it may have come across like 'how come Leigh's not reading. If you aren't hearing him read what are you doing then?' I was maybe coming across like that but what I meant was can he possibly have some extra time. Can someone hear [*sic*], for God's sake, give him some extra reading and let him get on because it's making my life harder. I was getting so anxious about him not reading cos I couldn't really help him. I'd get upset and frustrated and it wasn't doing Leigh any good because if he can't read what was happening. (Josie, Milner)

There is no need for me to explicate the subtext of inequity lurking beneath Josie's words, because Josie goes on to provide her own cogent summation of how increasing reliance on parental involvement within the British educational system is perpetuating educational inequalities:

> You need parental involvement. You need parents to be able to
> complement what you're doing but that's all it should be. It shouldn't
> be any more. You see not all people speak English, not all parents
> read and write so how can they help their children at home. They're
> at a disadvantage anyway so when they come to school they've got to
> have the help there. You should just be able to say to the teacher
> 'Look, I can't do it. You're qualified, can you do something about it?'
> without the teacher getting all upset about it. There's a lot of parents
> who can't, just can't do it.

Other mothers also resisted a construction of themselves as their children's
teachers. This ambivalence about assuming a teaching role was rooted in
mothers' differential access to dominant cultural capital. It was related to a
variety of factors; mothers' own negative experiences of schooling, feelings
that they lacked educational competencies, the refusal of some children to see
mothers as educational experts and the amount of time mothers had available
to undertake educational work with children.

Repairing children's perceived educational deficits was an easier process if
mothers had access to material and cultural resources. There was a strong class
difference in which middle-class mothers had access to a range of resources
which made repair work far less onerous than it was for working-class women.

Consequences for the Mother/Child Relationship

Training, including a degree of compulsion, is intrinsic to mothering (Ruddick,
1989). However, the tensions, which frequently emerge in all aspects of mothers' training of children, are exacerbated when mothers attempt educational
work with their children in the home. First, many of the working-class mothers' own negative experiences of schooling preclude any easy assumption of
the teacher role. Secondly, mothers' own desire to protect their relationship
with their child may mitigate against them persisting with educational work to
which their child does not readily assent. Thirdly, a number of both working-
and middle-class children resist any designation of their mother as an educational expert. As I outline later, this resistance was gendered. It was primarily
boys across class boundaries who were challenging their mothers' assumption
of a teaching role.

A majority of mothers raised the detrimental impact of undertaking
educational work with children in the home. Cathy told me 'I find it particularly
difficult with Shula because she's having problems with her reading. You can
get into a battle situation'. Lavinia and Lucy both talked of screaming at their
daughters, while Liliana and Josie described yelling at their sons. Christine,
Carmel, Jenny, Julie, Liz, Laura, Linda and Carol all mentioned their child's
recalcitrance in the face of maternal demands to do homework. However, it
was two working-class mothers, Joyce and Jill in Milner, who most clearly

elucidated the negative consequences for the mother/child relationship of undertaking educational work in the home. Both work with a conception of what constitutes the 'proper' mother/child relationship which stresses positive, non-coercive interaction, and views the assumption of a teacher role as a threat to harmony. For Jill, preserving the sanctity of the maternal role precludes her taking on a teaching role in the home, unless her daughter readily assents:

> I don't want to get into forcing her to do anything. I think your role as a mother is to encourage and help, not to force. I don't think it's for you to get upset and upset your child over schoolwork.

Similarly, the internal conflict between feeling responsible for her daughter's educational performance and a competing desire to protect the mother/child relationship surfaces in Joyce's words:

> I think I'd like to help her more but sometimes I worry about inter-fering too much. You can sit them down and say 'I think you should sit here and do this' and they say 'Why? I've been at school all day. I've learnt at school', I would love to say to her 'Let's sit down and do this.' but I don't want to force her. I don't want to pump her with education. If she wasn't doing so well I'd probably make her stay in and work regularly, but then again I don't know if that would be the right answer because would she hate me. If I'm keeping her in doing Maths would she start to hate me, you don't really know.

As I shall expand on later, most of the middle-class mothers were working with a very different construction of maternal intervention, which prioritized aca-demic achievement over individual volition.

Activating the repair part of the monitoring–repair sequence can also be problematic for reasons beyond those of the mothers' own doubts and insecu-rities. Jenny is engaged in a regular programme of supporting her son's aca-demic work, premised on her own perceptions of the educational level at which he should be working. She regularly monitors Andreas' work and inter-venes when she decides that he needs extra support. Although he is seen by the school as an able child, she identifies areas around grammar, punctuation and maths, where she feels he needs to improve. However, her efforts to implement a repair process are undermined by Andreas' refusal to acknowl-edge her as an educational expert:

> I have read through Andreas' work and there are no full stops. The only dots are on top of the i. I have tried to explain to him that you need to punctuate your work but he just says 'No, you've done it wrong because my teacher doesn't say anything, so you're wrong'. So what can you do? I think it's difficult saying you know better than the teacher. What can I do? Maxine knows and Maxine's the teacher so

> I am the one with the problem – that's the way it is with Andreas, his
> mum's the one who's wrong.

Jenny's intervention is proving problematic in so far as it brings her into
conflict with Andreas, who challenges her standards on the basis that they are
not those of the school.

The three middle-class mothers, Lavinia, Lucy and Lisa all mentioned their
daughters' 'tears', 'tantrums' or 'sulks' in response to repair work they had
initiated. Lucy told me that Sophie refused to speak to her for the rest of the
day after Lucy had told her that she could no longer attend computer club
because she needed to devote more time to Maths and literacy work. Many of
the mothers in both schools mentioned children's resistance to repair work.
Christine talked about how she had 'to battle with Matthew' to get him to do
his tutor homework. Sophie was engaging in a different form of resistance; one
of 'opting out'. Lucy told me anxiously 'I'm worried that she's just stopped
trying'. Although both boys and girls were resisting, to an extent compliance
with repair work was gendered. Girls' resistance, as in the cases of Riva,
Melinda and Sophie was episodic and intermittent. It was primarily boys who
were putting up a fight on a regular basis. Across class boundaries, Sergei,
Matthew, George, Andreas, Robert and Martin were all, in different ways,
engaging in an ongoing process of resisting 'the mother as teacher'. This
gender-differentiated response to mothers assuming a role as teacher was
almost as pronounced in middle-class as in working-class families. However,
there were class differences in the ways in which mothers responded to their
sons' recalcitrance. Working-class mothers, possibly because of their lower
feelings of confidence about educational matters, were far more likely to
reduce educational demands, while middle-class mothers persisted with theirs.

To conclude this section on the monitoring–repair sequence – in spite of
the many difficulties I have described, all the mothers attempted to monitor
their child's educational progress and many intervened when they identified a
problem. Intervention takes many forms. Mothers may attempt to repair
directly, they may try to get the school to modify the curriculum offer or they
may, like many of the Oak Park mothers, engage a tutor. Cultural capital is
most clearly visible in mothers' ability, or lack of ability, to choose between a
range of different practices in implementing the monitoring–repair sequence.
Mothers, like Jalil and Josie, bring to the contemporary educational field a
habitus structured by their experience as recently-arrived immigrants in a
strange educational system they have never really made sense of. Their bilin-
gualism clearly influenced this process (Corson, 1993). The consequences in
the present are that they feel inadequate to the task of undertaking repair
work themselves, lack the financial resources to pay someone else to do it and
feel desperate about the resultant dependence on the school. However, as I
discuss in more detail in Chapter 7, Jalil's social network has given her access
to a repair sequence which does not depend either on her own educational
resources or mainstream education:

I said to the teacher who runs the Saturday school that I'm concerned about Chantelle's reading, so they are going to work on that with her.

In working-class Milner, class is mediated by 'race'. Black mothers have access to an organized system of support for their children's education in the shape of Black Saturday schools and Black parents' groups.

'Complementors, Compensators and Modifiers': Cultural Capital and Mothers' Relationships to Schooling

I only found one direct reference to mothers' role in generating cultural capital in Bourdieu's work. In 'The Forms of Capital' Bourdieu writes:

> It is because the cultural capital that is effectively transmitted within the family itself depends not only on the quantity of cultural capital, itself accumulated by spending time, that the domestic group possess, but also on the usable time (particularly in the form of mother's free time) available to it. (Bourdieu, 1986: 253)

Here we have a recognition of the pivotal role mothers play in the generation of cultural capital. It is mothers' time that accrues profits. However, once mothers' time is harnessed to the acquisition of cultural capital, it is no longer free time. It becomes mothers' work time. Furthermore, while recognizing the importance of mothers' role, Bourdieu hints at, but fails to make explicit, the complexities of contemporary women's lives. It is more than an issue of time. In my study, some women on benefit had time on their hands, while a number of privileged women claimed to have 'no time'. Time can be, and, increasingly, is being bought by middle-class women with busy professional careers to pursue. As Bryan Adams suggests, it is not so much that time is money rather money is time (Adams, 1990). Time has little value if it is unsupported by resources. As Scott Lash and John Urry point out, 'time varies as to the differential possession of money, as well as to differentials of status and power' (Lash and Urry, 1993: 226–7). Women need to feel confident about tackling educational work in the home and to have access to material resources to support such work. Without these other essential ingredients of cultural capital, I found that in my study mothers' time did not count to anything like the same extent.

Most mothers conceptualized their relationship to schooling as one of complementing the education their children received. Working-class mothers like Jackie, Janice, Jane and Joyce in Milner, as well as Lesley, a middle-class mother in Oak Park, talked in terms of 'supporting the school' and 'backing the teacher up' to describe their relationship to schooling. However, a further group, in particular Leena and Lucy, saw their role as a compensatory one.

Annette Lareau uses the term in relation to her middle-class parents (Lareau, 1989: 169). Other mothers, primarily Josie in Milner and Liz in Oak Park, spoke about their efforts to modify the school provision. These three roles were by no means mutually exclusive. Middle-class mothers like Laura, Louise, Lucinda and Linsey moved in and out of different positions with regard to schooling. Laura's preferred practice was to complement her son's learning in the classroom, but she reluctantly compensated when she identified a need and at times intervened on the school site in order to try and modify the school's offer in her son's favour.

This weaving in and out of different roles was common in Oak Park where the combination of relative affluence, educational expertize and 'self-certainty' (Bourdieu, 1984: 66) gave mothers options most of the Milner mothers did not have. Middle-class mothers such as Lisa, Louise, Liz and Linsey compensated for what they perceived to be gaps in the state provision through the employment of tutors, as well as attempting to modify the provision the school makes for their child, all the while continuing to complement the school site offer through mothering work in the home. Liz elaborates two of those strategies very clearly:

> One is the support I give him at home, hearing him read, making him read every night, doing homework with him, trying to get the books he needs for his project. I see that as a support role. The other side, in the particular case of Martin, is where he has had difficulties and finds reading very, very difficult. So a lot of my time has been spent fighting for extra support for him and I mean fighting.

However, later on in the interview she discusses the tuition Martin receives:

> Well he just wasn't making enough progress in school so we decided we'd have to get him a tutor.

Linsey's account provides an example of how a developing sense of dissatisfaction has led to a move over time from complementing to broadening her interventions to include modifying, and compensating for, the school curriculum offer:

> I think I had too much faith in the system at the beginning that the system would educate my child. I feel ideally my role is to make sure they get the right education. It's really very important. In addition to that, because I know ideally what I would like, I have to fill in the gaps.

Below I explore in more detail compensating, modifying and complementing as maternal strategies.

Compensating

Although only Cathy, Jalil and Christine at Milner and Lucy and Leena in Oak Park used the term 'compensate' to describe their relationship to schooling, a majority of middle-class mothers compensated through the use of paid tuition. Similarly, six of the seven black mothers in Milner compensated for a perceived lack of basic skills work and the absence of a black perspective in the curriculum by sending their children to Black Saturday school. Leena at Oak Park not only employed a tutor for Negar and sent her to an Islamic Saturday school, but she saw her own role as pivotal in her daughter's education:

> Education starts at home, starts from her time after school actually. She's in her fifth year and I feel she has to do some serious work at home because she hasn't actually covered a lot of the stuff at school. I find I'm having to compensate despite the fact that according to the school she is doing quite well.

Four times over the course of the interview she uses the term 'compensate' to explain her rationale for the educational work she is carrying out in the home.

Lucy claimed that Sophie's educational attainment was the result of the provision she provided, both personally and through the employment of tutors, rather than anything emanating from the school:

> I have manufactured Sophie's educational success. Ask the school. Before I was made redundant Sophie was seen as an average ability pupil. Since I've been at home she has improved by leaps and bounds. That's down to me not the school.

Jalil told me:

> I know I have to make up for what she's missing out in school. I'm doing that now. I just wish I'd known how far behind she'd got earlier.

Complementing

By contrast, the majority of mothers in Milner positioned themselves as supporters in relation to their child's schooling. Jasbir told me 'I try and do what Sharoff's teacher asks', while Jackie said 'They expect you to hear your child read so we'll do that two or three times a week'. Carmel said 'They don't bring a lot of work home. There's the spellings and times tables you need to go over with them'. However, a focus simply on what mothers are doing does not tell the whole story. Conscientiously responding to school demands to support the curriculum translated into very different courses of action in the two schools. In the last chapter I discussed different components of institutional habitus, including the educational status of a school, its curriculum offer, teaching practices and teachers' expectations. The different institutional habituses of the two schools meant that the demands Milner made of parents added up to far less of mothers' time and energy than corresponding demands made of parents at Oak Park. Complementing in Oak Park was of a totally different scale to supporting the curriculum in Milner. There was regular homework three or four times a week, in addition to the spelling and dictionary work children were expected to undertake at home. Even so, few of the Oak Park mothers were content with simply complementing the school curriculum, preferring to draw on a mixture of all three strategies. The two mothers, Lesley and Jean, who were insistent that their role was one of simply supporting the school, still talked in terms of an hour a night being taken up with school issues:

> I do what I can. I find I'm regularly spending an hour going over things with her. They do seem to get an awful lot of homework. Like I said sometimes she'll be up until eleven at night . . . I can't spend all that time with her. I've got my own work to get on with but I do go over it with her. Last term she had to do a folder on explorers and encounters. I did help with that, embroidering the ships and putting together a collection of Roman coins. She spent ages on it. (Jean, Oak Park)

The messages mothers received about the educational support required to support the classroom curriculum differed enormously between the two schools.

'Providing the Trimmings'

Cultural capital played a crucial role in the extent to which mothers could provide their child with what Lelia defines as 'the trimmings':

> School is there to take the main responsibility for her learning and we provide the trimmings. (Lelia, Milner)

Many of the Milner mothers expressed the same sentiments:

> I expect them to teach her reading, writing and the basics of Maths. I mean I don't mind coming home and going over it with her but I expect them to do the foundation work. (Janice, Milner)

Only Lelia at Milner, who in spite of her self-designation as 'a complementor' of the educational system, was able to draw on the cultural capital to weave, seemingly effortlessly, between complementing, compensating for, and modifying her child's school-site provision. Naomi had had a Maths tutor for over two years. Lelia's intervention on the school site had resulted in Naomi's inclusion in a gifted writer's group, while Lelia read with Naomi every evening and actively supported the school's curriculum offer in other ways. Even in her account the assumption of ease and effortlessness are only on the surface. It becomes apparent that Naomi's current designation by the school as 'very bright' has been worked for:

> I see the parents' role as supporting the child's learning, but in a way that's fun. We used to be desperately earnest about it once, but we're much more relaxed now.

Other Milner mothers found assuming a range of strategies in relation to their children's schooling a much more conflictual process. Julie, whose interview displays her intense involvement in her children's education, attempts all three strategies, but with varying degrees of success. She proudly reveals how she persuaded the school to modify the curriculum provision:

> I've had them all into extra reading lessons actually because I think it's so important that they all learn to read early, with the school that is. Even Androulla had extra reading lessons because when she was six, I didn't think she was making enough progress. She didn't seem to be reading as good as she should be so I went to see her teacher. She was put in a reading group and she picked up straight away, it was fantastic, really fantastic. You could see the difference after a month or two. The same with Christina actually. She got extra reading in the infants and she picked up really quick as well. I went into school and because it made so much difference with Androulla's reading she was put in a group straight away.

However, Julie found compensating a much more difficult proposition, first, because of her lack of material resources and, secondly, because she found her compensatory role at odds with her understandings of what 'people like us should be doing' (Bourdieu, 1990a: 56):

> I shouldn't have to teach them, it's not my job. I did have a tutor but it was too expensive. It was taking up all my spare money. It got to the stage where it was either trainers for George or the tutor so we had to stop.

Much of Julie's account expresses the tension between feeling a compensatory role was required and not having the resources to provide it. Cultural capital was implicated in these mothers' ability to draw on a range of strategies in support their children's schooling. Financial resources, confidence in relation to the educational system, educational knowledge and information about schooling, all had a bearing on the extent to which mothers felt empowered to intervene in their child's educational trajectory and the confidence with which they embarked on such action. For Josie, whose account stresses over and over again the importance of education, her personal feelings of incompetence and lack of confidence mitigated against her embarking on any action with a sense of efficacy:

> I have tried, I really have. I knew I should be playing a role in getting Leigh to read but I wasn't qualified. Therefore it put extra pressure on me because I was no good at reading myself, it was too important for me to handle and I'd get very upset and angry at Leigh.

Attempting to modify the school's offer also had unpredictable and upsetting consequences:

> I always found if I went to the classteacher, she'd take it very personal and think I was attacking her. I wasn't. I was just bringing it to her attention in case she didn't know, you know, that in my opinion he's not progressing. The way I see him and from what I expect of him I don't see the progress. But I'd say 'I'm not saying that it's because you're not teaching my son. I do realise you have a class of 30 and you're only one person and you do so much and you're expected to do a lot of other things because the National Curriculum expects so much of you. I do understand about that. But what can I do about his reading?' But when I did go to the classteachers I think they took it too personal and felt I was attacking them when really it was that it is so important I couldn't let it go.

There are clearly articulated tensions in the accounts of mothers like Josie and Julie. They both feel inadequate to the task of compensating for what they perceive to be gaps in their children's educational provision. Josie, who attempts a different strategy of trying to get the staff to modify her child's curriculum offer, is only partially successful because the teachers view her as 'aggressive and over-emotional'. In contrast, the relative affluence of Oak Park mothers meant they had choices which were not available to Josie and Julie, choices which were productive of cultural capital. Most of the Oak Park mothers could range between all three strategies, compensating through the employment of tutors, at the same time successfully modifying the provision the school made for their child, while continuing confidently to complement the school offer through their mothering work in the home.

Conclusion

Women across the sample, regardless of class and 'race', were all involved in practical maintenance, emotional and educational work in support of their children's schooling. However, when cultural capital and habitus are used as conceptual tools to focus on what mothers are doing, the complexities of influences of social class and 'race' on the options available to mothers become much more apparent. Material resources, educational knowledge, women's own educational experiences and the amount of domestic and educational support mothers had access to all impacted on their relationships to children's schooling. Paradoxically, whilst mothers' work complementing the school curriculum appears to be the activity which is coterminous with continuity in schooling, it is modifying and compensating that require the greater cultural capital and generate the most profit. Both entail mothers taking the initiative, while complementing could simply be a process of responding to school requests.

Additionally, complementing means very different things in different educational contexts. As I have outlined earlier, responding to school requests in working-class Milner meant engaging in a fraction of the home-based educational work expected from Oak Park children and their parents. In a process paralleling that uncovered by research into class-specific expectations of pupils (Clarricoates, 1980; Brown, 1987; Haertel, 1987; Grant and Sleeter, 1988; Epstein, 1992), educational institutions seem to have widely differing expectations of children's parents, which are based on social class (Johnson and Ransom, 1983; Ashenden *et al.*, 1987; Wolpe, 1988; Holden *et al.*, 1994). In the next chapter differing expectations on the part both of teachers and mothers, and the interactions they generate, are explored in more depth through mothers' accounts of their contact with their children's teachers.

Chapter 7

'Just Talking to the Teacher?'

Talking to teachers is an important part of home–school relationships and yet research into parental involvement rarely includes any discussion of the vast range of communication between parents and their children's teachers. In this chapter the main focus is on oral communication between mothers and teachers, although I also analyze written communication sent from home into the two schools. It is in linguistic interaction that existing power dynamics between mothers and teachers become most apparent. Everyday communication between teachers and mothers is shaped by the differential social power that individuals bring to their interactions. Differences of social class make a difference both to how mothers communicate with their children's teachers and the ways in which their words are received.

Going into School: Mother-Initiated Contact

Making contact with teachers was a regular feature of maternal involvement across the sample and both groups of mothers initiated contact with teachers. There were, however, apparent social class differences. Contrary to Lareau's findings these differences did not lie in the reasons for making contact (Lareau, 1989). The working-class mothers I interviewed were just as likely to raise issues around academic matters as middle-class mothers. Unlike Lareau's working-class sample, who only came into school to discuss 'the peripherals' (Lareau, 1989: 58), they came into school just as often as middle-class mothers to engage in a dialogue about their child's academic work. Even so, cultural capital was the key to all dimensions of the process of contacting and communicating with teachers. Both social and cultural capital played a crucial role; knowing how to approach, present, mount a case, maintain pressure and make an impact all counted (Gewirtz et al., 1995). In Oak Park far more criticisms were communicated to teachers and they were delivered with a sense of certainty and entitlement missing from working-class women's accounts. When middle-class mothers came into school they were more likely than working-class mothers to make requests. Although some of the working-class mothers also made requests, middle-class women often asked for more than their working-class counterparts. As a consequence, a higher level of demand was made on the teaching staff in Oak Park than in Milner.

Mothers in both schools regularly chatted to classteachers as part of their monitoring work. Such contact, which was primarily to gather information, was far more likely to have a successful outcome than, for example, visits to ask for changes in a child's curriculum offer. The resource implications of the latter requests often proved a barrier to mothers achieving their objectives. Even so, a majority of mothers talked in terms of approaching a teacher with the aim of getting the school to take some sort of action. Twelve out of the 20 mothers at Milner reported such contact with the school over the period of my field work. In Oak Park, 10 out of 13 mothers had similarly initiated contact. However, there were far more complex issues enmeshed in the relationship between cultural capital and mother-initiated contact of this type than simply counting the number of visits. For some mothers making contact with teachers constituted an enormous psychological effort on their part, while for others it was much more a process of 'doing what comes naturally' (Bourdieu, 1990a). I would dispute that it was effortless for any of the women. All 22 mothers, regardless of social class, expended time and energy in initiating contact. For working-class women, in particular, it was the most stressful part of their mothering work in support of their child's education. Working-class women talked in terms of 'plucking up courage' and 'making myself go and see the teacher'.

The frequency of further contact depended on whether there was a successful resolution to an initial visit. Jackie had only to initiate one contact with Carly's classteacher to ensure her inclusion in a reading support group, while Liz was still trying, after five visits, to persuade the teachers at Oak Park to provide Martin with more remedial reading support. Consequently, she went on contacting the school on a regular basis in her attempt to achieve this goal. Failure to achieve objectives could lead to increased persistence, as in Liz's case. It could also lead to the adoption of a different strategy, as in the case of Leena who decided to teach her child at home rather than try and get the school staff to modify the curriculum.

Class does seem to have significant effects and appears to be linked to aspects of cultural capital such as confidence, information about available educational provision, assertiveness and a sense of entitlement. Middle-class Laura, Liz and Liliana had all managed to secure one-to-one special needs support for their sons. Liz and Liliana were fighting to obtain more of this scarce resource. In Milner, Jalil, Cathy and Josie also had children who were struggling with their reading. The provision they received was in a small group, rather than one-to-one, was less intensive and shorter-term than the support provided in Oak Park. This school difference raises important issues around school resourcing. Milner had a large number of Stage 1 English learners who were prioritized for special needs support and took up most of the special needs teachers' time. At Oak Park there were very few children who needed help with English language acquisition. Special-needs support was therefore given to children who would have been considered very low priority for such help in Milner.

Conducting a Dialogue or Talking Past Each Other?

Cultural capital enters the process of raising issues with teachers at many points. It is there in middle-class mothers' refusal to accept the school's verdict, in their persistence and their belief that they know better, in their feeling that they and their child are entitled to extra provision and in the sense of power and confidence they bring to exchanges with the teacher which results in teachers being persuaded to their point of view.

All these aspects of cultural capital make up the difference between Laura and Cathy's tales. Laura told me:

> They always said he was getting on fine. So they didn't really see any problems whereas I did. So I had regular contact with the teacher but we weren't really speaking the same language. I constantly had to ask when it was happening, go in and see the Headteacher, remind his own teacher. If I hadn't kept on going in it wouldn't have happened because of course the classteacher had all the other children's problems on her mind and then eventually he was tested but it was hard work getting to that stage. Then once they'd identified that he had Special Educational Needs I still had to keep on going in to make sure he got the extra support.

Although, as Laura emphasizes, at first she and the teachers were not speaking the same language, by repeatedly making a case for Richard's special needs, Laura gets the school-based provision she wants for her son.

Cathy, however, has a different version of the same story to tell:

> Teachers are more approachable. You can go in and talk to them, but I would have to say that I don't think it necessarily makes any difference. Like with Shula she needs a lot of support with her reading and I'm sick of talking to the school about it. They'll say they'll do this and it starts up for a little while then it disintegrates. Do I really have to keep on going back all the time? You go in and talk and somebody will appear to listen. They'll say they'll do A, B and C and A and B will never happen and C will happen for a little while and then you have to go back again. I've talked to the Head, I've talked to the classteacher but it's as if we are just talking past each other.

Clearly the mother is not the only agent in this exchange. There is a complex interplay between the confidence and self-assurance of the mother in interaction with teachers and the receptivity of teachers to parental requests.

Even when working-class women summoned up the courage to go into school to talk to teachers, they often ended up with less than they were asking for. June talked philosophically of asking for homework for Rosetta. She told me she had not wanted to boast about Rosetta's ability but because she had not, Rosetta had 'been set work below what she was capable of'. It is very difficult for mothers like June to make confident assertions about their children's ability when their own educational experience has been characterized by failure. She told me:

> I did try. I did ask for homework for Rosetta but you see they don't have homework here so I was asking for a favour. I wish they did have it. After I asked for homework for her she brought home these cards with numbers on them which were much too easy for her. She'd done the whole sheet in five minutes. I did mention it to Mandy but it made no difference the work she gave her was still far too easy.

June struggled in the interview to wrestle with a problem she did not know how to resolve. June was 'plucking up courage to go back and ask for harder work'. She told me that she did not want to boast about Rosetta's ability:

> What can I do? She is definitely too bright for the things that they teach her. But she can't do anything else because the other kids have got to catch up with her.

Although June said that it was very easy to talk to Rosetta's classteacher, she still found it extremely difficult to ask for what she wanted. The contrast with the words of another black woman, but one who is much more socially privileged, is stark:

> We are far more powerful now than in my parents day. Now we parents have opinions. If we don't like what is going on in school we say so. When I go into school what I say is taken into consideration and something is done about it. (Lola, Oak Park)

Confidence in relation to schooling, a key component of cultural capital, is crucially connected to women's own educational histories. It can also, as this example demonstrates, make the difference between being heard and not being heard.

Acting as Advocate: Extending Emotional Work to the School Site

While much of the emotional support of children's schooling took place in the home, occasionally mothers felt they needed to raise children's own concerns with teachers. Twice over the course of the fieldwork, Linsey came to see Sophia's teacher because Sophia was upset about her lack of team points. Both times she requested that Sophia be given more positive feedback because she was worried that 'Sophia was becoming dispirited about her school-work'. Lola talked at length about a racist incident when a younger boy had called Nancy 'chocolate face'. Lola had gone into the school to see the Headteacher the next morning and said 'she dealt with the incident very firmly straight away and there hasn't been a repetition'. However, as can be seen below in Carla's case, difficulties were not always resolved by talking to the teacher:

> I did go and talk to Lilly's teacher about how upset she was. It was not a successful meeting from my point of view because the moment I started explaining she suddenly said 'Oh dear' and called Lilly in. My mouth fell on the floor because I couldn't tell her what I had to say, not with Lilly there, so end of interaction. 'Oh, mummy tells me you have been crying, come and tell me what has been so awful'. You know, her eyes went blank, then she managed to pinpoint a couple of things to do with some boy, but I'm sure there was a lot more behind it that just didn't come out.

Often mothers stated, particularly when raising issues arising from bullying, that teachers were not really aware of what was going on when their backs were turned. Julie, Josie, Linda, Jalil and Jenny had all raised issues around playground interaction which they claimed had not been adequately addressed by Milner.

As I know from my own experience of undertaking Equal Opportunities work in school, school-based attempts to combat sexism and racism can also meet with resistance from parents. In Milner a number of mothers of boys, Christine, Jenny, Jackie and Josie, had been into school to complain about the gender groups the school ran. Jane had also made time to see the class teacher in order to ask for details about the work undertaken. All these visits were mothers' responses to their sons' frequently vocalized antipathy to the gender groups. Although my focus in the interview with Jackie was Carly, her nine-year-old daughter, she spent a third of the interview discussing Ricky, her eleven-year-old son, and his resentment about what he perceives to be a prioritizing of girls' interests over those of the boys:

> Ricky's always saying it's sexist at that school, that the teachers only like the girls. He sees the girls being praised and the boys aren't and he thinks 'arh'. They've got a notice in the playground that if a group

is playing champ it has got to have two girls in it. He'll point to it and say 'Look, I told you so'. He's always telling me the school's sexist. He's been wanting me to go into school and see Maggie. In the end I had a word with his teacher to try and calm him down, but she said it wasn't really possible for him to opt out. He still goes on about it though.

In Jackie's account she seems bombarded by Ricky's negative feelings about gender work in the school. There is a sad irony in anti-sexist work by teachers resulting in negative emotional consequences for mothers.

While Jackie's tone is conciliatory, other mothers described their sons and the gender groups in far more militant language. Jenny was very vehement:

On top of that they've got those gender groups which I'm totally against. It's all becoming political as well, you know. You know Andreas will say 'I had to discuss boys' things. They talk about respecting girls, bullying all that sort of thing but Andreas can't understand why he can't go down the football club with the girls cos the girls all do football training and he can't understand why he can't go. I've talked to his teacher about it. I said 'it's not fair, that they should let the boys go and have their turn'. Instead they feel they are being punished. Andreas feels it's not fair, he's always complaining about it.

However, Jenny's initial strong stance is undermined by her sense of not really being entitled to query the school's decisions. Unlike many of the Oak Park mothers who kept on going back if they did not get a satisfactory outcome from their contact with school personnel, Jenny is very clear that to make more than one petition on her son's behalf is to run the risk of being labelled 'a troublemaker':

The trouble is I've said what I think and obviously it was Maggie's decision so on one level whatever I say will not change it. Andreas wants me to talk to her about it again but I'll just be seen as a troublemaker.

The Influence of Children's Ability, 'Race' and Gender on Mother-Initiated Contact

Bauch, in her research in the USA, found that black parents were the most frequent communicators with teachers. In her article she writes about their high level of 'aggressive' contact with teachers (Bauch, 1993: 131). However, I found it was mothers whose children were perceived by them either to be struggling academically, or to be underachieving, who initiated the most contact, regardless of ethnicity and social class. Liz, Cathy, Julie, Josie and Liliana had all contacted the school or a local education service three times or more over the last year. That four out of the five had sons is perhaps unsurprising in view of boys' more visible academic difficulties at the primary stage.

'Aggressive' contact seems to be correlated far more with a combination of desperation and intense emotional investment in one's child's education than with 'race'. Josie was the one mother in Milner whom staff referred to as aggressive in interaction with teachers. Josie herself attributed her powerful emotions to her own extremely negative educational history:

> What was happening was I thought if my son can't read he's going to go through exactly the same thing as I went through and yet he's had a better start because he knows the language and that's what's really upsetting me cos if I was coming across heavy it was because of my anxieties. I thought oh no he's not going to go through what I went through.

Where 'race' did become an issue was in relation to Equal Opportunities policy. Black mothers were not only concerned that their child attend a school which was not overtly racist, they also wanted the curriculum positively to address questions around black self-identity. Cassie told me:

> I raised the issue around positive work around race with Maggie, but in the end I dropped it. Also I'd talked to Cathy and we were both very depressed about it in view of the current educational climate.

Contact with the Headteacher

Lareau (1989) found that only one working-class parent (a father) visited the Headteacher during the course of her field work. In Milner five mothers, Cathy, Josie, Julie, Jenny and Lelia, came to see the Head while I was observing in the school. Only one, Lelia, was accompanied by her partner, and she was the only one to make an appointment. Three working-class women came because of their concern about their child's academic performance. I have discussed Jenny's visit to raise concerns about the gender groups above. The agenda for Lelia and her partner, Mark, was their worries about peer-group interaction in the classroom. I do not know how significant the working-class women's avoidance of formality is, but failing to make an appointment appears to have contributed to their concerns being treated in a fairly casual way by teachers. In contrast, there was a deep intake of breath from Maxine, the classteacher, when she realised Lelia and Mark, Naomi's parents, had an appointment to see the Headteacher, and she commented anxiously to the Deputy Head 'Oh, no, what do you think it's about?'.

The working-class women approached the process of making contact with the Head very differently. They described their efforts to orchestrate informal contact with the Head:

> I hung around outside her office until she turned up and then just asked if I could have a quick word. (Josie, Milner)

> I was in school anyway because I'd come in to help sort out the publicity for the Family Supper. When Maggie came into the general office I asked if she had a spare minute because I needed to have a word about Shula. (Cathy, Milner)

Their strong sense of being in the right, of having justifiable grievances about their child's academic progress, which came through so powerfully in the interviews, does not seem to be there in their description of asking almost apologetically if they 'could have a word'. However, their very presence outside the Head's office was often the end-product of a tortuous process of prevarication, weighing up the costs and benefits of stating their case, which could extend for weeks:

> Carmel: 'Diane, I got so fed up with listening to them complain. I said "the only way you'll solve that is by going to see Maggie, it's no good standing at the school gates and telling us about it cos we already know all this. You have to go and sort it out and you have to make her aware of it so she will do something about it" and the next week they'd still be there complaining.'
> Diane: 'So, did they go and see her?'
> Carmel: (laughing) 'well some of them, eventually.'

In Oak Park just over half of the mothers visited the Headteacher over the course of my fieldwork, seven out of a total of 13. Gender is the key to deciphering their reasons for wanting to talk to Miss Richards. Lucy, Leena, Louise and Lucinda all raised issues around their daughter's academic performance being good enough for them to sit entrance exams for élite state and private sector schools. Lucy told me 'I don't want to put Sophie in for entrance exams she hasn't got a chance of passing. I wanted to know she was in with a chance. It seems from what Miss Richards told me she's got the best chance of all'. Leena said 'I needed to know what the gaps were so I saw Miss Richards in order to get Negar's test results. I also wanted her professional opinion on which entrance exams she thought I should put Negar in for'. Although, when I interviewed Lisa she had not yet made an appointment to see the Head, she commented that it was something she needed to do over the next few months 'in order to get a clear idea about Melinda's entrance exam prospects'. I saw her chatting animatedly to the Headteacher at the Christmas Fair, who, when I mentioned Lisa later, said 'She wants to talk to me about entrance exams. I get a steady stream of mothers with daughters in Year 5'.

In contrast, mothers of sons had a divergent agenda. Liliana, Liz and Laura all queried the adequacy of their son's existing school-based, special needs support. All three had a history of petitioning on their son's behalf. However, unlike in Milner where, for example, Jackie was satisfied with the school's offer of extra help, in Oak Park extra school help seemed to have the effect of escalating mothers' demands as in both Liliana and Liz's examples below. According to the Headteacher, Miss Richards, Liliana's first foray into asking for extra provision for Sergei had been meet with twice-weekly, one-to-one educational support. However, in Liliana's account that extra help becomes 'not doing anything'. Similarly, achieving one level of additional support, produces not a sense of satisfaction in Liz, but renewed attempts to gain yet more provision.

'Going over the Head's Head'

Visiting the Head often did not ensure a satisfactory outcome for mothers, any more than talking to the classteacher. A number of mothers at both schools spoke in terms of 'going over the Head's Head'. Two mothers, in particular, talked at length about their attempts to convey their concerns about their sons' unmet educational needs to educational personnel beyond the school. Liliana told me:

> I spent hours and hours talking to the Headteacher. She wasn't doing anything about his difficulties so eventually I went to the Borough authority and asked if there was any help for dyslexia. That is why the Headteacher was horrified and wanted to scratch me. She didn't like me going over her Head [laughing], but they sent someone and she assessed Sergei. That's why he has a special support teacher. But I got him assessed. It was recognized as a school assessment because even though I initiated it, it was done through the school. The lady who assessed him, she writes to me. We still send each other letters.

Although much of Liliana's interview was taken up with discussions about her difficulty in communicating with school staff, she found an alternative means of getting Sergei's needs met. While she lacks the extensive network of other middle-class mothers, which was the norm in Oak Park, she does possess the confidence to liaise with borough educationalists. This is a possibility for her because she can draw on her own status and resources as 'an educational expert':

> I have been to some lectures about the Maths curriculum. I contacted the Dyslexia centre again and as a result I went to a couple of conferences about how to teach children having problems in Maths and I came home and started to teach him this way.

'Talking to a Brick Wall'

However, 'taking it further' does not always produce positive results. Julie had also initiated contact with educational personnel outside the school. She had visited the Education Department to ask what extra help could be given to George, and to enquire what requirements the school had to meet with respect to homework:

> You can't say anything. You can't complain. It's like talking to a brick wall. You can't get anywhere. Choice, you've got no choice. I've spent so much time complaining about George not learning and I haven't got anywhere with it. I did try and take it further. I went up to the Education Department, but that was no good. They just told me 'You have to talk to the Head'.

Julie's account is infused with a sense of frustration coupled with urgency. Her cultural capital, like that of other working-class mothers and many of the women born in countries other than the UK, is in the wrong currency (Gewirtz *et al.*, 1994b). However, there is no passivity in her description of her relationship to her children's schooling. It is replete with her own agency. Concerned with her son's failure to progress, she visited the classteacher twice to ask for extra help. When help did not materialize she went to see the Headteacher. In her own words 'I got nowhere with them'. So she embarked on a different course of action. She employed a tutor and made an appointment to visit the Education Department:

> In the end I went to the Education Department and they told me it's up to the Headteacher so I got nowhere there either.

I have mentioned Cathy's feeling earlier that she and the teachers were talking past each other. Throughout the interview Cathy expressed her exasperation at what she perceives to be teachers' inability to respond to her requests for help:

> So far I've been up three times to see her teacher, apart from Open evening. In the end I went to talk to the Head but I might as well not bother. It's like facing a brick wall.

Like Julie she also uses the metaphor of 'a brick wall' when trying to explain how her concerns were received by the educational establishment. Both mothers draw very powerfully on understandings of how inequalities operate in contemporary society, in order to make sense of their failure to get their children's needs met within state schooling. The extent to which working-class mothers are trapped within wider societal perceptions of themselves and their children's potential are captured in Julie's wry comment:

> I mean it, they've just given up on our kids. What does that tell you about how they see the people they want to vote for them. I think it's got a lot to do with how they see the children. They think a lot of the children are slow and that's how they see us parents as well.

Dissatisfaction energizes both Cathy and Julie into taking action. However, that action is frustrated in the face of 'the brick wall' of the educational system. In the end both mothers attempt to repair their child's educational problem outside the educational system. For Cathy this strategy works better. She has the Black Saturday school, and her own salary as a school nurse to draw on in funding Shula's tuition. Julie, however, is on income support and can only pay for 10 weeks of tuition before she decides it is a course of action she can no longer afford.

Mothers Helping out in the Classroom: Easy Contact with Teachers?

I have briefly discussed volunteering in the previous chapter. Halfway through the period of fieldwork Lavinia began volunteering in Oak Park for two days a week. By the time I left the field she had been employed as a part-time helper for the two Year 3 classes, as well as being taken on as a lunchtime supervisor for five days a week. In Milner Janice had already been coming into school two half-days a week for the past year to help out in her daughter's and son's classrooms. However, Lavinia used her time in school very differently from Janice, who always sat very quietly in the staff room on the days we over-lapped in school, listening to, rather than initiating, conversation with teachers. I only heard her speak to the teacher once, about a freak storm which had occurred when she had been out in the playground with the children. On the occasions when teachers initiated conversations with her, she always answered briefly and never asked any questions in response. I have noted in my field notes that she appeared to be deferential towards the school staff.

Lavinia gave the appearance of deference too, but, from beneath that surface deference, she managed over the course of the fieldwork to ask at least six direct questions about her child's curriculum offer. The Head had a tacit policy of placing women volunteers in classes other than their child's, so I observed none of Lareau's middle-class surveillance of one's own child in the classroom setting (Lareau, 1989: 127). In one episode Lavinia inquired of Catherine, the school's special needs teacher, 'did she think Riva could possibly be dyslexic because when she heard her read at home she often made surprising reversals, for example "no" for "on"'. The teacher tried to be reassuring, involving a Year 3 classteacher who knew about dyslexia. At one point, Catherine went off to find her reading records for Riva in order to show them to Lavinia. Later in the course of the fieldwork I walked into the staff room to find Lavinia asking the Maths post/holder about binary Maths. 'What part exactly does it play in the National Curriculum?'. This time Mrs Symmonds, the classteacher, also became involved in the exchange, getting the Maths National Curriculum folder down from one of the shelves and showing it to Lavinia. After a few minutes Lavinia commented 'well you see I've bought a book on Maths key Stage 2 but don't really understand binary Maths. Could you explain it to me'. For the remaining 10 minutes of the break the Maths postholder sat down with Lavinia explaining the intricacies of binary Maths to her. There were other examples, but the point is what Lavinia considered to be appropriate behaviour was clearly not considered to be appropriate in Janice's eyes. She took up much less teacher time and attention than Lavinia, and consequently ended up drawing far less on teachers' educational expertize.

More Than Just Talking

Making the initial overture to teachers is only the first part of a multi-layered process. Self-presentation and self-confidence in relation to schooling clearly plays a crucial part in how concerns are communicated, and concomitantly how they are received. Mothers differed enormously in how they managed their contact with school personnel. There were social-class differences in the ways mothers presented both themselves and their concerns in dialogue with teaching staff. It was predominantly middle-class mothers who convinced teachers, and external educational personnel, of their entitlement to extra resources. Working-class mothers may have seen the school as a familiar site, but familiarity did not make a difference, as cultural capital did. It was middle-class women's confidence, their self-presentation as entitled, the certain conviction that their point of view was the correct one and their clearly-articulated knowledge of the system and how it worked, that counted.

Superficially, in spite of their social class differences, there were similarities between Josie and Liz. Both were seen by school staff as antagonistic towards the school. There were parallels in their situations in that both felt unable to work effectively with their child at home. However, Liz's reason lay in her full-time job as an educational advisor, which meant she lacked the time to spend regular, prolonged periods on Martin's cognitive development. Unlike Josie, she did have the financial resources to pay for tuition. In contrast to Josie who, on the occasions she managed to stay calm about Leigh's education, presented herself as a supplicant in relations with the teachers, Liz felt she had a right to support for Martin's education from the school:

> Liz: 'A lot of my time has been spent fighting for extra support for him and I mean fighting.'
> Diane: 'So does he get extra support?'
> Liz: 'Well he gets it but it's unofficial. Up to this term he's got it because every term I have been into school and kicked up such hell.

I think the Headteacher must dread seeing me come into school. She hides. I'm sure she ducks when she sees me coming. It's "Oh, my God, that woman's come to give me hell again." But I really have had to fight for it. Special Needs is such a scarce resource, she only comes in twice a week. There used to be two Special Needs teachers and he saw Mrs Webster regularly and every term he was told he had graduated, his reading was good enough for him to stop and every term I went in and said "Oh, no it isn't. He needs it. You get him back in there". The Head would say to me "Well, I've got other children who are worse". and I'd have to say "I'm not worried about other kids that are worse. I'm worried about my child and he needs it". Other parents have got to fight for their children. But don't tell me my child is behind and needs help but because he's not one of the worst don't bother about him. Can you believe it she told me they only give special support to children in Years 3 and 4 because if they haven't caught up by then they are not going to and it's just tough.'

But it was not tough for Martin because Liz's persistence and unswerving belief in her son's entitlement to scarce educational resources meant that he continued to receive one-to-one, special needs support, even though officially he did not qualify for the provision.

Written Communications to School

The greater formality of middle-class parents in initiating contact with school staff is documented in the flood of letters that poured into Mrs Symmond's classroom every week. During the period I spent in Oak Park, which spanned September 1993 until the end of March 1994, over a hundred letters, or more than five a week, were delivered by children to Mrs Symmonds. Apart from apologies for absences and requests for more time to complete homework, there were a number which raised substantive issues. The longest and most detailed was written by Lucy at the beginning of the Spring term. I reproduce it in full below:

Dear Mrs Symmonds,
I am sorry it is short notice but I would like to collect Sophie at 1.30 today. Would you please give her permission to meet me by her peg at that time–thanks. I would like to take this opportunity to mention that Sophie will not be able to attend computer club this term. Last term we were so 'choker block' with activities, we didn't know if we were coming or going.

As this is her last year before entrance examinations and she often has a very full weekend with visiting her father and one thing or another, I have decided weekday evenings will be dedicated to a little extra work and less of the dashing around. I must say though, she did thoroughly enjoy the lessons and is somewhat disappointed by my decision. I hope this has not inconvenienced you too much.

At some point I would like to discuss the National Curriculum. I would like to know a bit about the work plan you have adopted. I am sure you are aware this is the most important year in the junior academic period – it is the year that leads up to entrance examinations and I want to do everything possible to help Sophie without interfering with your procedures. I am particularly interested in Maths. I would like to know where Sophie is in National Curriculum terms, how much practice she gets in each topic and according to recommendations, where she should be at the end of the summer term.

Last term I was concerned by how much time was spent on Art activities. It seemed some of the projects went on for days with little time to do much else. I was concerned about the 26 page newspaper the children were asked to produce with what amounted to pages of squiggles with topic headings. Surely a six page newspaper with proper articles would have been more beneficial as a learning experience. I told Sophie not to complete her paper, but she insisted and sat for hours squiggling on every page. In future I must mention something at the time.

This academic year Sophie has lost her sincerity and discipline towards her work. She used to enjoy doing a good job. I only hope now she has had the time to get used to being a fifth former things will change.

Julia, I hope you do not mind me being frank with you about how I feel. If I bottle up my concerns they may not remain corked without a fizz for very long. I would appreciate it if you could suggest a day I can visit you,

Thanks

Lucy

P.S. We have an 'IOU' for a Christmas present for you. Sophie has been badgering me to get something. I have a particular idea in mind and it's not easily accessible – so you'll have to hang in there and wait.

The letter constitutes a challenge to Mrs Symmonds, her 'right to know best', that is very difficult to dismiss. Mrs Symmonds cannot reject it as an hysterical outburst, which was the term used to describe one of Josie's visits to Milner. It uses the language of educational professionals, while twice emphasizing that Lucy's own priority is entrance exams. It includes both veiled and overt threats of impending parental intervention: 'In future I feel I must mention something' and '(my concerns) may not remain corked without a fizz for very long'. There are explicit criticisms of Mrs Symmond's curriculum offer, namely 'the pages of squiggles', and examples of Lucy taking a leadership role not only in relation to her own child, but in relation to the curriculum Mrs Symmonds offers the whole class: 'Surely a six page newspaper with proper articles would have been more beneficial'. There is an illustration of an attempt to undertake a close surveillance of a child's progress and attainment in a specific area of the National Curriculum, namely 'I would like to know where Sophie is up to, how much practice she gets in each topic and according to recommendations where she should be at the end of the Summer term'. At the same time trenchant criticisms of Mrs Symmond's practice are framed by friendly familiarity, which I suggest is a device Lucy uses to emphasize her equality in dialogue with Mrs Symmonds. The letter weaves formality with informality in a formulation that makes it difficult for Mrs Symmonds to dismiss Lucy's criticisms of her. In accepting Lucy's more friendly overtures she is drawn into Lucy's construction of her as a teacher who both spends too much time on educational flippancies and who is letting Sophie down.

Lucy's letter is an example of the far greater power of parental judgments to influence teachers' self-assessments in Oak Park than in Milner. There were many parents like Lucy in Oak Park who felt entitled to articulate their often negative evaluation of teachers' practices. In Milner, on the occasions when criticisms were voiced they were frequently redefined by teachers as 'the parent's problem'. The only vaguely comparable letter received from a father in Milner was dismissed as the rantings of a bigot. I was in school on the day Mrs Symmonds received Lucy's letter. Her response was a mixture of fear and outrage. She clearly found it extremely difficult to reject Lucy's assessment. At lunchtime she commented to another teacher that 'perhaps she had spent too much time on the newspaper project'. We did not do the art work that I had been looking forward to after the break. Instead there was a formal Maths session with children working from text books. Before I left in the evening she confided that she 'was dreading the next time she saw Lucy' before commenting 'Well wouldn't you feel intimidated if you were me?'.

As a direct result of Lucy's letter Mrs Symmonds rescheduled the project she had planned to undertake the following term. Although Mrs Symmonds had intended to carry out an extremely ambitious animation project in the classroom, she changed the timing and location of the work and arranged with a local firm to use their facilities on Sundays. Much of the filming she had planned to do took place in her 'free time' over the course of eight consecutive Sundays as she collected small groups of children in the morning from their homes, took them to the office to film and then dropped them off in the late afternoon. When I expressed incredulity at her giving up so much of her own time, she laughed and said 'tell that to the parents, half of them didn't even thank me for looking after their child on a Sunday'. While I am not claiming that Lucy's letter on its own changed Mrs Symmonds curriculum offer, I am asserting that in Oak Park parental communications, both verbal and written, had an influence on teachers' practices that was largely absent in Milner.

The mothers in Milner did write letters to teachers, predominantly apologies for children's absences, and occasionally, requests for homework. However, while I was observing in Milner, there were no letters sent which engaged in detail with a child's curriculum in the classroom. Horror stories were told in the staff room of a letter from the father of a Year 6 girl, which was described as 'blatantly hostile to the school's sex education policy', but it was chiefly noteworthy because of its uniqueness. During the duration of the fieldwork neither of the Year 5 teachers received a letter which raised curriculum issues. By contrast, letters along the lines of the one sent by Lucy were an infrequent, but by no means unusual, occurrence in Oak Park. Although Lucy was the only mother among those I interviewed to send such a letter, Mrs Symmonds received two from mothers of other children in the class. It is important to underline that letters of all types were predominantly written by mothers at both schools, although Oak Park fathers occasionally wrote notes. Nancy's father sent a letter explaining the home circumstances, when Lola had to fly at very short notice to attend a family funeral in Nigeria. Martin's father also wrote a letter to confirm what had been agreed at Parents' Evening. Apart from these two, all the other letters were signed by mothers. In Milner there were no examples of written communications from fathers of Year 5 children.

How Maternal Involvement is Mediated by Power Relations between Mothers and Teachers

Although relations of power permeate all interaction between mothers and school staff, power imbalances were particularly highlighted through themes of infantilism, 'fobbing off' and the ways in which mothers were held accountable for their children on the school site. Although Liliana at Oak Park talked in terms of being made to feel like a child in relation to teachers, it was primarily working-class mothers at Milner who felt both reduced to the status of a child and blamed for aspects of their children's school-site behaviour. Carol Vincent's working-class respondents similarly spoke of being talked down to by teachers 'as if they were children themselves' (Vincent, 1996: 96).

Being on familiar territory did not compensate for a feeling that the school was operating with very different ground rules from the ones working-class mothers understood and were working with. The approachability of teachers, mentioned earlier by Cathy, figured in many of the Milner mothers' accounts. Milner teachers were on first name terms with children and their parents, while the ethos of the school was actively to encourage mothers to come into school. Jasbir and Linda worked in the school, Jalil ran a Mother and Toddler group on the school site, while Claire, Josie, Janice, Julie, Jenny and Joyce were regular visitors to both the playgroup and the school. Milner was, therefore, a very familiar site to these women, and this clearly contributed to their sense of entitlement in approaching their child's teacher. It seems that the frequent informal contact that working-class mothers, such as Jalil, Josie, Jenny and Joyce, experienced was in some sense enabling for them and facilitated approaching teachers when they had concerns. These four had all raised issues with the classteacher at least three times over the course of the fieldwork.

For Josie and Jalil, in particular, however, this sense of entitlement did not permeate their delivery of their problem. For these two mothers there was rarely any satisfactory outcome from initiating contact. Talking to school staff often led to a feeling of being 'fobbed off' and, as Josie commented, 'you often came away thinking they were speaking a different language' (something which could have plunged her straight back into her own school experience). While there was a 'profit' in that the confidence these mothers had in approaching school staff was enhanced, and any image of teachers as distant experts was tempered by their regular access, school was still a site in which the power imbalance worked firmly in favour of teachers.

'Fobbing off' was a term five of the mothers at Milner used when discussing contact with teachers. The term captures the pervasive sense of dissatisfaction these mothers felt with the educational system generally, while conveying an underlying theme of unmet needs. 'Being fobbed off' raises complex issues about who is the expert on the child and in which context. Oak Park mothers retained a sense of being the expert on their own child, regardless of context. The working-class mothers were far more ambivalent about 'knowing best' and appeared to be dealing with difficult internal contradictions. Many, including those who saw themselves as having minimal educational skills, expressed unease about handing over the expert role to the teacher even on the school site. Yet, at the same time, working-class mothers also felt disqualified to challenge educational assessments they viewed as partial and inadequate. These tensions seemed to be articulated in their feelings of being 'fobbed off'. Cathy told me:

> I don't think it's helpful telling you 'They'll catch up', it's just fobbing you off because what you want to know is what they're going to do to make sure it happens.

In addition to children not having their educational needs met, the parents' need for accurate, detailed information was also not being met:

> I do find, you know, when I go to Parents' evening that all you're told is 'he's doing well, he's doing well, he's doing well'. That's it, just fobbing me off and I want the information to be there. I mean his maths, his reading, his writing, you know, his spelling all need to be improved, but they don't tell you. Like with punctuation the kids don't do that, they don't even know what it is [laughing] honest, they don't even know what it is. (Jenny, Milner)

Even when there was no direct reference to the term 'being fobbed off', it was implicit in what other Milner mothers said. It seemed to encapsulate women's sense of frustration and relative powerlessness in the face of educational expertize.

Many of the working-class mothers wanted to challenge teachers' evaluations, but stated that they felt unqualified to do so. A few saw the school staff as actively engaged in a process of dissemblance they felt ill-equipped to counter:

> Maggie said 'Let me tell you I can promise you Leigh will leave this school being able to read fluently and if he doesn't you have every right to come back and tell me'. But it will be too late by then and I thought she's fobbed me off and I said 'That's really good of you' but I thought to myself what's the good of telling me 'I promise you he will read'. (Josie, Milner)

Although many of the Milner mothers challenged teachers' assessments in dialogue with me, they often seemed to approach teachers with the class deference evident in Josie's communication of a gratitude she did not really feel. Even Linda, who was a teacher in the school, stated 'I do think in Milner the parents are fobbed off a little too easily'. However, this was not the case in Oak Park, where two mothers used the term in order to demonstrate what they would not allow to happen in interaction with teachers:

> I wouldn't be fobbed off for sure, but I would be worried about being aggressive. (Lesley, Oak Park)

Valerie Walkerdine and Helen Lucey write of a process in which working-class mothers are redefined as pupils in need of instruction, alongside their own children:

> The whole discourse of parental involvement assumes that teachers must teach parents (almost always mothers) how to prepare and help their children in the right ways. The target is, almost always, black and white working-class parents. (Walkerdine and Lucey, 1989: 181)

This process was apparent in interactions between teachers and mothers in Milner. As I discuss below, this process of infantilization operated most powerfully when mothers were summoned into school to account for some aspect of their child's behaviour. However, it could also occur when mothers initiated contact. Jalil told me that when she went into school to discuss Chantelle's continuing lack of progress in reading the Headteacher made her feel 'like a naughty school girl'. Jenny laughed about the reversal she had to deal with when she finally plucked up the courage to query the compulsory nature of the gender groups:

Then after getting nowhere with the gender group thing I really got my knuckles rapped. Maggie told me she'd heard I was thinking of putting Marina's name down for a church school. 'I'm really disappointed in you'. [laughing] Really that's what she said. (Jenny, Milner)

Christine, who in her own words, 'made the mistake of going in to see the teacher without my husband' said that, as the agenda shifted from her concerns to those of the classteacher, she began to panic 'about what she had done wrong'. It appears from the accounts of Milner mothers and that of Liliana in Oak Park that, sometimes, teachers assume a manner of relating to them that is based on their model of interaction with their pupils, rather than one of relating to another adult.

Feelings of being treated like a child often surfaced when mothers were asked to go into school to discuss problems which their child was experiencing. Mothers talked of being asked to go into school to discuss aspects of their child's behaviour, and, less frequently, their progress, with either the class teacher or the Head. These requests were made far more often in Milner than in Oak Park. When I asked the Oak Park Head why there was a relatively low level of requests for parents to come and talk to school staff, she laughed and said 'Don't you think we see enough of them as it is?'. Certainly in Mrs Symmond's classroom it was parents seizing the initiative and contacting the teacher rather than the other way round. In contrast to mother-initiated contact, there was a large disparity in teacher-initiated contact between the two schools. In Milner, almost half – nine out of the 20 mothers – had been asked to go into school to talk to the teacher since their child had been in the juniors, while in Oak Park there had only been one such request – made to Liliana.

The way a number of mothers spoke of being addressed by staff was redolent of the process of being reduced to a child, as I have mentioned earlier. If, sometimes, mothers felt they were being treated as children when they approached teachers, this sense of being infantilized was even more intense when teachers initiated contact. Liliana said:

I was scared to death of the Headteacher because she said 'I don't know what we are going to do with Sergei'. When she speaks to me I feel as if I have been very naughty and she is going to tell me off. Now whenever she comes towards me I think 'Oh, no'.

There were also examples of being treated like a child beyond the confines of formal contact between mothers and teachers. Jalil told me:

I was chatting to some other mother downstairs in the hall, waiting for Chantelle and you know me Diane how I get the giggles. I think the infants were doing games in the hall and Maggie came down. She just looked at me and pointed her finger 'Out Jalil' and I had to go out.

Carol and Cathy both linked school identification of problems that staff considered serious enough to warrant contacting them to their status as lone mothers. Carol, who raised issues around her own status as a lone mother and the sex of her child, was particularly vehement:

> The contact with the school has been about behaviour problems, not to do with his academic work. Nine times out of 10 it was just because he's a boy. I think they overreacted a lot of the time. Whenever there's the slightest problem they drag me up 'Is there anything wrong at home? Have your circumstances changed?'. Well we both know what that's code for. I'll say 'No, it's fine nothing's changed'. Assumptions are made that everything's related to you being a single parent when all children have their ups and downs and nine times out of ten things settle down without you making a big issue out of it. It's become much more intrusive all this partnership with parents. I mean I've been phoned up at work, but always to do with behaviour, never about schoolwork. His schoolwork has always been excellent, they can't complain about that because I've done masses of work with him.

Cathy talked about the letter she received from the Headteacher asserting that Shula had been involved in the victimization of another girl in the playground. She said:

> I think they tend to home in on children from single parent families. They think they are bound to have problems and then they are half way to finding them.

That was far from the case, however, in Oak Park. One of the few children from a single-parent family was Sophie, the cleverest child in the year on the basis of the NFER (National Federation for Educational Research) test results. While I was observing in the classroom, there was a major falling out between Robyn and Sophie, one consequence of which was Robyn's mother coming into school to complain that Sophie had been bullying her daughter. Mrs Symmonds did not even consider contacting Lucy. She told me 'there is no need, she will be in here tomorrow and if not tomorrow, the day after'. Sure enough, the next day Lucy came into school, requesting to see the Headteacher with a counterattack about Robyn and her friends excluding Sophie. In Oak Park the relative privilege of mothers, regardless of their marital status, put them in a position vis-a-vis teachers where it was primarily the mothers who were on the offensive.

The working-class mothers at Milner were held accountable for their child's school-site behaviour through a process of school-initiated contact which was far less prevalent at Oak Park. Mothers often expressed resentment about being held responsible for their children's behaviour at school. Cathy told me:

> The letter the Head sent me very definitely put the responsibility back on me as the parent to deal with the problem. I mean I can talk to her yes but I'm not at school and I'm not seen as the disciplinarian at school. It's a different context. I think parents should support the school, that's fine, but not to take on the responsibility. That's another whole area we are expected to deal with, those kind of problems as well – discipline problems at school as well as the educational ones.

It is difficult to disentangle the factors that contributed to this difference between the two schools. I have discussed the very different institutional habituses of the two schools in Chapter 5. There were more discipline problems at Milner. The school's version was that they could only deal with the weight of discipline problems by sharing the burden with parents. However, mothers did not feel they were simply being asked to 'share', they also felt they were being made accountable for their child's school-site behaviour in ways which were implicitly judgments of their parenting:

> Well I had to go in and see the Headteacher about his playground behaviour and she was making out he was rough and you know me I am strict with my kids. I'd never hit them but I have rules about their behaviour and there she was telling me how I should bring up my own son. (Julie, Milner)

Contact between mothers and teachers is mediated by power differentials. Among many other things, cultural capital generates certainty, self-assurance and the ability to reject opposing views. From the teachers' perspective, contesting the viewpoint of someone who knows they are right is a very different proposition from contesting the viewpoint of someone who is tentative and uncertain as to whether they are correct. The working-class women brought to their interaction with teachers a habitus often shaped by educational failure. Reinforcing their negative educational experiences was their own and their parents' lack of experience in dealing assertively with professionals. As a consequence, working-class women were much more hesitant, more questioning of their own stance, and far more likely to qualify and at times contradict themselves in interaction with school staff. While middle-class women talked of making direct criticisms of teachers, the difficulty many of the working-class women had in criticizing people they saw as having higher status than themselves resulted in situations where they felt teachers 'didn't seem to hear what I was saying'. Their ambivalence in assigning blame led them continually to qualify their criticisms. After talking for half an hour about how the school was failing her son, Julie told me 'George's teacher is a good teacher, I will say that she's a good teacher, but then you see she's got a very difficult situation'. Josie explained to me that, although the classteacher was 'strict' with Leigh, she was 'a good teacher. You can't expect her to get on with all of them'. Many of the Oak Park mothers had no such compunction. There, some mothers recited a litany of how hopeless, inadequate and inexperienced some teachers were. Even those mothers who did not engage in direct criticisms of teachers saw themselves as having the power to define what made a good teacher:

> Well I expect certain standards from teachers. For one I expect them to be professional, but I'd expect a bit more than that, I'd want for want of a better word moral obligations as well. (Lucinda, Oak Park)

An elaboration of the power balance between teachers and parents is crucial to understanding relative outcomes from mother-initiated contact. In Milner the power to define in interaction lay with the teachers. This imbalance is encapsulated in Julie's comment:

> They'll do these tests with the children and they'll see half the class can't read or write properly but they still won't do anything because it will be the child's fault. That's why I disagree with the SATs because teachers are going to say this 7 year old can't read or write, it's his own fault.

In Oak Park the power to define lay more often with the parents than the teachers. Mrs Symmonds told me:

> Teachers can't win in schools like ours. If the children are doing well then it's all down to the home, if they're not then it's our fault.

This right to define, to locate the blame elsewhere, is characteristic of elites across society. The power of naming (Bourdieu, 1992; Spender, 1980) lay predominantly with the teachers in Milner and with the parents in Oak Park. This is not to suggest that this *status quo* was not contested and challenged on both sites, but in the sphere of home–school relationships as elsewhere in society, 'right' resides with the more powerful. As Bourdieu asserts:

> Linguistic exchanges are also relationships of symbolic power in which the power relationships between speakers and their respective groups are actualised. (Bourdieu, 1992: 37)

Many of the teachers working in Milner, however, felt enormous tensions and conflict about their involvement in a chain of events they frequently felt they had little power to affect. Interaction between mothers and teachers at Milner raises a difficult and complex issue: the difficulty of telling black and white working-class parents the truth about their children's educational prospects. As Walkerdine points out in her discussion of girls and mathematics, 'the problem is not teachers for . . . they are ensnared too' (Walkerdine, 1989: 208). The teachers, particularly those who were themselves from working-class backgrounds, often found the contact they had with working-class mothers painful. Maggie, the Headteacher told me:

> What can we do? They want us to make their children middle-class. We can't do that. It's out of our hands, it's just not possible, Diane.

Just as women primary school teachers are caught up in processes over which they feel they have little control in the classroom (Reay, 1991), so they often felt their interaction with parents demanded the impossible of them. Mandy said 'the thing I hate most about teaching is the emotional blackmail involved in teaching other people's children. They expect miracles.' Mandy, Maxine and Maggie all at different times over the course of the fieldwork agonized about the failure of schooling to alleviate social inequalities and the difficulties of being honest with parents.

Time and time again mothers at Milner raised the issue of 'telling the truth':

> It's very difficult to get an honest opinion. (Christine, Milner)

and:

> I think what it is is the conflict teachers have between being positive about a child and giving you detailed information, I don't know. Perhaps that is why they find it so difficult telling you the truth. (Cassie, Milner)

and:

> You get this wonderful report at the end of the year and your child's doing wonderfully when you think your child's not doing anything. Every report my children have had has been lovely and great and I find they're not reading properly, you know, there's no truth in it. (Josie, Milner)

As they skirted around black and white, working-class mothers' demands for information, for extra resources and, above all, for educational outcomes that transformed their children's life chances, teachers seemed to be caught up in a dance of denial over which they had little control.

If the language I have used in discussing both mother- and teacher-initiated contact is replete with military terminology, that is because that is often how these interactions appeared. The descriptions of teachers in Oak

Park often conveyed the impression that they were under siege, while the language of a number of mothers at Milner who spoke of initiating contact was couched in terms of battling against an impervious system. In addition some Oak Park mothers, like Liz and Liliana, talked in terms of fighting for their children's rights. Sari Knopp Biklen in her research into the relationship between elementary school teachers and middle-class mothers found both groups 'often feel great hostility towards each other' (Biklen, 1993: 155), while Carol Vincent describes relationships between primary teachers and working-class parents 'as often marked by wariness and in a few occasions, outright hostility' (Vincent, 1996: 79). I found 'fighting talk' was a feature of both working- and middle-class mothers' speech. Middle-class Lucy and Liz conceptualized their involvement, in part, as 'fighting to ensure their child got an appropriate curriculum offer'. Working-class women's 'fighting talk' was often qualified. Joyce told me you 'have to keep on fighting against the changes you don't agree with even if you're not going to win'. Mrs Symmonds, particularly in her interaction with Lucy, resolved 'not to be defensive and meet fire with fire'. To conclude, while there are many positive aspects of parent–teacher relationships, they are a far more complex mixture of negative and positive features than the harmonious partnerships between parents and schools described in the texts on parental involvement.

Conclusion

Cultural capital permeates all interaction between home and school. Working-class mothers at Milner may have seen the school as a familiar site, but familiarity did not make a difference. Cultural capital did. The middle-class mothers displayed a confidence, self-presentation and self-belief that was often effective in convincing teachers to their point of view. By contrast, the ambivalent and self-deprecating attitude most working-class women assumed when approaching teachers, and their misgivings that they were not being listened to indicate a very different 'sense of one's place' (Bourdieu, 1985b) to that of the middle-class women. Bourdieu writes about the practical intuition of the habitus which 'permits us to sense or to comprehend the conduct of people familiar to us' (Bourdieu, 1996: 13). I found that an effective dialogue was far more likely to be instituted between teachers and middle-class mothers than between teachers and their working-class counterparts.

All the same, I am not asserting the existence of unitary class groupings. Bourdieu's different fragments of the middle-class are represented here (Bourdieu, 1984). Oak Park mothers do not constitute an homogeneous class grouping. Liz has to go in and fight, albeit with a certainty about her son's entitlement that Cathy's, Josie's and Julie's 'fight' lacked. Other mothers, like Louise and Lucinda, used far more subtle strategies. They insisted politely and charmingly that they knew better than the teacher, and so succeeded in getting what they wanted without the physical and emotional costs involved in Liz's techniques. Similarly, in Milner those mothers I have described as 'on the boundaries of social class' were slightly more confident about making demands on the school than mothers who were firmly rooted within the working class. In the next chapter I explore more intra-class, as well as inter-class, differences in an investigation of the social lives of mothers and their children. The chapter explores the ways in which class differences in both mothers' social networks and children's out-of-school activities are mediated by 'race', gender and ethnicity.

Chapter 8

Social Whirls and Domestic Routines

This chapter examines the social life of mothers and their children and the differences 'race', gender and social class make to socializing and social networks across the two schools. The first part of the chapter looks at mothers' social networks, while the second focuses on children's social activities.

Mothers and their Networks: Generating Social Capital?

> there is a whole realm of work performed by mothers outside the home, in their neighbourhoods and communities. This work revolves around mothers' responsibilities to provide their families with the contacts, services and supports which they deem appropriate and enriching ... In short, this is the work mothers do to get things for their own. (O'Donnell, 1985: 117)

Implicit in O'Donnell's quotation is an assumption of agency. If this work is inadequate it is the (ir)responsibility of the mother. However, habitus can be understood in terms of the options delimiting choice (Calhoun, 1993: 74). These social options available to mothers are heavily dependent on women's material and cultural resources. As I outline below, access to these resources is influenced by social class, and, according to my evidence, to a lesser but still important extent, by 'race'.

Middle-class Parents and Collective Action: Not Such a Contradiction in Terms

In the Oak Park transcripts and the relevant field notes it seems as if the process of social networking is coterminous with middle-class mothers' support of their children's education. Their children's access to the wide range of out-of-school activities is heavily dependent on elaborate mutual arrangements about which mother drops off and which mother collects the small group of children attending the same maths class or English tutor. 5S parents, like most class groups in the school, have organized their own telephone chain which is distributed to every family. There is lots of evidence in the transcripts that they talk to each other on a regular basis, and also to parents of children in other years. In Oak Park a number of mothers told me that, if there was a problem with their child's schooling, they would phone one of the school governors. At Milner such an option was widely viewed as inconceivable. No mother mentioned it and when I did suggest it in conversation with a mother who had told me she only had her own mother with whom to talk through problems, she laughed incredulously and said 'I don't know any school governors'. By contrast, five of the Oak Park mothers spontaneously raised contacting school governors as one of the first things they would do if there was an educational problem.

The impression in Oak Park is of the teacher being on probation and it seems that mothers saw the process of evaluation as a collective one. Similar processes were evident in the practices of Cohen's sample of middle-class mothers (Cohen, 1981: 281). Lisa gave the most overt articulation of the process of assessing the teacher:

> Well it's too early to make up our minds really. She has only been in Mrs Symmond's class for five weeks. Another of the mothers has already approached me and said 'What do you think?' But it's too early to make a judgment.

Weaknesses and strengths are discussed with other parents of children in the class and also with parents of children, who had been in the class last year. Sieber found that middle-class parents in the American elementary school in which he conducted his research, acted collectively to marginalize working-class parents and prevent them from influencing school policy (Sieber, 1982). Unlike Sieber's middle-class parents, mothers' actions were not directed against the working-class parents (possibly there are just not enough of them to constitute any sort of a threat – in 5S only two out of the 29 children are working-class). Instead the teachers seem to be the target of discussion and activity. There was also a precedent in the successful action of last year's 5S parents. On hearing that their children had been allocated a newly-qualified teacher for Year 6, they got together and organized a petition in protest which 24 out of the 30 parents signed. They achieved their aim. The Headteacher assigned the Deputy Head to that class group, while the parallel group of less well-organized parents got the new teacher. Such demonstrations of collective social power were unheard of in Milner where mothers' attempts to specify which teacher they wanted for their child were all individualized and largely unsuccessful.

On closer inspection, however, this seemingly united front of parents is riven with divisions. The parents, in spite of being predominantly white and middle-class, are by no means an homogeneous group. Laura, Richard's mother, deliberately distanced herself from the majority parental group at the very beginning of her interview: 'Most of the mothers at Oak Park are very pushy', and 'Nearly all the parents have got tutors for their children, not me of course, it's mainly the parents with daughters'. Louise clearly endorses other ways of learning from the 'by rote/cramming mode' a lot of the mothers favoured. Jean, the only working-class mother in the Oak Park sample, was a lot more acquiescent towards the teachers and openly distanced herself from those mothers 'who are always moaning about the teachers', while Lesley and Liz are positioned very differently in relation to the school and its staff because of their sons' special educational needs. In addition Lesley made at least three statements about her left-wing political commitments, and used these to signify differences between herself and other parents. When these mothers are subtracted from the parental group 'the majority view' is reduced to a vociferous minority. Cleopatre Montandon found in her research into primary schools in Geneva that teachers were continually dealing with competing demands from parents (Montandon, 1993: 62). In Oak Park mothers' very different requirements of the learning environment are structured by the children's gender and ability.

Despite the educational field for these mothers being one of individualistic, competing needs rather than the collective, harmonious ones that mothers like Lucy, Lisa, Leena and Lavinia initially presented in their accounts, there are clear benefits of social capital from mothers' regular interaction with each other, and with professionals in the field. Social capital is evident in the these mothers' transcripts to a far greater extent than it appears in white, working-class women's accounts. Bourdieu writes that social capital is 'generated by a particular form of social labour, which presupposes expenditure of money, time and a specific competence and which tends to ensure the reproduction of social capital' (Bourdieu, 1993a: 33). Middle-class mothers were working at both their own and their children's social connections. There were regular references to telephone conversations with members of the governing body and informal access to experts in the educational sphere, ranging from classteachers to educational advisors, educational psychologists and Head-teachers of other schools.

There were also regular dinner-parties where parents socialized with educational professionals and each other. While I was observing in Oak Park, Lucinda invited the Headteacher to a dinner-party where a number of other mothers were present. Linsey mentioned attending dinner-parties hosted by other parents in Oak Park. During the course of being interviewed Lesley told me 'I hate dinner-parties – all the other couples seem to talk about is their children's education', while Linsey said in response to my query about whether she discussed education with other mothers: 'It often comes up at dinner-parties'. It seems that for these middle-class mothers children's education is an important topic for conversation, even when they are socializing outside the school context.

Social Capital with a Difference

Both working- and middle-class black women at Milner also had social networks which generated educational profits for their children. Mothers at Milner, but in particular black mothers, talked of being involved in an information-gathering process before making a decision about primary schooling for their child. Cathy had attended Milner, an experience she stressed she had enjoyed in spite of 'anything to do with Equal Opportunities being appalling'. When deciding on a school for Shula 20 years later, she had talked to other black mothers, as well as utilizing the professional network she has established as a school nurse. She had purposefully chosen Milner because 'since the new Head it had a reputation for being a caring school with an excellent Equal Opportunities policy'. During the course of the interview Cathy reminded me about how she had quizzed me as a mother with two children at Milner about my views on the school. Shula had been three at the time. She talked about the wide range of different sources of information, including other mothers and educational professionals, which she had drawn on before coming to a decision.

Jalil, June, Jasbir, Cathy, Carmel and Cassie, all had access to black networks which supplied educational information and knowledge of alternative educational provision that they could afford. Cassie and Carmel were involved in a Black parents' group that was based in an adjoining local educational authority, while all six mothers sent their children to one of four Black Saturday schools operating in the borough (see also Reay and Mirza, 1998). Cassie was very clear about the benefits that accrued to her son from attendance:

> The first time I took him to Saturday school it was amazing. We discussed the Saturday school a lot. I saw Saturday school as at times a black home, you know, feeling 'oh my god I can't cope with looking at a book', 'Oh Akin just go away and read' and I knew that really was not fair to him, he should be able to be motivated all the time. I feel that if someone else is able to do that with him it would be great and I feel the Saturday school will develop that interest in him – the sort of things I'm not able to do because of the pressure on my time. When I came back with him from Saturday school Akin was jumping all over the place and saying 'Mum why can't I go to this school five days a week?'. He loved it, he was really really excited. He said I know all about so and so and about so and so, all these people from Black history. He was fascinated and up to now if he's going to do Black history he's really excited.

Jane was unusual in this group of mothers in not having a social network of other black mothers, but even she, towards the end of my fieldwork, had been taken 'under Jalil's wing' and told me that on Jalil's advice she had put Delroy's name down for Black Saturday school.

The accounts of the black mothers at Milner raise complex and difficult issues. Black women seem to have learnt an awareness of the need for social support and collaborative action through their experience of dealing with a white racist society. In *In Other Words* Bourdieu writes that habitus 'can also be controlled through the awakening of consciousness and socioanalysis' (Bourdieu, 1990b: 116). It seems possible from black women's actions that this awakening of consciousness and socioanalysis could be triggered in response to living in a racist society. Wendy Luttrell writes of the ability to deal with racism as a type of 'real intelligence', which she asserts black women acquire by virtue of being a black in a white society (Luttrell, 1992: 185). I found examples of articulate, politicized understandings of racial oppression and its potential impact on their children in the black women's words, nearly always accompanied by an outline of preventative measures:

> I suppose I see because of the National Curriculum that I have to support him in learning which he probably won't get at school which is actually to talk about his background, his own identity, his blackness and the pitfalls that face him as a black boy. I think the National Curriculum have pushed that off the agenda. I know that schools like Milner probably would have been progressive and probably still are progressive in a certain sense but are no longer able to deal with that part of it, the part of identity. Those very things that tackle the identity of children and address their vulnerability as Black people, I think there's going to be less and less of that as the National Curriculum develops because the Government see it as a threat and see it as politics so those teachers who go on doing it are seen as subversive. I think that's the reason they have put this emphasis on parents because they see parents as coming in and taking over from those sort of teachers, teachers who are political. It's an appeal to white parents. That's why I've sent Akin to Saturday school. (Cassie, Milner)

Many of the white working-class women did not articulate a sense of class inequalities in their accounts, although issues around class thread their way through their transcripts. While, at points in black women's transcripts, a process of awareness leading to action could be traced through the women's words, there were few examples in the white, working-class women's accounts. Although Jill, talking about moving her elder daughter from Grasmere to Milner, explained her decision in terms of class prejudice in much the same way as black mothers explained their educational decision-making by reference to racism:

> That's why I moved Gemma from Grasmere they were only interested in bright pupils from the right background.

Both she and Julie linked their understanding of how the educational system works to issues of class inequalities. However, for most of the white women, regardless of class location, any overt articulation of class inequalities was missing from their accounts.

While Nash (1993: 192) found that it was professional parents who were more likely than working-class parents to perceive inequalities in the system, this was not the case with my sample. Apart from Cassie, Lola, and Lesley, middle-class women took their class privilege for granted. That two of these three middle-class women were black is perhaps unsurprising in view of their experiences of inequalities operating in relation to 'race'. Lola, without once mentioning 'race' or class, expounded a view of inequality that mixed a recognition of unfairness with an implicit acceptance of the *status quo*:

> You have to beware of being so strict that you repress what is good in a person. Hopefully, so far I have done it well because she has got a lot of kindness in her, as well as being confident. She gets a lot of input at home, you know, you don't laugh at other people's discomforts. If it happened to you and somebody laughed at you you wouldn't like it. We try and make her realize those things that even though it's a fact of life that we are not all equal, some have more than others, we all have to live together so we have to respect others, that better off doesn't mean better. If she wants to laugh at some one who has less than her, well put yourself in their position.

Except for Lesley, on the other hand, the white middle-class women queried neither the *status quo* nor the inequalities it produced. There was an unexplored assumption, underlying most of the white middle-class women's words, that the educational system should be working to secure their ambitions for their offspring without any contextualization of what that implied in terms of opportunities for other people's children. It was only the black women and a small number of white working-class women who conceptualized the educational system as operating in ways which resulted in inequalities.

You cannot act on inequalities you are not aware of, but then I am not in a position to speculate about most of the white women's levels of awareness, because they were often unexpressed in the interview. Discourses of meritocracy may have a differential impact on black and white women. They seem to have contradictory effects for black mothers because, on the one hand, they can see inequalities operating in relation to 'race' and, as a consequence, are more likely to reject prevailing political discourses which present children as 'having an equal chance'. On the other hand, black women, regardless of social class, were all strongly committed to their child's academic success and in the interviews placed a greater emphasis on academic achievement than white working-class women. Superficially, they seemed to be complying with discourses of meritocracy, in spite of their awareness of inequalities of 'race'.

Bourdieu writes of the paradoxical consequences of compliance with the educational system, and rejects the dichotomy between submission and resistance inherent in accounts of working-class schooling such as Paul Willis' *Learning to Labour* (Bourdieu and Wacquant, 1992: 23). As he points out:

> Resistance may be alienating and submission may be liberating. Such is the paradox of the dominated and there is no way out of it. (Bourdieu, 1990b: 155)

I would suggest that the messages black women were giving their children, that they needed to work hard, were strategies to mitigate the effects of living in a racist society (see also Mirza, 1992; 1995).

It may have been that the majority of white working-class women did not view a discussion about their involvement in their children's education as an appropriate forum to raise issues around class inequalities. Some of the black mothers did, however. The most explicit articulation of class inequalities was expressed by Cathy:

> A lot of people from Aston are sending their kids to Maddon now, you know very middle-class so what hopes have the likes of me got. These parents are the ones with choice. I work in the school and have to deal with them. They expect to get what they want. You should hear some of them talk to me, as if I was nothing, just a servant, or else they are friendly, but in a really condescending way. When the Government talks about parents it means parents like that. It's all about cutting down on the social mix not increasing it. It's about segregated education without paying for it. I think when it comes down to it that's what Major's classless society is about.

In the process of attempting to understand and deal with the dynamics of a racist society some black women seem to have developed an awareness and agency which was not matched by their white, working-class counterparts. What I do think is important to point out is that when that awareness and agency is placed in the balance with the countervailing effects of living in a racist society, it is the constraints rather than the opportunities that still seem to weigh the heaviest.

Bourdieu's work has been criticized for presenting cultural capital as something the working-classes lack (Jenkins, 1992: 146; Szczelkun, 1993: 108). 'Race' and ethnicity do not even enter the frame of the debate. However, Hirabayashi (1993) has argued that the Zapotec migrants in Mexico City create their own cultural capital in response to the day to day challenges of city life. The migrant associations they form constitute a form of social capital, while the solidarity they develop – *paisanazgo* – is a form of embodied cultural capital:

Specifically, when mountain Zapotecs find themselves in a mega-
lopolis such as Mexico City, where they are at a disadvantage –
in competing for jobs and other resources, paisanazgo provides a
familiar context and a means for obtaining provisions, information,
resources and political power. (Hirabayashi, 1993: 113)

I am arguing that a similar process was operating in respect to black women
and their children's education in Milner, particularly with regard to information and resources such as black schools and black parents' groups.

Slipping Away

Social change meant many of the white working-class women were struggling
with a disjuncture between habitus and the social field. Their own experience
of entering a buoyant labour market in the 1960s and 1970s had led to expectations that there should be jobs for young people. Half the working-class
women expressed either resignation or anger that there were no longer
'proper' jobs for their children. Jill told me 'it's all training schemes, they
expect them to go on some training scheme'. while Josie said 'there aren't any
proper jobs for our kids'. These women clearly felt that they were operating in
a context of reduced social capital. There was a pervading sense that the social
capital accruing from their immediate and extended family had been slipping
away since they had been adolescents seeking work. Julie, Jenny, Jean and
Jackie had all 'walked into jobs' arranged by one or both of their parents.
Their views about the current local labour market situation were based on an
understanding that in the recessionary nineties jobs were scarce and no longer
available through working-class family networks to anything like the extent
they had been in the 1960s and 1970s:

> Well there's nothing out there for them is there Diane. It's totally
> different from when I left school. Then I just walked into a job. Both
> my mum and dad worked in the shoe factory and they put a word in
> for me and that was it. They more or less got the job for me. Now
> there's nothing out there for our children. If they get a job it's a
> Youth Training Scheme and they're thrown out of it when someone
> cheaper comes along. (Julie, Milner)

and:

> Carly will have to stay at school as long as possible. It's not like in my
> day. My mum got me a job with her firm and I started the next week.
> (Jackie, Milner)

This awareness of the constraints imposed by the wider economic context had
paradoxical consequences to the extent that all the working-class mothers

strongly emphasized the importance of staying on to gain further qualifications. Jean told me 'nobody gets a decent job nowadays without qualifications'. However, this realization that 'qualifications are essential' (Julie) intensified the pressure and anxiety mothers had to deal with in relation to their children's schooling. Allatt and Yeandle identify a similar process of social capital slipping away in the context of local labour markets:

> The changing character of the local labour market meant that the affective networks of kins and friends was both becoming scarce and losing its currency. (Allatt and Yeandle, 1992: 41)

On one level the effects of the current economic recession could be viewed as setting working-class mothers up to fail. In order to ensure that her child negotiates the passage to adulthood successfully, I suggest that 'the good mother' increasingly has to make sure her child is academically successful. She has to achieve this in an educational context where the material and social resources she often lacks are of growing importance.

It is constraints which characterize working-class women's socializing. Working-class women's material circumstances and those of their social networks often mitigated against frequent social contact with friends and relatives who lived outside the locality. Josie was one of a number of women who told me she could not afford to go out socially. It is clearly difficult maintaining friendships on a low income. There were times when Jalil and Josie could not afford to attend the aerobics classes at the local sports centre. The classes cost £1.80. While Linsey mentioned travelling across London to go to a dinner-party, the friends the working-class mothers saw regularly invariably lived 'round the corner', as in the case of Jalil and Jenny and Josie and her friend, Dorothy. Contact with parents and extended family was much easier if they lived within walking distance. Joyce and June, who both lived across the road from their parents, saw them daily. Jenny used to see her mother every day when they were living on the same estate. Since her mother had been rehoused in another borough she said 'I can sometimes go two or three weeks without seeing her'. This situation was not presented sanguinely by Jenny, but as a cause of regret – the inevitable outcome of budgetary constraints and the restricting timetable imposed by her children's schooling. I discovered that working-class women frequently found themselves dealing with a situation in which lack of money and transport constrained opportunities for generating social capital. These constraints affected not only their own possibilities but also the range of choices they could provide for their children.

After School: Free Time versus Packed Timetables

Lack of resources seriously impinged on working-class women's ability to organize after-school activities for their children. While mornings for mothers

across the sample are similar experiences, the time after school is characterized by striking differences. Cultural capital is central to understanding differences regarding how time was spent after school. Miriam David has written
about the mothering work entailed in extra-curricular activities, 'both in organising them and often in acting as unpaid chauffeur to children in order for
them to attend these activities' (David, 1984: 198). However, it was middle-
class children who were caught up in a whirl of extra-curricular activities. Few
of the working-class children were involved in organized activities after school.
Bourdieu stresses the importance of extra-curricular activities which, although
not taught in schools, are highly valued in the academic market. Such activities
generate a form of cultural capital which yields high symbolic profits
(Bourdieu, 1984: 63). From the evidence of my research it was middle-class,
not working-class children, who had access to this form of cultural capital.

The Milner playground at 3.30pm was always full of mothers, milling
around in small groups, laughing and chatting. Most mothers came on foot and
took their children straight home after school. Fathers were a rarity. Brendan
collected Matthew and his sister twice a week, while Naomi's father picked her
up every Wednesday. Out of my sample of 20 children, four, Shula, Stuart,
Lucy and Fola stayed for playcentre, paying the £1 per evening charge which
had recently been introduced.

It was also predominantly mothers collecting children at Oak Park. Martin told me in passing one day 'Today's a miracle day'. When I asked him why
he said 'because my father's collecting me'. However, here there was no
loitering: mothers turned up in cars, usually exchanging no more than waves
with each other, before speeding off, often with two or three children in the
back. Most mothers were members of organized networks, collecting their
children on a rota basis, a system which rewarded women with 'days off'.
Lucinda only collected Jessica twice a week, while Louise collected Amy three
times.

Intricate social arrangements were a feature of Oak Park. The norm was
not to go straight home, but to attend an organized activity, have tuition, or
visit a friend. It was mothers who arranged, co-ordinated and serviced these
out-of-school activities. The only father involved on a regular basis was Neil.
The one Milner child to have anything approaching the structured leisure time
which was characteristic of Oak Park was middle-class. Naomi went to gymnastics on Monday, saw her tutor on Tuesday, had free evenings on Wednesday and Thursday, attended a trampolining class on Friday and a Hebrew class
on Saturday. Attendance at a range of out-of-school activities was crucial to
the generation of cultural capital in Oak Park. There appeared to be a shared
objective of ensuring that children gained accomplishments. The average Oak
Park child learned to play a musical instrument, attended drama and/or dance
classes and had extra paid tuition in preparation for entrance exams. Some
mothers that I interviewed listed five organized activities that their child
attended every week. Tutoring was widespread. Out of the 29 pupils in the
class where I did my participant observation 19 had a tutor. However, within

this overall percentage of 62, there were clear gender differences – 71 per cent of the girls had a tutor, but only 37 per cent of the boys.

In fact, participation in social activities generally was gendered. It was primarily girls who were attending four or five paid activities a week. Louise and Amy are typical of mothers and daughters in the school. On Monday Amy is collected by a friend's mother and dropped off after 6 pm. On Tuesdays, Louise takes Amy and her friend to dancing classes. On Wednesday, the English tutor comes to the home. On Thursday Amy has her guitar lesson and is taken home by one of the other mothers. Friday is a free evening and Louise picks Amy up and takes her home via the supermarket. At the weekend there is a further tuition session, this time in Maths, and Amy has a piano lesson. Louise summed up her early evenings and weekends as 'all about chauffeuring'. Miriam David raises the influence of children's sex. Maternal protectiveness results in continued collection of girls long after boys are allowed to travel on their own (David, 1984). Mothers of daughters at Oak Park spent from two to six hours a week chauffeuring their daughters from one activity to another.

Lydia O'Donnell found that in over half the families she studied mothers 'spent between three and five hours a week chauffeuring' (O'Donnell, 1982: 124). While she does not discuss gender differences, there were specific reasons for the gender differences in Oak Park. These differences were explained by the Headteacher as a consequence of 'Ambitious parents of boys having already moved them across to the private sector by Year 5'. There were boys, like Martin and Oliver, whose after-school timetable resembled that of the girls. However, there were also boys, like Sergei and Simon, who were involved in only one or two after-school activities. When the focus is on girls, it is difficult to avoid the impact of social class. Susan, the only working-class girl in 5S, had a schedule which was much closer to that of children in Milner than to other girls in her class. She did no out-of-school activities. Jean told me 'She keeps asking for a tutor because all the other girls have got one, but no way with five children and only one income coming in'.

As mentioned earlier, by far the most common thing for mothers and children to do at Milner was to go home, even if this involved stopping off at the shops on the way. A social whirl of organized activities was beyond their financial and geographical reach. Only two out of the 20 children in the Milner sample went home by car, and only three out of the 20 lived in families with an income of over £20000 a year. A few of the mothers had organized after-school activities for children. Linda took Mark to swimming class once a week. Lelia had enrolled Naomi at Hebrew class, and she had a Maths tutor, in addition to attending two gymnastics classes a week. Matthew went two evenings a week to the sports centre where Brendan, his father, worked and, at least once a week, took part in sporting activities there as well as having weekly tuition. In these cases the link with income becomes very apparent. Mark, Matthew and Naomi were the three children in families with incomes of over £20000. More surprisingly, Cathy and Jasbir paid for their children to have weekly tuition, while Julie had recently abandoned tuition sessions for George because 'the costs were crippling'.

The nearest to organized out-of-school activities most Milner children got was attendance at playcentre. Four of the children attended daily. However, as the title implies, emphasis was on play rather than learning or the acquisition of accomplishments. Even playcentre, since the introduction of the £1 an evening charge, had become outside the financial range of some mothers. Ann told me:

> Nicholas would like to stay for playcentre but financially, if he stayed then Matthew would want to stay as well and it would all mount up. It's too much money with two children, to be fair I'd have to let Matthew stay. I can do quite a lot with £10, you know, for them. Things are a bit tight these days.

A large part of many Oak Park children's afternoons and early evenings are taken up with activities of one sort or another. When they finally arrive home time has to be made for homework. Just how pressurized this time often is is evident in Liz's comment:

> I have to help him with his homework. It's usually this time, around eight when I get a minute, after they've finished their activities.

The workload of some Oak Park children, especially the girls, was immense. The classteacher estimated that she set the children approximately two to two-and-a-half hours of homework a week, but it was clear from the work that they brought into school that some children spent far longer than that. In addition, they had tutor homework, music practice and, for girls like Sophie, Negar and Riva, additional educational work set by their mothers. Leena told me 'for an hour every night Negar does some work that I set her', while Lucy said that Sophie had to do at least half an hour every night on Kumon Maths techniques and then additional work she set daily on 'essay writing techniques, grammar, spelling and punctuation'. Lavinia not only got up early every morning to hear Riva read, she also devoted her evenings to academic work with her daughter. She described the time the two spent together in the home as primarily devoted to Riva's educational progress. After collaborating together on work set either by the teacher or herself, she insists on Riva reading and then polices the activity:

> Every evening I have to literally go into her room and say 'Riva come on, what will you read tonight?'

The consequences are there in these three girls' estimation of the time they spent on homework. Negar's total was nine hours of homework and an additional four hours of reading, while Sophie has listed 12 hours a week, of which school homework is a three-hour component. Riva had distinguished between nine hours of studying and seven hours a week of reading. For all three girls this mother-directed work was squeezed into a timetable already packed with organized out-of-school activities. Even mothers who did not impose their own academic work programme spent a lot of time ensuring that their children met the school's homework requirements:

> I think I'd been through the spellings three or four times with Sophia and I was getting cross because she wasn't really concentrating. She was insisting she needed to take a little break so, you know, it was 'You can't watch "Top of the Pops" because you haven't learnt your spellings'. (Linsey, Oak Park)

Some mothers ended up introducing a degree of coercion into the process:

> He is too tired even to do his homework. My husband said to me 'Just let him be', but I have to force him, I have to force him. I know it's awful, but I have to and he hates it. (Liliana, Oak Park)

Because of a combination of factors – Milner's no-homework policy and the lack of money for organized activities – Milner children's evenings were characterized by free time and the semblance of choice, in direct contrast to that of many of their mothers who, as I have discussed in Chapter 6, often talked of domestic responsibilities taking up all their time in the evenings. No child told me, as did three or four children in Oak Park, that they 'did not have a free evening'. Instead, a number of children, four girls and one boy, had chosen to do homework and, on their own initiative, had set up a special arrangement with their classteacher. Jane told me:

> Delroy wanted to do homework. He actually asked Mandy for some and she put him off because she had too much on that week, but he did ask again if he could bring some home. I helped him with it but really it was too easy for him. He still brings some home but not so often. I think he finds it too easy for him.

Delroy was not the only child to arrange a personalized homework programme for himself. Lucy had organized with Mandy, her classteacher, to bring work home on a regular basis:

> Lucy brings these cards that they have in the classroom, Maths and English cards. She went through a stage last term when she was bringing them back every night. She loves it. She actually enjoys it, getting it done. She gets a real sense of achievement with the cards. As soon as she's finished them she says 'Mum tick them'. I have to do it there and then. So she gets a lot from it. (Jill, Milner)

A few children at Milner, namely Naomi, Andreas and Stuart, had to complete homework in the evening set by their mothers. However, many children were left to entertain themselves after school. The most the school asked in terms of home-based work was for children to read for ten minutes every evening and, occasionally, to learn spellings and times tables. So it was a voluntarism which characterized the majority of Milner children's evenings, a voluntarism which was totally absent from the Oak Park transcripts and fieldnotes. The two groups of mothers were working with very different conceptualizations of free time. For all the children in the sample, apart from Susan, free time at Oak Park came under the ambit of mother's organization with mothers exercising a tight control over how children used their time. Children's compliance rarely seemed to be questioned. Linsey told me that Sophia had wanted to stop ballet classes. Linsey said she had insisted that Sophia continue until the end of term, but that then they would discuss the issue again. Sophia decided to continue. Oliver told me how much he hated his Kumon Maths classes:

> going is the worst thing in the world, really the worst thing in the world, if you don't believe me ask Sophie.

When I asked if he could stop going, he confided that he had to go because it was good for him: 'Maths is my weak area'.

Although there were fragments of compulsion in working-class women's accounts – for example, Julie and Josie insisting their sons read to them – compulsion was shot through with enormous ambivalence. There was a strong sense that 'it was not good for children'. Although mothers in both schools use the terms 'force' and 'make them', in the working-class women's accounts the juxtaposition of compulsion with 'academic work' has powerful negative connotations that are absent in those of middle-class women. Joyce pointed out to me more that once in the interview that she felt that forcing children to do educational work jeopardised the mother-child relationship:

> I don't think children should be pressurised. I think if you sit a child down and say 'Do this, do that' then they can hold it against you.

Jill, Jackie and Janice all expressed similar views. I have explored earlier the powerful links which these attitudes had to women's own experience of education. Suffice to say this 'fear of forcing' combined with a general 'no-homework' policy and lack of funds meant many of the children at Milner had long stretches of unstructured time. The downside of having periods of free time is the resulting boredom a number of Milner children expressed.

Although most Oak Park weekends did not feature the social whirl of Oak Park weekdays, they were characterized by regularity and regulation. Negar attends an Arabic school from 9am until 2pm on Saturdays and then goes to poetry class for one and a half hours from 4pm until 5.30pm on

Saturday afternoon. On Sundays mornings she claimed to spend two hours reading, followed by a piano lesson on Sunday afternoon. A lot of the other girls used weekends for socializing, but many also had tuition and music lessons spilling over into the weekend period. So did some Oak Park boys, but they were more likely to list sporting activities on Saturdays and Sundays. It was at weekends that 'race' made a difference in Milner. Six out of the eight black children attended Saturday schools, while the vast majority of white children had no organized activities.

Socializing

Oak Park children's socializing was built around their acquisition of cultural and educational accomplishments. Small groups of children would go to one child's home for a snack before all attending drama class together. Three of the children in 5S attended the same Kumon Maths class and spent social time together both before and after the class. Girls, in particular, shared tutors and attended the same dance and drama classes. Over and above this social contact, however, the children at Oak Park socialized regularly. Allatt (1993) identifies 'the asset of sociability' as an integral part of social capital. It is clear from what Linsey, Lavinia, Leena, Lisa, Louise, Lucinda and Lucy told me that these women were actively fostering in their daughters:

> the skills necessary for the creation of their own social capital-sociability and an understanding of the mechanisms of social networking. (Allatt, 1993: 143)

Socializing was accentuated in both the Oak Park children's and their mothers' accounts. While I was observing in Oak Park, the children in 5S did some work on the 24-hour clock for which they had to produce a typical timetable for a week in the school term. Some children, in particular the girls who made up 'the gang of four' listed up to 10 hours of socializing. However, the norm was much nearer to Riva's four hours a week. The girls, in particular, regularly discussed their social life in the classroom, telling me about plans for 'sleepovers' involving four or five girls all staying at the same friends' house on Friday or Saturday night. Planning parties and producing lists of who was to be invited was a regular occurrence in 5S. Riva and Magda spent all of one lunchtime compiling a list of guests for their joint party. All the girls, apart from the two working-class girls, Susan and Temi, were to be invited. Socializing seemed to be intricately bound up with the existence of high-status groups. Riva told me:

> I know Dee, Jessie and Bella aren't my friends in school but we go to each others' houses. They're coming to our party.

That she should mention these three girls' names out of all the ones she is inviting is significant, as they are the three most influential members of the pupil peer group. It is also significant that the two girls with the lowest status among the girls were the only ones to be excluded.

While in Oak Park free evenings and weekends were often times for socializing, in Milner no-one used the term 'socializing' or described a process of children regularly seeing friends out of school. Although it was clear neither Milner mothers nor their children were operating with extensive social calendars, many of the women described seeing regularly members of their extended family. Jill's parents were leaving as I arrived on Tuesday evening. Joyce's mother popped round at least two evenings a week, and her husband's parents travelled five miles across London every Thursday to spend the evening with their grandchildren. Cathy, Carmel, Josie, Janice and June all talked of regularly spending an evening with their parents. Jalil's father came for supper on Thursdays, while Jean's sister came to visit once a week. For these women socializing did not have the instrumental quality of much middle-class socializing in Oak Park. It was rooted in emotional support. For the children it seemed to be more about bonding with members of the extended family than part of a process of acquiring social contacts. As Jill explained:

> It's to do with morals. Lucy has been very good but I had to sit Gemma down and explain to her about being caring about her family. Her aunt and her grandparents come every week, but all she seems to want to do is go off gallivanting with her friends. So I had to say to her 'It's wonderful to have lots of friends and a social life outside the home but you should never forget your family. It's important to show you value them whatever else is going on in your life'.

As I have touched on earlier, there was no evidence of extensive social networking among the children at Milner. There was no conceptualization of social hierarchy to be found in either mothers' or their children's accounts. By contrast, the existence of high-status groups is a continuing theme across many of the Oak Park mothers' interviews, as well as being the key to many of the girls' social manoeuvrings within the classroom. The one main exception to this was the accounts both the Jewish mothers and their children gave me of the importance of regular contact with their extended family. Martin said 'Friday night is family night, my grandparents come and we have a family dinner'. Other Jewish children in the class talked similarly of family nights which incorporated grandparents and sometimes aunts, uncles and cousins.

The vast majority of Milner mothers never mentioned socializing or the importance of developing social skills. The only mother to do so was middle-class. Lelia raised the issue of social skills in relation to middle-class survival in working-class contexts:

Naomi had a hard time socially. She's very caught because she's from a middle-class family and that's not helped. She hasn't got the right credentials, she doesn't quite fit in so she's worked on being socially acceptable and that's created its own problems. I mean she's got this split way of talking, one for her friends and one for home. I mean you are torn because there are so many positive things. Naomi is so strong about issues to do with race and gender. She's very good at working as a member of a team. They're all very good skills and they come from being a middle-class child in a predominantly working-class school, and having constantly to negotiate your acceptability.

However, this absence in women's accounts was sometimes contradicted by what I found in the course of the field work. Jalil's flat was full of other women when I arrived to do the interview. She sent these three women away, but two more turned up while she was talking to me. Cassie was very involved in refugee support groups, and had a steady stream of refugees who she helped and befriended, passing through her flat, while Josie popped in to see Jenny as I was leaving.

John Hood-Williams, writing about power relations in children's lives, states that:

> What appears to be distinctive about these controls over the child's life is their reference to space, body and the child's time. (Hood-Williams, 1990: 163)

The activities at Oak Park, from tuition to timetabled social interaction, and the absence of such activities in Milner, added up to a significant difference. Middle-class mothers managed their children's time far more heavily than working-class mothers. As a consequence, the leisure time of middle-class children had a very different pattern and regularity from that of their working-class counterparts. Lynne Chisholm *et al.* (1990) comment that 'children's lives are busier than in the past'. From the evidence of my research, however, that busyness is class-specific. Working-class children were far less likely to be caught up in a whirl of out-of-school activities than their middle-class counterparts. Chisholm *et al.* assert that 'leisure activities and life-style join education and training as the mediators of competitive and individualised acquisition of cultural "credentials" both formal and informal' (Chisholm *et al.*, 1990: 7). A comparison between the out-of-school activities of these working- and middle-class children illustrates that the two groups have very differing possibilities for acquiring 'socially valued' cultural capital.

An acceleration in the tempo of life (Buchner, 1990) was far more a feature of middle-class than working-class children's experience. There is an interesting interaction between mothering practices in Oak Park and their children's lack of time, the one using up the other in an attempt to generate cultural capital. A recognition of the effect that regular, organized leisure has on the amount of time available to children is there in middle-class mothers' interviews. Linsey, talking of her daughter's best friend, said 'They used to see each other regularly, but now they're so busy she doesn't get a chance'. While Leena told me 'She sees her best friend regularly, at ballet class'.

One consequence is that some of the children's accounts mimic the themes of pressurized time found in their mothers' accounts. Buchner describes a process experienced particularly by urban and middle-class children, in which the tempo of their lives accelerates to such an extent that children are left feeling they have no time (Buchner, 1990: 80). A sizeable minority of children in Oak Park expressed similar sentiments. Martin told me 'I don't have a free evening', while Robyn confided 'I'm busy doing something every evening and at the weekend'. In a book she made in the classroom as part of a project on 'myself', she starts off her description of herself with the sentence 'I am happy, shy and busy'.

Middle-class mothers were engaged in an extensive, systematic programme of generating cultural capital for their children, whether it was straightforwardly educational capital through tuition, cultural capital through art, dance, drama and music classes, or social capital through orchestrating regular slots for their children to develop their own social networks and practice their social skills (Bourdieu, 1984). In doing so, they were, in part, responding to a range of external pressures – familial, neighbourhood and the pupil peer-group. Dance, drama and music lessons were 'what people like us do' (Bourdieu, 1990a: 64–5). However, this was mothers rather than their children, deciding on involvement in out-of-school activities. Although some mothers occasionally let children have a deciding voice, more often children had no choice. Oliver and Sophie both expressed their intense dislike of Kumon maths classes, but they had to go in spite of their negative feelings. Similarly, the three mothers who put their children's names down for a prestigious drama school when they were all under three could not have engaged in any process of shared decision-making with their offspring. Rather, a rhetoric of shared decision-making served to mask the ways in which mothers controlled children's time. Riva was not enjoying one of her two drama classes. However, Lavinia had 'discussed with her the importance of continuing to go until she gets to the stage of being one of the most experienced in the group, then she can make up her own mind'.

A number of middle-class mothers made a connection between the energy and time they had to expend and their child being in the state system. Leena, Lisa, Lavinia and Lucy pointed out most of the work they had to undertake would be unnecessary if their daughters attended private schools, while Linsey commented:

> What you pay for in the private sector is for your child not to fail and for you not to have to make an enormous investment of your own time and energy. I realize that's what I'm doing because for the last

three years I've been teaching. When I went back to work I realized that I was doing the same thing at home as I am at work, which is educating, and I really feel that wouldn't have been the case if I had sent them to private schools.

The inequalities that permeated the transcripts and the field notes were those between middle-class and working-class women and, mediating these, those between black and white mothers. However, in the middle-class stories the focus on inequality, if it was there at all, was far more likely to be on the mothers' own invidious position in relation to other middle-class mothers who send their children to private schools. The five mothers I mentioned had managed to redefine inequalities in their narratives so that they become the 'disadvantaged'.

That, however, was not my reading of their texts. Middle-class mothers were planning, co-ordinating and executing enrichment programmes for their children. In monopolizing scarce resources within the state sector, deploying financial resources to secure children's educational advantage and drawing on useful social networks which excluded working-class mothers, many of the middle-class women were ensuring that the outcome of the educational competition was resolved in their children's favour. They were bringing habituses shaped by educational success and a sense of entitlement to the field of primary education, and, consequently, were not dealing with anything as ephemeral as the working-class women's hopes and desires. They were guaranteeing their children's educational success. My study provides support for Dorothy Smith's view that middle-class mothers:

> by reason of occupying positions, from which, in varying degrees, power is exercised, can be seen to both actively organise the internal relations of their own classes to maximise their advantage, and to actively manage the working-class in their interests as well. (Smith, 1989a: 112–113)

In contrast, many of the working-class mothers were unaware of the rules of the educational game in which they were caught up. Information about how the educational system operates is a vital component of cultural capital. Although there was evidence of awareness of wider educational contexts than that of Milner and the secondary schools it fed into, the majority of working-class women seemed blissfully unaware of just how many resources middle-class mothers were investing in their children's primary schooling. Jill and Joyce both asserted that 'their children did a lot more homework than other children their age', while Josie told me 'I'm seriously going to have to do something about Leigh's school work once he gets to secondary school'. However, most of the middle-class mothers had been 'seriously doing things' for at least the past five years, some for much longer:

Amy started school just before she was three. I had done simply masses of learning activities with her at home before she went so she was exceptionally advanced academically. (Louise, Oak Park)

Conclusion

In this chapter I have tried to illustrate through the accounts of middle-class women and their children the myriad ways in which they were able to generate social capital in support of their children's schooling. In contrast, working-class women lacked the resources to enable their children to undertake similar social activities and often felt their access to useful social networks was slipping away. The exception was black, working-class mothers who appeared to have much more politicized and aware social networks to draw on. In particular, the black communities of which they were part provided resources such as Black Saturday schools and Black parents' groups. In the next chapter I examine the absence in my text so far; fathers, and what mothers have to say about the involvement of male partners in children's schooling.

Chapter 9

Men on the Margins

Gendered habitus generates a view of the world in which the division of labour between men and women is seen as 'natural' and much domestic labour is rendered invisible. The 'ontological complicity' (Bourdieu, 1981: 306) of female habitus results in mothers feeling made for their mothering. One consequence is that women across the sample either take their partners' limited involvement for granted, or reluctantly accept it as inevitable. The division of labour between women and their male partners in relation to parental involvement is rarely problematized in women's accounts. There seems to be a general acceptance of fathers' marginality. Although there is very little research which looks at fathers' involvement in their children's schooling (Lareau, 1989; 1992; Ribbens, 1993), the little that does exist confirms that fathers are often distant from the day-to-day maintenance of home–school relationships.

I found that lack of paternal involvement was a feature in women's accounts which crossed class differences. Just under half of the 22 women living with a male partner saw them as uninvolved in their children's education. Of these nine, five were working-class and four middle-class. According to Linsey, Leena and Janice their partners had little time for involvement because they left for work before 8am and rarely arrived home before 7.30pm. Over half of this group of women were full-time carers, while only two worked full-time in the labour market, which would suggest that these more traditional arrangements tend to be reproduced within the sphere of parental involvement. When I asked Jackie who else is involved in Carly's education she said 'No one', so I probed 'What about your husband?'. 'No, he's not.' 'At all?' 'No.'. She went on to tell me about the help she got from Carly's elder sister. Janice's explanation was a common one among this group of women:

No, he's not really involved. He'll maybe sit and listen to them read once in a while if I haven't got time. But he doesn't really get involved on his own initiative. He works long hours and I think he feels if I do it he doesn't need to.

On occasions women's versions of paternal non-involvement were confirmed by their male partners. Paul happened to be at home when I was interviewing

Linda. He initially asked if I was interviewing fathers as well, but before I could reply, commented 'I suppose most dads are only involved at a distance'.

Helping Hands and Public Personae

Twelve mothers described their husbands as 'involved', seven from Oak Park and five from Milner. However, it soon became apparent that involvement can mean many different things. Jasbir's husband sometimes helps with Sharoff's homework but never goes into school, whereas Lesley and Lavinia both have husbands who were very involved in the public sphere of home school interaction – for example, chairing the Parent–Teachers' Association, organizing fundraising events and producing the parents' school play. At the same time, both had no role in their child's home-based educational work. Evans (1988) in his research into primary schooling in Australia describes a similar process in which:

> In equating parenthood with these forms of school activity, fathers are able to shift their parental responsibility from the home, to the more masculine territory of maintenance work at school or attending meetings. Within their families such fathers are able to absent themselves from what little parenting they do at weekends or during evenings, in order to perform what are recognized as important tasks. (Evans 1988: 87)

However, it was not only Evans' fathers who present their limited involvement as central. There were shades of Hochschild's 'family myths' in Lavinia and Lucinda's statements that they 'share the parental involvement with their partners'. Hochschild and Machung (1989) describe a process in which women redefine an unequal familial division of labour as equitable. Beneath both mothers' taken-for-granted assumption of paternal involvement lies a very different variant of involvement to that of their own. Lucinda initially tells me that Peter is 'involved, yes, I'd say he was very involved'. However, the only example she gave me of his involvement told a different tale:

> If there has been a bit of tension between Anna and me, you know what it's like, they often say 'mummy tell me if this is right'. That's OK, but if I then want to explain how to do it, it's more difficult. It's easy to say parents ought to be supportive but children don't always make it that easy there's an emotional tension and sometimes that can be dissipated by me saying 'go and ask daddy' or whatever, so we can split it that way.

Lucinda's was far from the only example when paternal involvement meant relieving the pressure of educational work on mothers.

Male involvement, where it did exist in the home, was primarily focused at the two ends of the scale of parental involvement. Men either helped out when women were too busy, or else their intervention was at the level of decision-making and advice-giving. Liliana told me that she 'desperately wanted to employ a tutor for Sergei' but :

> My husband said 'No, you must just leave him because he is too tired. If you get him another teacher after a whole day at school it will make him worse. A new person will be too much'. So I will teach him and then we can stop when he gets too tired.

Louise outlined a very clear division of labour in which she undertook the day-to-day educational work with her daughter while:

> Of course any important decision we will sit down and decide together.

Only Lisa and Lola talk about a gendered division of labour in relation to the child's curriculum, both husbands taking responsibility for maths and science homework. But there was little evidence in any of the women's accounts of men being involved in monitoring or repairing their child's educational performance. Intense, repeated daily work with children was very much the province of the mother, they were the ones with 'the finger on the pulse'. Geoffrey, who within my sample counts as an involved father, tells me that 'I've never found children very forthcoming about what they are doing and what they are thinking'. However, his wife Lisa clearly does not trust 'hands-off' methods of waiting for the child to volunteer information and tells me that she often 'spends a lot of time worming information out of Melinda about what she's done at school'.

Marion Tolbert Coleman (1989) has highlighted the subtle, yet important difference existing between 'taking responsibility for' and 'helping with'. She points out that there is a significant difference between taking responsibility for a task without being asked, and having to make your male partner aware that something needs doing and then asking if he will do it. Brendan, Christine's husband, was one father perceived to be involved in his children's education on a regular daily basis. When Linda suggested that I should interview Christine, she added 'because then you'll get a father who's really involved in his children's education'. However, unlike many of the academic texts on parental involvement, there is no conceptualization of sharing or partnership in Christine's account. Christine describes what Brendan does as 'help, Brendan helps a lot'. Christine reiterated many times over the course of the interview that she could not have coped without Brendan's willingness to take some responsibility for co-ordinating the children's school day, and even pointed out how much more skilled he was at hearing the children read than she was:

He's always very positive with what he writes in the comment book. He writes it very quickly, you know 'she's not using phonics'. He's very good at it.

It is difficult to surmize if this help that Brendan provides would have continued if Christine's work circumstances had changed. In the current situation, however, it was the only way in which the two of them could juggle work commitments without incurring child-minding costs. Christine's work schedule included two evenings when she worked until 8pm in the Beauty Salon, and so on Tuesdays and Wednesdays Matthew and his younger sister walked the 5 minute journey from school to the Sports Centre where their father worked.

> Christine: 'Brendan's very good, two nights a week I don't finish until 8 then they actually go round to the Sports Centre where he works and actually do sports after school.'
> Diane: 'Every week?'
> Christine: 'Yes.'

However, when Christine relayed the details of the prior week, she told a slightly different tale:

> Tuesday they went to Brendan's work. I think they stayed at work for a little while then they came home. When I got back I got Sarah to read to me and made sure Matthew did some reading on his own . . . Wednesday Brendan runs them round to his sister's. I work on a Wednesday until eight.

One of the two evenings when Brendan is responsible for the children he delegates that responsibility to another woman, his sister, while Christine still retains the overall responsibility for ensuring that the children read.

I am not trying to minimize Brendan's role in his children's education. Within my sample Brendan, like Geoffrey, counts as an involved father. Rather, I have tried to demonstrate through Christine's account some of the ways in which paternal and maternal involvement differ. Jordan *et al.* (1994) found in their study of middle-class couples that women constructed their family role as including overall responsibility for child-care 'whereas men construe "supportiveness" to mean occasional assistance' (Jordan *et al.*, 1994: 47). Similarly, it is the construction of Brendan in Christine's account as 'special' and herself as 'lucky' that highlights the inequalities operating within the parameters of parental involvement. While mother's educational work can be 'taken-for-granted', fathers' involvement occupies the realms of the 'not to be expected', it is something to be grateful for (Hochschild, 1987).

Adding to Rather Than Subtracting from Mothers' Work?

In some cases men could be viewed as adding to the range of roles women had to assume in relation to their child's education. All the mothers elaborated in great detail the minutiae of getting children up. However, fathers did not figure in their constructions of what happened, except as peripheral figures. For instance, Lola talked about having to get her husband up as well as Nancy. The job of making sure children got up, got dressed, fed and ready for school was clearly designated as women's work until children were able to take on the responsibility themselves. Men, when they did feature, were there as people with important priorities, whose timetable took precedence over that of mothers and children. Work schedules often meant that they left home earlier than the children did. In the few instances where men combined going to work with dropping children off at school, extra tensions and conflicts could arise:

> Neil has a strictness in the morning. If he has an appointment at nine he has to have everything sorted out. If it's not done then he starts to get very agitated. He starts screaming and shouting. 'How come this is not done?' 'How come that's not done?' He has to be out of the house by 8.30. If she is not ready by 8.30 then we are both to blame and there is usually a panic. (Lavinia, Oak Park)

Claire, Jenny and Jackie acted as buffers between their child and the father. Jackie, who had first said categorically that her husband was not involved, later explained to me:

> You see he gets cross with Carly if he thinks she's not doing well. It's best he doesn't try and help with her school work. He's got no patience, you see. He just gets angry with her.

While Claire told me:

> Well Ron's interested, he's interested in what Nick's covering at school. He's not anything like as involved though, he's interested. Nick irritates him, so I'll end up saying 'Let me help you with that Nick', no he's not anything like as involved as me.

Mediating between father and child increases women's work. Jenny talks about taking a protective stance in relation to Andreas, bolstering his self-esteem in the face of his father's criticisms, in addition to carrying out the necessary repair work:

> Last term he brought home all his times tables to learn. It was terrible he just didn't know them, honestly, the one times table was the best.

His dad came down, he thought his son was totally, you know, a dunce. I said 'It's no good getting cross with him, that won't help. It's just that he doesn't understand it, that's what it is. He does not understand what he's supposed to do. He needs help with it, not yelling at. You have to explain it to him'. Do you know it took ages, about three months before he grasped it all, we'd been over it so many times before it clicked.

Jenny provided the most explicit example of men adding to rather than sharing educational work. She told me that Costas had not given Andreas any encouragement with his schooling – rather, she said he becomes angry 'and tells me off'. However, he had insisted that she undertake more work herself:

> Costas has made sure Andreas goes to Greek school. Andreas goes every Saturday. It is a real drag I have to go all the way to Richmond Road. Then I have to collect him again at 1.30. It has been good for him, he's really enjoyed it, but as far as his father being involved, well he isn't.

Oak Park Fathers – a Gendered Generation of Cultural Capital

The presence of fathers in school influenced how families were perceived by teachers. Teachers in both schools linked 'real' interest in children's schooling to fathers' attendance at school events. It was unsurprising then that some women talked about trying to ensure either that male partners came with them or, more rarely, in their place. As Christine told me:

> I made a bad mistake I was so wound up about Matthew I felt I needed to see Maggie as soon as possible but it was Brendan's night on and he couldn't come with me. I should have waited until he had an evening off.

While Liliana commented:

> It is much better my husband go to parents' evening. He is very authoritative. He will not be intimidated by the teacher.

This is not to rob men of agency. Obviously, many fathers came of their own volition. However, it suggests that masculinity is seen as a resource in dealing with teachers. At the same time masculinity is not an undifferentiated notion – it appears to be primarily middle-class masculinity which impresses teachers. The one working-class father who had any concerted contact with teachers over the study period was a working-class father of a Year 6 girl. He both wrote a letter and came into school to see the Milner Headteacher in order to complain about the sex education programme. While Maxine, one of the Year 5 teachers told me he was 'mad', Maggie, the Headteacher dismissed him as 'just a stupid man'.

Attendance at parents' evenings fitted in with middle-class perceptions that the role of fathers was one of overseeing, rather than working at, children's educational progress (Lareau, 1989). However, it is important to point out that a number of women 'stage managed' their partner's presence on the school site. Liliana sent her husband into school on his own on parents' evening because she felt he dealt with school staff more effectively than she did, while a number of other middle-class mothers felt that their male partner's presence added weight to their own words or provided a more powerful alternative. These middle-class strategies raise interesting issues around the relationship between gendered habitus and linguistic capital, in which what men have to say is seen as more important not only by the men but also by their female partners.

Regardless of home-based involvement, Oak Park fathers were much more visible at parents' evening than the fathers at Milner. At parents' evening in Milner only 12 per cent of the parents who turned up for consultations with Mandy, the Year 5 classteacher, were fathers. These fathers, a total of three, all came with their female partners. In contrast, in Oak Park, which boasted a 96 per cent attendance at parents' evening, the norm was for both parents to attend. Mrs Symmonds saw 15 couples, nine mothers and four fathers. While 85 per cent of mothers of children in 5S attended, so did 68 per cent of the fathers.

Two Oak Park fathers, Geoffrey and Neil, both went on the 5S class outing, along with one of the mothers. Neil, in particular, was viewed by the school as a very involved father and so he was – on the school site. He dropped Riva off and shared the task of picking her up with Lavinia. As a consequence, he was the one father who was involved in the otherwise totally female network of parents delivering to, and collecting children from, a range of out-of-school activities. The children in the class all knew him and clearly enjoyed his company. However, Lavinia had talked to me about the complex decision-making process concerning Riva's education in which she and Neil had engaged when Riva was in the infants, and the events which led up to it:

> I remember this occasion very clearly. I had broken my knee. I had a bad fracture but I still had to go to work because they were sending me back and forth in a cab. So I had to be at work, my husband was very busy with his business. In the meantime we were trying to juggle all these things and still get Riva to and from school. There were elaborate baby-sitting arrangements in the evening. I took Riva from home. I brought her in a cab because I was paid by work. I took her to the school gates. I left her there. I saw that she went into the school compound and she was lost. To me that was OK because I didn't worry about that but I remember the Headteacher either giving me

a call at home or making some reference in a PTA meeting because Riva must have gone and said 'I went to school alone'. So she made a rude comment, she made reference to Riva coming alone and my husband got very wild and he said 'How can you even think that we sent Riva to school on her own?' But when we looked back and analyzed why she could have made that statement, it came out to be that occasion where we went in the cab. In fact even now some of the other parents have said 'Are we considering sending Riva to school alone and we still say no'. You see there was that one experience and a really bad misunderstanding. You know the school telling me 'Riva came to school alone'. It was like 'How can we do this', and it caused a lot of aggravation. It is frightening to think what your child may be saying in school and what the staff may be thinking like 'This mother sends a 5 year old to school on her own'. Things can grow all out of proportion. The thing was I had a full-time job, my husband was not available to pick up Riva. He did collect her from school and drop her at this after school club. Then at 6pm he would pick her up from after school club. It was easier for him than for me because I was working in the West End. I had to travel to and from work so he was the one who would pick her up but one particular day he had to go in his car to the West End and got stuck in the traffic. Riva was to be picked up from after school club at 5.30. Then Neil makes me a call to say it's impossible he is stuck in the traffic at Hammersmith. So I quickly make arrangements to say I have to leave right now. Even if I leave right now I am going to be late. The whole experience was so traumatic. I knew Riva would not be alone that there would be an adult with her. But knowing we had not done what we were meant to do, to pick her up at 5.30. I got there by 6.15. The Headteacher was there 'How can you do this sort of thing?' I apologised, I pointed out it doesn't happen every single day. That it had been most unexpected. But again that sort of feeling–guilt, guilt, guilt, terrible feelings of guilt. From then on we decided that he must organize his business so that he could accommodate Riva. It was possible for him because he is his own boss, whereas I have not been able to, so he has always worked so that he has time to collect Riva in the middle of the afternoon and of course the family finances have suffered through him being flexible. He turns down work if it means he will be too busy to collect Riva.

None of the other mothers talked in terms of an extensive period of consideration, culminating in decision-making, which in effect resulted in the family prioritizing the child's education over the father's work.

Neil was far more involved in his child's education than any other father in my sample. The Headteacher commented that Neil was very involved, much more involved than Lavinia was. Her assessment serves to underline the invisibility of much mothering work. When the time Neil spent in dropping Riva at school, collecting her two evenings a week and fulfilling his obligations as secretary of the PTA are added up, he still spent less than half the time devoted by Lavinia to educational work in the home.

Male visibility in school did not indicate involvement in educational work in the home. As stated earlier, sometimes it was the result of a familial division of labour, as in the case of Lavinia and Lesley. More often it was orchestrated by mothers, such as Liliana and Leena, who were both very clear about the 'gravitas' men bring to social interaction with school staff. A number of other mothers, Christine, Linda and Liz, talked about bringing men to parents' evening with them for 'back up' when they felt their own concerns would not be heard. It was clear from listening to these women that they viewed men's distance from the child's education as an asset in interaction with the school. They saw their own, often intense, involvement as a barrier to communication with school staff.

The Influence of Changes in Labour Market Participation on Patterns of Involvement: All Change or Just Women

There already exists a substantial body of research which suggests that women's employment in the labour market does not significantly affect men's contributions within the home (Berk and Berk, 1979; Fenstermaker Berk, 1985; Coverman and Shelley, 1986; Morris, 1990; Ross and Mirowsky, 1990; Arber and Gilbert, 1991). Janice started work full-time in a local supermarket in February 1994, while Lavinia was made redundant two weeks before I interviewed her in November 1993. I spoke to both of them about their changed circumstances and how it impinged on their established pattern of parental involvement. For Janice there had been minimal impact on the allocation of responsibilities for parental involvement within the home. When referring to home-based educational work she spoke of 'squeezing it in':

> Janice: 'Well of course I can't go into school anymore but I do try and make sure I hear both of them read every evening.'
> Diane: 'Does Fred help?'
> Janice: 'Well like I said, it's difficult for him because he works such long hours.'
> Diane: 'Aren't you working long hours?'
> Janice: 'Well, I try and squeeze it in.'

Lavinia, whose changed circumstances should have afforded her more time, was rapidly propelled into a situation where her already extensive educational work in the home was expanded to encompass school-site involvement as well. Two months after losing her job, Neil volunteered her as treasurer of the PTA. Simultaneously, she became a regular helper in the school working with the two Year 3 classes. In addition to these new unfamiliar roles for someone whose parental involvement had always been firmly located in the home, Lavinia began to undertake far more educational work with Riva:

> I used to pay Riva very disciplined attention. She got my attention the moment I got back from work and I knew I was really tired because I used to work a really full day, more than a full-time job. So I knew she'd got my attention because I was the one to teach her at home. So I gave her a very strict regime, you know, always an hour. Then we would shop or cook, but she got that attention from me on a very strict basis. These days it is different and I don't know whether it is good or bad, but I give her my attention all the time, now we often seem to spend the whole evening on her work and I'm not sure whether that is good or bad.

In her interview Lavinia elaborates a division of labour in which she is the parent responsible for both planning and then executing educational work. However, she presents the differences between her own and Neil's input as 'natural':

> There is the homework to organize and like tonight she is having an evening with her friends so I have to think ahead, but usually because I have a very organized way of working I have usually worked out what Riva needs to do and what she needs to have for the morning in advance. My husband is much more spontaneous, he is lively and on the spot. He doesn't think about planning ahead. So where the week is concerned I do the planning and organizing. I will sort of sit with her and work it out with her in the evening to make sure her work gets done.

Within a construction of difference as natural there seems little possibility of change. In fact all the changes are made by Lavinia who increases both the range of tasks undertaken in relation to Riva's schooling and the amount of time taken in carrying them out. These two stories of Neil, an unadaptable man, and Janice, an adaptable woman, highlight a marked gender difference in the data. Mothers and fathers have very different priorities in relation to labour market participation and involvement in their children's schooling. The elasticity of women, the stretching of their time and attention, is a common theme across all the accounts.

Off Stage!

David *et al.* (1994) found that some ex-partners of lone mothers were involved in educational decision making around issues of secondary school choice.

However, I found little evidence of involvement in primary schooling within my own sample. Four of the lone mothers, Carol, June, Carmel and Jenny, spoke in terms of talking difficulties through with their child rather than another adult. When other adults were mentioned, it was primarily women friends (Jalil, Lucy, Cassie and Josie), own mother (Cathy) or sister (Jill). The one lone mother who mentioned consulting an ex-partner was Lucy, who said she often talked to Sophie's father about the resources necessary to support Sophie's education. The week before I spoke to her she had negotiated that he pay for a maths computer package after discussions about how useful it would be. Social class, and concomitantly, level of material resources, plays a part here. Middle-class Lucy was the only lone mother to receive financial support from her ex-partner and talking to him generated financial support for Sophie. This was not the norm for other lone mothers.

Lone mothers' accounts of the breakdown of their heterosexual relationships stands in contradistinction to the elevation of fathers as an unmitigated good in both right and left political discourses. Five of the 11 lone mothers had separated from their partner because of his physical violence, and this clearly had a bearing on their lack of contact. Current public and political opinion focuses on the negative and 'harmful' aspects of lone motherhood. However, there is a different version in the narratives of lone mothers like Jill and Josie in which the absence of abusive male partners is a bonus. Furthermore, as is evident in many of the accounts above, the presence of a male partner often had little impact on the amount of work women were undertaking in relation to children's schooling.

Issues of Power

Mothers operate with widely varying constraints on their involvement in schooling, but they all share the constraint of working within a patriarchal society. Women's explication of men's roles within the sphere of parental involvement resonates with vibrations of unequal power between men and women. This imbalance emerges in their explanation of what men actually do, which is predominantly helping women out with daily tasks that are primarily seen by both parents as her responsibility. It is there in men's more central involvement in decision-making about their children's education and the ways in which some of the mothers deferred to male partners' judgments. This power imbalance is also there in tales of persuading men to intercede 'powerfully' on the school site. It permeates accounts, expounded by Lavinia and Lesley, of a very clear division of labour which leaves them both with the day-to-day task of teaching the child in the home, and their husbands with a public role in the school setting. It also emerges in the way some mothers have to mediate not just between children and school, but between children and their fathers about issues of school work. Parental involvement is gendered. It means very different things for the woman of the house and her male partner.

This difference is most vividly illustrated in women's descriptions of the early morning. It is primarily women who get children up, dressed, fed and ready with all their equipment to go to school. Men disappear from these tales of getting things done, mostly to leave early for work.

Research into parenting in the 1990s found that many men played little part in the care of their children and that middle-class men working long hours are the group least likely to help with child care (Ferri and Smith, 1996). Similarly, I would like to suggest that for many of these women anything more than nothing seems a bonus, a gift to be grateful for (Hochschild, 1987). The underlying assumption by both parents that parental involvement, especially in the home, is women's work meant both men and women operated with a norm of men's non-involvement, unlike the texts on parental involvement which make a very different assumption – that of both parents' equal involvement. In fact a sizeable proportion of male presence in the school was managed and co-ordinated by women. As Liliana told me when I asked her why only her husband had attended parents evening 'I decided it was best he went so I made him go'. So, in a number of instances there was a level on which male presence in the school was, paradoxically, the accomplishment of invisible maternal work. Catherine Snow and her colleagues, although they began with the premise that both partners were involved, found in their research that it was mothers who were:

> the ones who helped with homework, selected reading material, answered questions, read bedtime stories, enforced TV rules, and in many other ways served the educating family functions. (Snow *et al.*, 1991: 68)

It is primarily women who are undertaking the day-to-day labour of parental involvement, not their male partners:

> You've got to be joking. Vassos does not get involved. Well he may tell me what to say to the teachers and if I'm lucky he may drop me off at the school gate but I don't call that getting involved in your children's education. (Julie, Milner)

The mother is also the parent who is emotionally involved in their child's education. Fathers rarely make the same emotional investment as their female partners. Anthony Giddens writes that:

> With the development of modern societies, control of the social and natural worlds, the male domain, became focused through 'reason'. Just as reason, guided by disciplined investigation, was set off from tradition and dogma, so it was also from emotion. As I have said, this presumed not so much a massive psychological process of repression as an institutional division between reason and emotion, a division

which closely followed gender lines. The identifying of women with unreason, whether in serious vein (madness), or in seemingly less consequential fashion (women as the creatures of caprice), turned them into the emotional underlabourers of modernity. (Giddens 1992: 200)

As Giddens points out, relationships within families need to be located within wider cultural understandings which recognize the unequal power relationships which exist between men and women, and the damaging consequences, for both sexes, of the ways in which they are played out within the private sphere of the family. One of the consequences, as we have seen in Chapter 6, is the intensity of some women's emotional involvement in their children's education in which women experience a whole gamut of powerful emotions – guilt, anxiety, frustration, as well as empathy, in relation to children's schooling.

Gendered habitus in the form of a taken-for-granted, sexual division of labour was evident in many of the women's words and their actions (Krais, 1993). I would suggest that Bourdieu's 'subjective vocations' (Bourdieu, 1981: 306) are just as applicable to gender as they are to social class. In the realm of parental involvement it was women, not men, who were operating with 'a fit' between what they feel 'made for' and what is expected of them (Bourdieu, 1981: 308). The consequence is that all three components of parental involvement – practical, educational and emotional – become women's work. Bourdieu writes of 'a toleration of exploitation' which infuses some habituses (Bourdieu, 1981: 315), and in an article, which focuses specifically on male domination, stresses the collusion of women with male oppressors (Bourdieu, 1990c). However, Leslie McCall argues that, while the most obvious reading of gendered habitus in Bourdieu's work depicts women as complicit in viewing gender divisions as natural and universal, a second, more feminist reading is possible (McCall, 1992). She suggests that the operations of gendered habituses and gendered capitals can be viewed as constitutive, rather than derivative, of social structure. As such, Bourdieu's conceptual framework provides possibilities for studying:

the complex process of enacting patterns of gendered social practice in a world that is at once rigid in its enforcement of gender symbolism and inventive in its capacity to challenge such symbolism in everyday life. (McCall, 1992: 852)

While there is little challenge to conventional gender symbolism in Bourdieu's own work, his concepts hold the potential for more feminist interpretations.

Tensions between reinforcing and challenging gender hierarchies as normative were evident in the stories that five of the lone mothers told of deciding to leave abusive male partners and, to a lesser extent, in the exasperation mothers like Jenny, Julie and Lelia expressed when describing their male partner's limited involvement. I would also suggest that sometimes apparent complicity with male power masked potentially effective strategies for getting fathers to do more. For example, that was one outcome from the actions of mothers who engineered their male partners' attendance at parents' evenings. Furthermore, the 'toleration of exploitation' of these mothers needs to be contextualized within the wider frame of male social power which operates powerfully to constrain women's choices. Mothers and fathers were both making sense of parental involvement in education, and their respective roles and responsibilities within a political climate in which both the Conservative and the Labour parties were actively promoting traditional family arrangements. In their accounts of the roles they and their male partners played in supporting children's education, women across the sample were revealing a gendered distribution of power in which women are positioned as the parent responsible for the children, and male activities outside the home continue to be more valued than female caring within it.

Chapter 10

The Conclusion

> Starting with this assumption that we are not a racist society and now with John Major that we are a classless society, the problems are actually being swept away so no one has to deal with these issues. People are no longer privileged because they are white, they are no longer privileged because they are middle-class. It's scary, it's frightening. What also frightens me is that after one hundred years of state education we are still not really sure why we are educating the working-classes. There are no jobs for them and the Government doesn't want thinkers. They just need pupils to be controlled in the classroom, to keep them busy, churning out a whole lot of facts, keep them so busy they don't have time to analyze, no time to question the way things are. Schools are becoming like firms and a firm is nothing to do with all those things we have been talking about. It is about efficiency, money, productivity and so things like human relations and social justice go right off the agenda. (Cassie, Milner)

Cassie's words rehearse a number of important issues in relation to the contemporary education field, in particular, the ways in which current educational policy is exacerbating inequalities of 'race' and social class (see also Gewirtz *et al.*, 1995; Vincent, 1996). While Cassie does not mention gender, this book has argued that there are no ungendered class and 'race' relations and has described through the accounts of 33 mothers the myriad ways in which gender, 'race' and social class are intertwined in home-school relationships.

There is an irony when collective action is almost always associated with the working classes (Hoggart, 1957; Seabrook, 1982), that effective class action within the educational field has always been the province of the middle-classes. I would argue that the individualistic and self-interested activities of the privileged in society add up to a specific form of collective class action. Within the educational field contemporary collective *middle-class* action has led to increasing class and racial segregation both between and within schools, from pressure for streaming, on the presumption that their children will be allocated to top sets (Reay and Ball, 1997; Gewirtz *et al.*, 1995), to the avoidance of schools with a sizeable cohort of black and/or white working-class pupils who might hinder their own child's learning (Vincent, 1992; Bagley, 1996).

A further irony lies in who it is who is doing this dirty work of class. It is primarily mothers who help children with schoolwork, talk to teachers and network in order to uncover relevant information which will 'give their child a Head start'. This is not to imply moral judgment. Middle-class mothers are often juggling intense anxieties about their children's education together with the pursuit of their educational advantage. On one level they are 'trapped in affluence' (Jordan *et al.*, 1994) and are subject to constraints, albeit very different constraints to those of the working-class mothers (David *et al.*, 1997). At the same time, the self-interest, instrumentalism and individualism which permeate many middle-class mothers' practices need to be analyzed in terms of their consequences for other, less privileged mothers and their children. In *Unhealthy Societies* Wilkinson has convincingly demonstrated how the pursuit of self-interest has damaged the health of the nation (Wilkinson, 1996). A similar argument can be made concerning the education of the nation where middle-class monopolization of increasingly scarce resources continues to contribute to a huge wastage of working-class educational talent.

This empirical study of mothers' work in support of children's education within the state system suggests a very different relationship between women and social class from orthodox perspectives which view their activities as largely peripheral. Because it uses social and cultural processes rather than occupational status to look at class relations, it allows for women rather than men to be the starting point for investigation. Over 20 years ago Basil Bernstein suggested that changes in the composition of the middle-classes were transforming the mother 'into a crucial preparing agent of cultural reproduction who provides access to symbolic forms and shapes the dispositions of her children so they are better able to exploit the possibilities of public education' (Bernstein, 1975: 131). The mothers in this study, in particular middle-class mothers, are at the front line of cultural reproduction, investing heavily in time and mental and emotional labour. Mothers have a relationship to the generation of cultural capital and, concomitantly, social class which is different from that of fathers. It is mothers who are making cultural capital work for their children. It is they, far more than men, who appear to be the agents of social-class reproduction. In particular, it is mothering work which bridges the gap between family social class and children's performance in the classroom. Maternal practices demonstrate that class is much more than materiality (Reay, 1997a). It is played out, not only in mothers' activities in support of children's schooling, but also in women's attitudes, assumptions and confidences about their children's education.

Annette Lareau found that her most active working-class families were less involved in their children's education than the least involved middle-class families (Lareau, 1989: 145). However, my research suggests that class differences are far more complex than a clear-cut dichotomy between middle-class activity and working-class passivity in the context of schooling. All the mothers were actively involved in supporting children's schooling. Women across the sample were engaged in practical, educational and emotional work in support of their children's education. They were monitoring their children's progress and attempting to repair any educational deficits they discovered (Griffith and Smith, 1990). Many mothers in both schools were initiating contact with teachers. As I have mentioned earlier, the majority of women, regardless of social class, were undertaking this work with little support from their male partners. Furthermore, the range of different responses to schooling, namely complementing, compensating and modifying children's curriculum offer were represented among both groups of mothers. What made a difference was not women's activities but the context in which they took place and the resources underpinning them. Although many of the working-class women had fewer cultural resources than middle-class mothers, including far lower incomes, fewer educational qualifications, less educational knowledge and information about the system, this did not indicate lower levels of involvement in children's education. What it did mean was less effective practices, as working-class women found it difficult to assume the role of educational expert, were less likely to persuade teachers to act on their complaints and were ill-equipped financially, socially and psychologically to compensate for deficits they perceived in their child's education.

They also had to deal with an inequitable state schooling system in which standards and expectations were shaped by the class character of school catchment areas. Lareau found that teachers in her two schools made similar, and at times identical, requests for involvement (Lareau, 1989: 104). However, the exposition of teachers' practices and school differences in Chapter 5 depicts a very different educational landscape to that described by Lareau. While her ethnography suggests an undifferentiated educational provision in schools, regardless of their social class intake, I have tried to capture those differences through the concept of institutional habitus. My research points to considerable disparities in school expectations of parental involvement, which are profoundly influenced by pupils' social class. I would suggest that Lareau's typology of separation between working-class homes and schooling and interconnectedness between middle-class homes and schooling misses out too much. There is a reciprocity between the middle-class home and primary schooling, in the sense that the school's impact on the home is matched by a significant impact of the home on schooling. However, Lareau's understanding of the relationship between working-class families and schools as one of separation ignores the enormous impact contemporary schooling has on family life across social classes. As I have tried to illustrate throughout this research, working-class mother's lives are powerfully organized by their children's school day. What they do not share with middle-class women are comparable resources and the power to influence their children's schooling directly. From the evidence of my research the standards of schools are shaped by their catchment areas through dynamic processes in which the relative social power of parents and teachers play an important part.

Frequently used indicators of social class, namely occupation and educational qualifications, only tell half the tale of parental involvement. Understandings of the resources women activate in daily practices need to be much richer. It is here that cultural capital provides a very useful concept for unravelling the processes of everyday life, as it spans economic, social, cultural and psychological aspects of people's activities. Differences between mothers are complex and multi-faceted. They are more completely understood in terms of the degree of confidence and entitlement that accompanies women's practices, the amount of educational knowledge and information about the system underpinning actions, and the social networks informing and supporting them. I have also outlined the wide spectrum of emotions women experience in their mothering work. Mothering needs to be understood in terms of the emotions, both positive and negative, that infuse mothers' activities. In particular, the concept of emotional capital (Nowotny, 1981) opens up a central role for women within Bourdieu's conceptual framework.

However, it is in conjunction with the concept of habitus that cultural capital demonstrates the greatest efficacy. My feminist reworking argues for an understanding of habitus as both gendered and 'raced' as well as classed, and illustrates the potential that habitus offers for tying together the macro trends and the micro details of social change within the sphere of home–school relations. I would maintain from my own analysis that utilizing the concept of habitus alongside that of cultural capital enhances the analytical strength of research, because of its incorporation of a historical perspective, its focus on change and its emphasis on trajectory across time and space. This potential of habitus is explored in Chapter 5 in the section 'habitus as history'. Middle-class women could be seen to be engaging in a process of replicating habitus within the sphere of involvement in schooling. Their working-class counterparts were attempting a much harder task; that of transforming habitus. Habitus provides a means of responding to the troublesome distinction between macro- and micro-levels of society. As I argue in my analysis of both women's personal histories and themes of generational continuity and discontinuity in maternal practices, habitus allows structure to be viewed as occurring within small-scale interactions and activity within large-scale settings. As such, it is a powerful analytical tool for revealing the power dynamics of everyday interaction.

Habitus can be understood as the interplay of agency and structure. Although this research is a feminist qualitative study which has sought to avoid categorizing and compartmentalizing women, the tables in Appendices 1–3 demonstrate in a more quantitative fashion how 'race' and class have shaped women's actions (see p. 168–72). The tables on the extent of formal education outside state schooling in Milner and Oak Park highlight the powerful influences of 'race' in Milner and of relative degrees of affluence in both Milner and

Oak Park. All the children in Milner currently receiving tuition are either black, white middle-class, or in Christine's case, defining herself as 'classless' and on a high income. In Oak Park four of the five children involved in four or more out-of-school activities are from families with incomes over £40000 a year. Women's activities are powerfully circumscribed by structure. Being black or white, working-class or middle-class, had a strong influence on what women did. Equally important was the level of resources to which they had access. I would argue that, taken together, habitus and cultural capital form a useful method for focusing on the intricate and complicated association of activity, structure and situation that make up social class. Furthermore, it is a method that allows differences within social class groupings to be taken into account.

Mothering in the Context of the Educational Marketplace

Class practices are historically specific. At the end of the twentieth century class processes within families are linked integrally to the operations of the wider marketplace. First, we need a recognition of mothering work. Then, we need to develop understandings of mothering which engage with the complex interplay between mothering work and educational markets. An analysis which conceptualizes mothering work as strategically located in relation to schooling systems allows for an understanding of mothering work as generative of social-class differences. Within a capitalist society in which market forces are ascendent (Wilkinson, 1996; Hutton, 1995; Jordan *et al.*, 1994), 'acting in their child's best interests' inevitably means middle-class mothers acting simultaneously against the interests of the children of other, less privileged, mothers. As I have pointed out earlier, this is not to blame middle-class mothers, but rather to see all mothers as caught up in educational markets which operate on the (il)logic of 'to her who has, yet more shall be given'. Educational success becomes a function of social, cultural and material advantages in which mothers' caring within the family is transmuted by the operations of the wider marketplace to serve its competitive, self-interested, individualistic ethos. Mothers' practical maintenance, educational and emotional work underpins the workings of educational markets, contributing to a culture of winners and losers within which one child's academic success is at the expense of other children's failure.

Theorizing about such social inequalities has become increasingly problematic within a contemporary educational marketplace underpinned by a rhetoric of classlessness. Current discourses of classlessness perpetrate the fantasy that ungendered parents only have to make the right choices for their children for educational success to follow automatically. As the words of the women in this research study illustrate, the reality is far more complex. It is one in which gender, 'race' and class continue to make significant differences. In Britain class infuses everyday practices and social interactions:

> It is evident in speech . . . in the sharp class divisions between resi-
> dential areas . . . in types of education, in clothing and in everything
> that can be included under the concept of 'lifestyle'. (Beck, 1992:
> 102)

Implicit within the concept of 'a classless society' are more equitable social
relations and enhanced mobility. However, despite all the talk of classlessness
and increased social mobility (Saunders, 1995), in 1990s Britain class differentials in educational attainment remain the same as they were 25 years ago
(Egerton and Halsey, 1993; Blackburn and Jarman, 1993). This book has
explored, through a focus on the home–school relationship, some of the ways
in which these class differentials are sustained.

It has also challenged 'the historical construction of putatively genderless
but in fact exclusively or overwhelmingly male discourse of scientific understanding, public sphere and economy' (Calhoun, 1995: 187). As Calhoun
points out, the gendered construction of social life generates a discourse in
which a range of ruling apparatus, including the educational system, appear as
if they are actorless systems. Furthermore, as I have argued in Chapter 2, the
discursive construction of home–school relationships operates with a norm of
the genderless parent. When, as in this book, there is an account of the human
activities which constitute these systems, and the ways in which human beings
exercize power in and through them, the classed, 'raced' and gendered nature
of the social world is revealed. Middle-class mothers may be making the
educational system work for their children in ways that working-class mothers
were unable to, but what both groups of mothers shared was the hard labour
of involvement in schooling; work largely unshared with male partners. The
marketization of education is 'a dense social phenomenon crucially invested
by relations of power' that co-opt and work through social class, 'race' and
gender (Hey, 1996: 358).

The Difficult Relationship Between Feminisms and Social Class

This book raises a difficult issue for feminisms; that of the involvement of
women in the perpetuation of social-class inequalities. Women's implication in
the transmission and perpetuation of social inequalities has always been a
thorny issue for feminism to engage with and, as a consequence, has consistently been overlooked in feminism's preoccupation with gender oppression.
But, as Lareau suggests, 'it seems that the reproduction of crucial aspects of
social inequality falls heavily to women' (Lareau, 1992: 222). Feminisms still
need to retain analyses in which women, in many different ways, and to
varying degrees, are seen to be 'subject to systems of power, oppression and
exploitation' (Weir, 1996: 184).

The abandonment of class within feminisms has been understandable. As
recent feminist and post-structuralist debates have made clear, social-class

categories ignore the multiplicity of women's positionings within contemporary social life (Barrett, 1991; 1992; Mahony and Zmroczek, 1997). While feminist theorizations now engage with a plurality of differences, social-class theory has remained trapped within binaries. However, it is not simply that much social-class analysis still operates with a dichotomy between 'working' and 'middle' class, it has also remained rooted in conceptualizations of class as position at the expense of developing understandings of class processes. It can be argued that the inadequacy of social class for feminist theory is a consequence of such one-dimensional theorizations which focus on social class as location in the labour market.

The relationship between gender and class will remain a difficult one for feminists to theorize about as long as conceptualizations of class are rooted in paid-employment status (Stacey, 1993). Position in the labour market tells us very little about how social-class processes are played out in social relationships. Beverley Skeggs writes that:

> The term 'class' has been so heavily criticised for its universalising pretences, reductionism and inapplicability to the complexity of difference that it has almost disappeared from feminist theory. (Skeggs, 1996: 13)

At the same time jettisoning class has led to middle-class female experience becoming the assumed norm within feminist work, displacing working-class, female experience as deficient, lacking in one way or another. Middle-classness remains part of the taken-for-granted within existing frameworks of feminist analysis (Opie, 1992). Within feminist work such tendencies both contradict, and struggle in tension with, transformative efforts to counter 'malestream' perspectives which conceptualize gender issues as women's problems (Burman, 1996). Without an understanding of how class continues to contribute to social inequalities, feminist theory will fail to engage adequately with the intricate web of social injustice, competitive individualism and divisiveness which constitutes society at the end of twentieth century.

This book has illustrated through the accounts of 33 mothers some of the ways in which inequalities of gender, 'race' and social class are embedded in the home–school relationship. Shifting understandings of social class from those rooted in location to encompass understandings embedded in activity reveal the crucial part mothers play in social-class reproduction. Feminisms, as well as research which is concerned more generally with the complex and multi-faceted relationship between social justice and education, need to recognize this 'class work'.

Appendix 1

Educational Qualifications and Material Circumstances of Mothers at Milner

Name	Housing Tenure	Own Job	Own Education	Father's Job	Father's Education	Marital Status	Family Income Band
Cassie	Council flat	Charity worker f/t	Private School/ University	–	–	Lone mother	Approx. £15 000
June	Council flat	Houseworker/ benefit	Left 15/no qualifications	–	–	Lone mother	<£10 000
Jasbir	Council house	School helper/.5	Left 16/no qualifications	Railway worker	Left 15/no qualifications	Married	£15–20 000
Jalil	Council flat	Houseworker/ benefit	Left 15/no qualifications	–	–	Lone mother	<£10 000
Jane	Council flat	Shop assistant/.2	Left 15/no qualifications	Service engineer	Year 1 p/t degree	Lives with partner	£15–20 000
Carmel	Council flat	F/t Student/ P/t Cleaner	Year 2 degree	–	–	Lone mother	<£10 000
Julie	Council house	Houseworker/ Income Support	Left 15/no qualifications	Tyre fitter	Left 15/no qualifications	Married	Approx. £15 000
Joyce	Council flat	Cleaner/.3	Left 15/no qualifications	Electrician	Left 16	Married	£15–20 000
Jill	Council flat	Clerical worker f/t	Left 15/no qualifications	–	–	Lone mother	Approx. £10 000
Jackie	Council flat	Houseworker	Left 17/5 CSEs	Lorry driver	Left 15/no qualifications	Married	Didn't know
Claire	Council house	Houseworker/ Income Support	Left 18/2 A Art Diploma	Supply Teacher	Teaching Certificate	Married	Approx. £15 000
Josie	Council flat	Houseworker/ benefit	Left 15/no qualifications	–	–	Lone mother	<£10 000
Jenny	Council flat	Houseworker/ benefit	Left 16/ 4CSEs	–	–	Lone mother	<£10 000
Janice	Private rented flat	Shop assistant f/t	Left 16/5 Os	Plumber	No information	Married	£15–20 000
Carol	Council flat	Clerk f/t	Grammar to 16/5 Os	–	–	Lone mother	Approx. £18 000

Name	Housing Tenure	Own Job	Own Education	Father's Job	Father's Education	Marital Status	Family Income Band
Lelia	O/O semi-detch	Social worker/.8	Private–16 professional qualification	Director of Charity	Private School/ University	Married	>£30 000
Christine	O/O terraced	Beauty therapist f/t	5 Os/1 A City&Guild	Sports instructor	Left 16	Married	>£30 000
Linda	O/O terraced	Teacher/.8	6 Os/2As Teacher Training	Health & Safety Officer	Private School/ University	Lives with partner	>£30 000
Carla	Council flat	Houseworker/ benefit	University +RADA	–	–	Lone mother	<£10 000
Cathy	Private rented flat	School nurse f/t	5 Os/1 A Nursing Qualification	–	–	Lone mother	Approx. £15 000

Note: Under 'Own Job', f/t means full-time, while a number is the hours worked part-time.

Appendix 2

Educational Qualifications and Material Circumstances of Mothers at Oak Park

Name	Housing Tenure	Own Job	Own Education	Father's Job	Father's Education	Marital Status	Family Income Band
Laura	O/O Semi–detached	University Lecturer f/t	University MA/PhD	Computer Analyst	University	Married	>£30000
Lesley	O/O Semi–detached	Child Therapist/.6	University Prof Qual.	Marketing Executive	Private School/ University	Married	>£40000
Lucinda	O/O Semi–detached	Education Officer .8	University	Lawyer	Private School/ University	Married	>£40000
Louise	O/O Semi–detached	Manager/ National charity f/t	Private School/ University/ PhD	Lawyer	Private School/ University	Married	>£40000
Lola	O/O Terraced	Lawyer f/t	University	Graphic Designer	University	Married	£40000
Liliana	O/O Flat	Teacher/tutor translator f/t	University/ PhD	Computer Analyst	University/ PhD	Married	Approx. £30000
Linsey	O/O Semi–detached	Dance Lecturer .8	Art College PGCE	Film Editor/BBC	Private School/ University	Married	>£40000
Leena	O/O Detached	Houseworker	University MA	Accountant	University	Married	>£30000
Lucy	O/O Terraced	Self-employed f/t	FE College Degree	Film Producer	University	Lone Mother	Would not disclose
Jean	Caretaker's house	Houseworker	City&Guild Diploma	Caretaker	Left 16	Married	<£20000
Liz	O/O Detached	Education Advisor f/t	Teacher Training/ B.ED	Businessman	University	Married	>£40000
Lisa	O/O Detached	Secondary teacher f/t	Teacher Training/ B.ED	Redundant Engineer	Private School/ University	Married	Approx. £20000
Lavinia	O/O Terraced	Redundant FE Teacher now F/T school helper	Private School/ University/ MA	Self-employed Businessman	Left 16	Married	Approx. £20000

Note: Under 'Own Job', f/t means full-time, while a number is the hours worked part-time.

170

Appendix 3

Teacher Assessment of Children's Ability and Extent of Formal Education Outside State Schooling

Milner

Mother's name	Child's Name	Ability Level	External Education
Cassie	Akin	Band one	Black Saturday School
June	Rosetta	Band one	Private school/Caribbean 90–92
Jasbir	Sharoff	Band three	Muslim Saturday school/ Tutor
Jalil	Chantelle	Band three	Black Saturday School
Jane	Delroy	Band two	
Carmel	Fola	Band two	Black Saturday School
Julie	George	Band three	Tutor (stopped after ten weeks)
Joyce	Cerise	Band two	
Jill	Lucy	Band one	
Jackie	Carly	Band three	
Claire	Nicholas	Band two	
Josie	Leigh	Band three	
Jenny	Andreas	Band two	
Janice	Gemma	Band two	
Carol	Stuart	Band one	
Lelia	Naomi	Band one	Tutor/Hebrew class
Christine	Matthew	Band two	Tutor
Linda	Mark	Band one	
Carla	Lilly	Band one	
Cathy	Shula	Band three	Tutor/Black Saturday school

Appendix 4

NFER Test Results and Extent of Formal Education Outside State Schooling

Oak Park

Mother's Name	Child's Name	Ability Level	External Education
Laura	Richard	108	music class
Lesley	Simon	109	
Lucinda	Anna	132	Tutor × 2/music + dance class
Louise	Amy	132	Tutor × 2/music + dance class
Lola	Nancy	106	
Liliana	Sergei	99	
Linsey	Sophia	101	Tutor × 2/music + dance + spanish
Leena	Negar	116	Tutor/Islamic class/ art + poetry
Lucy	Sophie	134	Tutor × 2
Jean	Susan	115	
Liz	Martin	92	Tutor/Hebrew class/ drama + music
Lisa	Melinda	115	Tutor
Lavinia	Riva	109	dance + drama + music class

References

ABBOTT, P. A. (1987) 'Women's Social Class Identification: Does Husband's Occupation make a difference?', *Sociology*, 21:1, pp. 91–103.

ABBOTT, P. A. and SAPSFORD, R. J. (1986) 'The Class Identification of Married Working Women: A Critical Replication of Ritter and Hargens', *British Journal of Sociology*, 37:4, pp. 535–549.

ABBOTT, P. A. and SAPSFORD, R. J. (1987) *Women and Social Class*, London, Tavistock Publications.

ACKER, J. R. (1973) 'Women and Social Stratification', *American Journal of Sociology*, 78:1, pp. 2–48.

ADAMS, B. (1990) *Time and Social Theory*, Cambridge, Polity Press.

ALLATT, P. (1993) 'Becoming Privileged: The Role of Family Processes', in BATES, I. and RISEBOROUGH, G. (Eds) *Youth and Inequality*, Buckingham, Open University Press.

ALLATT, P. and YEANDLE, S. (1992) *Youth Unemployment and the Family: Voices of Disordered Times*, London, Routledge.

ANDREWS, M. (1991) *Lifetimes of Commitment: Aging, Politics Psychology*, Cambridge, Cambridge University Press.

ANGUS, L. (1993) 'The Sociology of School Effectiveness', *British Journal of Sociology of Education*, 14:3, pp. 333–345.

ANYON, J. (1980) 'Elementary Schooling and Distinctions of Social Class', *Interchange*, 12:2–3, pp. 118–132.

ANYON, J. (1981) 'Social Class and the Hidden Curriculum of Work', *Boston University Journal of Education*, 162, pp. 67–92.

ARBER, S. and GILBERT, G. N. (Eds) (1991) *Women and Working Lives: Divisions and Change*, London, Macmillan.

ASHENDON, D., CONNELL, B., DOWSETT, G. and KESSLER, S. (1987) 'Teachers and Working-Class Schooling', in LIVINGSTONE, D. *et al.* (Eds) *Critical Pedagogy and Cultural Power*, London, Macmillan.

ATKIN, J., BASTIANI, J. with GOODE, J. (1988) *Listening to Parents: An approach to the improvement of home–school relations*, London, Croom Helm.

ATKINSON, P. (1983) 'The Reproduction of Professional Community', in DINGWALL, R. and LEWIS, P. (Eds) *Sociology of the Professions: lawyers, doctors and others*, London, Macmillan.

Class Work

BAGLEY, C. (1996) 'Black and White Unite or Flight? The racialised dimension of schooling and parental choice', *British Educational Research Journal*, 22:5, pp. 569–580.

BAKER, D. and STEVENSON, D. (1986) 'Mothers' Strategies for Children's School Achievement: Managing the transition to High School, *Sociology of Education*, 59:2, pp. 156–166.

BALL, S. J. (1993) 'Education Markets, Choice and Social Class: the market as a class strategy in the UK and USA', *British Journal of Sociology of Education*, 14:1, pp. 3–21.

BALL, S., GEWIRTZ, S. and BOWE, R. (1994) *School Choice, Social Class and Distinction: the realisation of social advantage in education*, Markets in Secondary Education Project Paper.

BARNARD, H. (1990) 'Bourdieu and Ethnography: Reflexivity, Politics and Praxis', in HARKER, R. MAHAS, C. and WILKES, C. (Eds) *An Introduction to the Work of Pierre Bourdieu*, London, Macmillan.

BARRETT, M. (1991) *The Politics of Truth: From Marx to Foucault*, Cambridge, Polity Press.

BARRETT, M. (1992) 'Words and Things', in BARRETT, M. and PHILLIPS, A. (Eds) *Destabilising Theory*, London, Polity Press.

BARRETT, M. and PHILLIPS, A. (1992) (Eds) *Destabilising Theory*, London, Polity Press.

BASTIANI, J. (1989) *Working with Parents: A Whole School Approach*, Windsor, NFER-Nelson.

BAUCH, P. (1993) 'Improving Education for Minority Adolescents: Towards an Ecological Perspective on School Choice and Parent Involvement', in CHAVKIN, N. F. (Ed.) *Families and Schools in a Pluralistic Society*, Albany, State University of New York Press.

BAXTER, J. (1988) 'Gender and Class Analysis: The Position of Women in the Class Structure', *Australia and New Zealand Journal of Sociology*, 24:1, pp. 106–123.

BAXTER, J. (1991) 'The Class Location of Women: Direct or Derived?', in BAXTER, J. *et al.* (Eds) *Class Analysis and Contemporary Australia*, London, MacMillan.

BECK, U. (1992) *Risk Society*, Cambridge, Polity Press.

BELL, L. and RIBBENS, J. (1994) 'Isolated Housewives and complex maternal worlds? The significance of social contacts between women with young children in industrial societies', *Sociological Review*, 42:2, pp. 227–262.

BERK, R. A. and BERK, S. F. (1979) *Labor and Leisure at Home: Content and Organisation of the Household Day*, Beverly Hills, CA, Sage.

BERNSTEIN, B. (1975) *Class, Codes and Control volume 3: Towards a Theory of Educational Transmissions*, London, Routledge and Kegan Paul.

BHACHU, P. (1991) 'Culture, ethnicity and class among Punjabi Sikh women in 1990s Britain', *New Community*, 17:3, pp. 401–412.

BHAVNANI, K. K. (1993) 'Tracing the Contours Feminist Research and Feminist Objectivity', *Women's Studies International Forum*, 16:2, pp. 95–104.

174

BIKLEN, S. K. (1993) 'Mothers' Gaze from Teachers' Eyes', in BIKLEN, S. K. and POLLARD, D. (Eds) *Gender and Education*, Chicago, University of Chicago Press.

BLACKBURN, R. M. and JARMAN, J. (1993) 'Changing inequalities in access to British universities', *Oxford Review of Education*, 19:2, pp. 197–215.

BOURDIEU, P. (1967) 'Systems of education and systems of thought', *Social Science Information*, 14:3, pp. 338–358.

BOURDIEU, P. (1974) 'The School as a Conservative Force: Scholastic and Cultural Inequalities', in EGGLESTON, J. (Ed.) *Contemporary Research in the Sociology of Education*, London, Methuen.

BOURDIEU, P. (1977a) 'Cultural Reproduction and Social Reproduction', in KARABEL, J. and HALSEY, A. H. (Eds) *Power and Ideology in Education*, New York, Oxford University Press.

BOURDIEU, P. (1977b) 'Symbolic Power', in GLEESON, D. (Ed.) *Identity and Structure: Issues in the Sociology of Education*, Drifford, Nafferton Books.

BOURDIEU, P. (1977c) *Outline of a Theory of Practice*, Cambridge, Cambridge University Press.

BOURDIEU, P. (1981) 'Men and Machines', in KNORR-CETINA, K. and CICOUREL, A. V. (Eds) *Advances in Social Theory and Methodology: Towards an Integration of Micro and Macro-Sociologies*, London, Routledge and Kegan Paul.

BOURDIEU, P. (1983) 'The Field of Cultural Production or the Economic World Reversed', *Poetics*, 12, pp. 311–356.

BOURDIEU, P. (1984) *Distinction*, London, Routledge and Kegan Paul.

BOURDIEU, P. (1985a) 'The Genesis of the concepts of "Habitus" and "Field"', *Sociocriticism*, 2:2, pp. 11–24.

BOURDIEU, P. (1985b) 'Social Space and the Genesis of Groups', *Theory and Society*, 14:6, pp. 723–744.

BOURDIEU, P. (1986) 'The Forms of Capital', in RICHARDSON, J. G. (Ed.) *Handbook of Theory and Research for the Sociology of Education*, New York, Greenwood Press.

BOURDIEU, P. (1987) 'What makes a Social Class? On the Theoretical and Practical Existence of Groups', *The Berkeley Journal of Sociology*, 32:1, pp. 1–17.

BOURDIEU, P. (1988) *Homo Academicus*, Cambridge, Polity Press.

BOURDIEU, P. (1990a) *The Logic of Practice*, Cambridge, Polity Press.

BOURDIEU, P. (1990b) *In Other Words: Essays towards a reflexive sociology*, Cambridge, Polity Press.

BOURDIEU, P. (1990c) 'La domination masculine', *Actes de la recherche en sciences sociales*, 84, pp. 2–31.

BOURDIEU, P. (1992) *Language and Symbolic Power*, Cambridge, Polity Press.

BOURDIEU, P. (1993a) *Sociology in Question*, London, Sage.

BOURDIEU, P. (1993b) 'Concluding Remarks: For a Sociogenetic Understanding of Intellectual Works', in CALHOUN, C., LiPUMA, E. and

POSTONE, M. (Eds) *Bourdieu: Critical Perspectives*, Cambridge, Polity Press.

BOURDIEU, P. (1993c) *La Misere du Monde*, Paris, Seuil.

BOURDIEU, P. (1996) 'On the Family as a Realised Category', *Theory, Culture and Society*, 13:3 pp. 19–26.

BOURDIEU, P. and SAINT MARTIN, DE, M. (1974) 'Scholastic Excellence and the Values of the Educational System', in EGGLESTON, J. (Ed.) *Contemporary Research in the Sociology of Education*, London, Methuen.

BOURDIEU, P. and PASSERON, J.-C. (1977) *Reproduction in Education, Society and Culture*, London, Sage.

BOURDIEU, P. and BOLTANSKI, L. (1981) 'The Educational System and the Economy: Titles and Jobs', in LEMERT, C. (Ed.) *French Sociology: Rupture and Renewal since 1968*, New York, Columbia University Press.

BOURDIEU, P. and WACQUANT, L. (1989) 'For a socioanalysis of intellectuals: on Homo Academicus', *Berkeley Journal of Sociology*, 34:1, pp. 1–29.

BOURDIEU, P., CHAMBOREDON, J. C. and PASSERON, J. C. (1991) *The Craft of Sociology*, New York, Walter de Gruyter.

BOURDIEU, P. and WACQUANT, L. (1992) *An Invitation to Reflexive Sociology*, Chicago, University of Chicago Press.

BOURDIEU, P. and SAINT MARTIN, DE, M. (1994) 'The Meaning of Property: Class Position and the Ideology of Home Ownership', in RYAN, M. and GORDON, A. (Eds) *Body Politics: Disease, Desire and the Family*, Boulder, Westview Press.

BOWE, R., GEWIRTZ, S. and BALL, S. J. (1994a) 'Captured by the discourse? Issues and concerns in researching "parental choice"', *British Journal of Sociology of Education*, 15:1, pp. 63–78.

BOWE, R., GEWIRTZ, S. and BALL, S. J. (1994b) '"Parental Choice", Consumption and Social Theory: The Operation of Micro-Markets in Education', *British Journal of Educational Studies*, 42:1, pp. 38–53.

BRAH, A. (1994) 'Time, Place and Others: Discourses of Race, Nation, and Ethnicity', *Sociology*, 28:3, pp. 805–813.

BRATLINGER, E. (1985) 'What low-income parents want from Schools: A different view of Aspirations', *Interchange*, 16:4, pp. 14–28.

BRATLINGER, E. (1993) *The Politics of Social Class in Secondary School: Views of Affluent and Impoverished Youth*, New York, Teachers College Press.

BRATLINGER, E., MAJD-JABBARI, M. and GUSKIN, S. L. (1996) 'Self-Interest and Liberal Educational Discourse: How Ideology Works for Middle-Class Mothers', *American Educational Research Journal*, 33:3, pp. 571–597.

BREEN, R. and ROTTMAN, D. (1995a) *Class Stratification: A Comparative Perspective*, London, Harvester Wheatsheaf.

BREEN, R. and ROTTMAN, D. (1995b) 'Class Analysis and Class Theory', *Sociology*, 29:3, pp. 453–474.

BRITTEN, N. (1984) Class images in a national sample of women and men', *British Journal of Sociology*, 15:3, pp. 406–434.

BRITTEN, N. and HEATH, A. (1983) 'Women, Men and Social Class', in GAMARNIKOW, E., MORGAN, D., PURVIS, J. and TAYLORSON, D. (Eds) *Gender, Class and Work*, London, Heinemann.

BROWN, P. (1987) *Schooling Ordinary Kids*, London, Tavistock Publications.

BRUBAKER, R. (1985) 'Rethinking Classical Theory: The Sociological Vision of Pierre Bourdieu', *Theory and Society*, 14:6, pp. 745–775.

BRUBAKER, R. (1993) 'Social Theory as Habitus', in CALHOUN, C., LIPUMA, E. and POSTONE, M. (Eds) *Bourdieu: Critical Perspectives*, Cambridge, Polity Press.

BUCHNER, P. (1990) 'Growing up in the eighties: Changes in the social biography of Childhood in the FRD', in CHISHOLM, L., BUCHNER, P., KRUGER, H.-H. and BROWN, P. (Eds) *Childhood, Youth and Social Change: A Comparative Perspective*, London, Falmer Press.

BURMAN, E. (1996) 'Introduction: Contexts, contests and Interventions', in BURMAN, E. (Ed.) *Challenging Women: Psychology's Exclusions, Feminist Possibilities*, Buckingham, Open University Press.

BURNS, A. and HOMEL, R. (1985) 'Social inequalities and adjustment to school', *Australian Journal of Education*, 29:1, pp. 79–91.

CALHOUN, C. (1993) 'Habitus, Field, and Capital: The Question of Historical Specificity', in CALHOUN, C., LIPUMA, E. and POSTONE, M. (Eds) *Bourdieu: Critical Perspectives*, Cambridge, Polity Press.

CALHOUN, C. (1995) *Critical Social Theory*, Oxford, Blackwell Publishers Ltd.

CALHOUN, C., LIPUMA, E. and POSTONE, M. (Eds) (1993) *Bourdieu: Critical Perspectives*, Cambridge, Polity Press.

CAVENDISH, R. (1982) *On the Line*, London, Routledge and Kegan Paul.

CHARLES, N. (1990) 'Women and Class – a problematic relationship?', *Sociological Review*, 38:1, pp. 43–89.

CHISHOLM, L., BUCHNER, P., KRUGER, H. H. and BROWN, P. (1990) *Childhood, Youth and Social Change: A Comparative Perspective*, London, Falmer Press.

CLARRICOATES, K. (1978) 'Dinosaurs in the classroom – a re-examination of some aspect of the "hidden curriculum" in the primary school', *Women's Studies International Quarterly*, 1, pp. 353–364.

CLARRICOATES, K. (1980) 'The importance of being Ernest, Emma ... Tom ... Jane ...', in DEEM, R. (Ed.) *Schooling for Women's Work*, London, Routledge and Kegan Paul.

COHEN, G. (1981) 'Culture and Educational Achievement', *Harvard Educational Review*, 51:2, pp. 270–285.

COLEMAN, J. S. (1987) 'Families and Schools', *Educational Researcher*, 16:1, pp. 32–38.

COLEMAN, M. T. (1989) 'The Division of Household Labor: Suggestions for Further Empirical Consideration and Theoretical Development', in BLUMBERG, R. L. (Ed.) *Gender, Family and Economy: The Triple Overlap*, London, Sage.

COLLINS, J. (1993) 'Determination and Contradiction: An Appreciation and Critique of the Work of Pierre Bourdieu on Language and Education', in CALHOUN, C., LiPUMA, E. and POSTONE, M. (Eds) *Bourdieu: Critical Perspectives*, Cambridge, Polity Press.

COLLINS, P. H. (1990) *Black Feminist Thought*, London, Harper Collins.

COLLINS, P. H. (1994) 'Shifting the Center: Race, Class and Feminist Theorising about Motherhood', in BASSIN, D., HONEY, M. and KAPLAN, M. M. (Eds) *Representations of Motherhood*, New Haven, Yale University Press.

COLLINS, R. (1979) *The Credential Society*, New York, Academic Press.

CONNELL, R. W. (1983) *'Which Way is up?': Essays on Class, Sex and Culture,* Sydney, George Allen & Unwin.

CONNELL, R. W., ASHENDEN, D. J., KESSLER, S. and DOWSETT, G. W. (1981) 'Class and Gender Dynamics in a Ruling-class school', *Interchange*, 12:2–3, pp. 102–117.

CONNELL, R. W., ASHENDEN, D. J., KESSLER, S. and DOWSETT, G. W. (1982) *Making the Difference*, Sydney, George Allen and Unwin.

CORSON, D. (1993) *Language, Minority Education and Gender: Linking Social Justice and Power*, Clevedon, Multilingual Matters.

COVERMAN, S. and SHELEY, J. F. (1986) 'Men's Housework and Child-Care Time, 1965–1975', *Journal of Marriage and the Family*, 48, pp. 413–422.

COYLE, A. (1984) *Redundant Women,* London, Women's Press.

COXON, A. and JONES, C. (1978) *The Images of Occupational Prestige*, London, Macmillan.

COXON, A. and JONES, C. (1979) *Class and Hierarchy*, London, Macmillan.

CROMPTON, R. (1989) 'Class, Theory and Gender', *British Journal of Sociology*, 40:4, pp. 565–587.

CROMPTON, R. (1994) *Class Stratification: An Introduction to Current Debates*, London, Polity.

CROSS, G. (1993) *Time and Money: The Making of Consumer Culture*, London, Routledge.

DAUBER, S. and EPSTEIN, J. (1993) 'Parents' Attitudes and Practices of Involvement in Inner-City Elementary and Middle Schools', in CHAVKIN, N. F. (Ed.) *Families and Schools in a Pluralistic Society*, Albany, State University of New York Press.

DAVID, M. E. (1984) 'Women, Family and Education', in ACKER, S., MEGARRY, J., NISBET, S. and HOYLE, E. (Eds) *Women and Education: World Yearbook of Education*, London, Kogan Page.

DAVID, M. E. (1993) *Parents, Gender and Education Reform*, Cambridge, Polity Press.

DAVID, M. E., EDWARDS, R., HUGHES, M. and RIBBENS, J. (1993) *Mothers and Education: Inside Out? Exploring Family-Education Policy and Experience*, Basingstoke, Macmillan.

DAVID, M. E., WEST, A. and RIBBENS, J. (1994) *Mother's Intuition: Choosing Secondary Schools*, London, The Falmer Press.

DAVID, M., DAVIES, J., EDWARDS, R., REAY, D. and STANDING, K. (1996) 'Mothering and Education: Reflexivity and Feminist Methodology', in MORLEY, L. and WALSH, V. (Eds) *Breaking Boundaries: Women in Higher Education*, London, Taylor & Francis.

DAVID, M., DAVIES, J., EDWARDS, R., REAY, D. and STANDING, K. (1997) 'Choice within Constraints: Mothers and schooling', *Gender and Education*, 9:4, pp. 397–410.

DAVIES, K. (1990) *Women, Time and the Weaving of the Strands of Everyday Life*, Aldershot, Gower.

DELAMONT, S. (1989) *Knowledgeable Women: structuralism and the reproduction of elites*, London, Routledge.

DEPARTMENT FOR EDUCATION. (1992) *Choice and Diversity: A new framework for schools*, Cm 2021, London, HMSO.

DEVAULT, M. L. (1991) *Feeding the Family: The Social Organisation of Caring as Gendered Work*, Chicago, University of Chicago Press.

DEVINE, F. (1992) 'Social identities, class identity and political perspectives', *Sociological Review*, 40:2, pp. 229–252.

DUNCAN, I. (1990) 'Bourdieu on Bourdieu: Learning the Lesson of the Leçon', in HARKER, R., MAHAR, C. and WILKES, C. (Eds) *An Introduction to the Work of Pierre Bourdieu: The Practice of Theory*, London, Macmillan.

DUNCOMBE, J. and MARSDEN, D. (1993) 'Love and Intimacy: The Gender Division of Emotion and "Emotion Work": A Neglected Aspect of Sociological Discussion of Heterosexual Relationships', *Sociology*, 27:2, pp. 221–241.

EDGELL, S. (1980) *Middle Class Couples: A Study of Segregation, Domination and Inequality in Marriage*, London, George Allen and Unwin.

EDWARDS, R. (1993) *Mature Women Students: Separating or connecting Family and Education*, London, Falmer Press.

EDWARDS, V. and REDFERN, A. (1988) *At Home in School: Parent participation in Primary Education*, London, Routledge.

EGERTON, M. and HALSEY, A. H. (1993) 'Trends by social class and gender in access to higher education in Britain', *Oxford Review of Education*, 19:2, pp. 183–196.

ENDERS-DRAGASSER, U. (1987) 'Mothers' unpaid school-work in West Germany', in SCHMUCK, P. A. (Ed.) *Women Educators. Employees of schools in Western world countries*, Albany, State University of New York Press.

ENDERS-DRAGASSER, U. (1991) 'Childcare: Love, Work and Exploitation', *Women's Studies International Forum*, 14:6, pp. 551–556.

ENGLER, S. (1990) 'Illusory equality: The Discipline-based Anticipatory Socialisation of University Students', in CHISHOLM, L., BUCHNER, P., KRUGER, H. H. and BROWN, P. (Eds) *Childhood, Youth and Social Change: A Comparative Perspective*, London, Falmer Press.

EPSTEIN, E. H. (1992) 'Social Paradoxes of American Education', *Oxford Review of Education*, 18:3, pp. 201–212.

ERIKSON, R. and GOLDTHORPE, J. H. (1992) *The Constant Flux: A Study of Class Mobility in Industrial Societies*, Oxford, Clarendon Press.

EVANS, G. (1996) 'Putting Men and Women into Classes: An Assessment of the Cross-Sex Validity of the Goldthorpe Schema', *Sociology*, 30:2, pp. 209–234.

EVANS, T. (1988) *A Gender Agenda*, Sydney, Allen and Unwin.

FARKAS, G., GROBE, R., SHEEHAN, D. and SHUAN, Y. (1990) 'Cultural Resources and School Success: Gender, Ethnicity, and Poverty Groups within an Urban School District', *American Sociological Review*, 55:1, pp. 127–142.

FEATHERSTONE, M. (1987) 'Leisure, Symbolic Power and the Life Course', in HORNE, J., JARY, D. and TOMLINSON, A. (Eds) *Leisure, Sport and Social Relations*, London, Routledge and Kegan Paul.

FENSTERMAKER BERK, S. (1985) *The Gender Factory: The Apportionment of Work in American Households*, New York, Plenum.

FERRI, E. and SMITH, K. (1996) *Parenting in the 1990s*, London, Family Policy Studies Centre.

FINE, M. (1987) 'Silencing in Public School', *Language Arts*, 64:2, pp. 157–174.

FINE, M. (1991) *Framing dropouts: Notes on the politics of an urban high school*, Albany, SUNY Press.

FINLEY, M. K. (1992) 'The Educational Contest for Middle- and Working-class Women: The Reproduction of Inequality', in WRIGLEY, J. (Ed.) *Education and Gender Equality*, London, Falmer Press.

FRANKENBERG, R. (1993) *White Women, Race Matters: The Social Construction of Whiteness*, London, Routledge.

FRAZER, E. (1988) 'Teenage Girls talking about Class', *Sociology*, 22:3, pp. 343–358.

GASKELL, J. and McLAREN, A. (1987) *Women and education: a Canadian perspective*, Calgary, Alberta, Detselig Enterprises.

GEWIRTZ, S., BALL, S. and Bowe, R. (1994a) 'Parents, Privilege and the Education Market Place', *Research Papers in Education*, 9:1, pp. 3–29.

GEWIRTZ, S., BOWE, R. and BALL, S. (1994b) 'Choice, competition and Equity: lessons from research in the UK', Paper presented at The Annual Meeting of the American Educational Research Association, New Orleans, 6 April 1994.

GEWIRTZ, S., BALL, S. and BOWE, R. (1995) *Markets, Choice and Equity in Education*, Buckingham, Open University Press.

GIDDENS, A. (1992) *The Transformation of Intimacy: Sexuality, Love and Eroticism in Modern Societies*, Cambridge, Polity Press.

GLASER, B. G. and STRAUSS, A. L. (1967) *The Discovery of Grounded Theory: Strategies of Qualitative Research*, London, Weidenfeld and Nicolson.

GLATTER, R. and WOODS, P. A. (1993) 'Parental choice and school decision-making operating in a market-like environment', in WONG, A. K. C. and CHENG, K. M. (Eds) *Educational leaders and change*, Hong Kong, Hong Kong University Press.

GOLDTHORPE, J. H. (1980) *Social Mobility and Class Structure in Modern Britain*, Oxford, Clarendon Press.

GOLDTHORPE, J. H. (1983) 'Women and Class Analysis', *Sociology*, 17:4, pp. 465–488.

GOLDTHORPE, J. H. and MARSHALL, G. (1992) 'The promising future of class analysis: A response to recent critiques', *Sociology*, 26:3, pp. 381–400.

GRAHAM, H. (1993) *Hardship and Health in Women's Lives*, London, Harvester Wheatsheaf.

GRANT, C. A. and SLEETER, C. E. (1988) 'Race, Class, and Gender and Abandoned Dreams', *Teachers College Record*, 90:1, pp. 19–40.

GRAUE, E. (1993) 'Social Networks and Home-School Relations', *Educational Policy*, 7:4, pp. 466–490.

GRIFFIN, C. (1993) *Representations of Youth*, Oxford, Polity Press.

GRIFFIN, C. (1996) 'Experiencing Power: Dimensions of Gender, "Race" and Class', in CHARLES, N. and HUGHES-FREELAND, F. (Eds) *Practising Feminism: Identity Difference Power*, London, Routledge.

GRIFFITH, A. (1992) 'Interviewing Mothers: The Social Organisation of Interview Data', Paper presented at the Ethnography in Education Forum, Philadelphia, University of Pennsylvannia, February 21–23.

GRIFFITH, A. (1994) 'Insider/Outsider: Epistemological Privilege and Mothering Work', Unpublished paper, University of New Orleans.

GRIFFITH, A. and SMITH, D. E. (1987) 'Constructing Cultural Knowledge: Mothering as Discourse', in GASKELL, J. and MCLAREN, A. (Eds) *Women and Education: A Canadian Perspective*, Calgary, Alberta, Detselig Enterprises.

GRIFFITH, A. and SMITH, D. E. (1990) ' "What did you in School today?": Mothering, Schooling and Social Class', *Perspectives on Social Problems*, 2, pp. 3–24.

HAERTAL, E. H. (1987) 'Comparing public and private schools', in HAERTAL, E. H., JAMES, T. and LEVIN, H. M. (Eds) *Comparing Public and Private Schools volume 25, Student Achievement*, New York: Palmer.

HALSEY, A. H., HEATH, A. F. and RIDGE, J. M. (1980) *Origins and Destinations: Family, Class and Education in Modern Britain*, London, Clarendon Press.

HALSEY, A. H., HEATH, A. F. and RIDGE, J. M. (1982) 'Cultural Capital and Political Arithmetic: a response to the review symposium on "Origins and Destinations" ', *British Journal of Sociology of Education*, 3:1, pp. 87–91.

HAMMERSLEY, M. (1992) *What's Wrong with Ethnography*, London, Routledge.

HARKER, R. (1984) 'On reproduction, habitus and education', *British Journal of Sociology of Education*, 5:2, pp. 117–127.

HARKER, R., MAHAR, C. and WILKES, C. (1990) *An Introduction to the Work of Pierre Bourdieu: The Practice of Theory*, London, Macmillan.

HAYES, B. and JONES, F. L. (1992) 'Marriage and Political partisanship in Australia: Do wives' characteristics make a difference?', *Sociology*, 26:1, pp. 81–102.

Class Work

HENRIQUES, J. and HOLLWAY, W., URWIN, C., VENN, C. and WALKERDINE, V. (1984) *Changing the Subject: Psychology, social regulation and subjectivity*, London, Methuen.

HEY, V. (1996) ' "A Game of Two Halves" – A Critique of Some Complicities: between hegemonic and counter-hegemonic discourses concerning marketisation and education', *Discourse: studies in the cultural politics of education*, 17:3, pp. 351–362.

HIRABAYASHI, L. R. (1993) *Cultural Capital: Mountain Zapotec Migrant Associations in Mexico City*, Tucson, The University of Arizona Press.

HMSO (1995) *Social Trends Jubilee Edition*, London, HMSO.

HMSO: DEPARTMENT OF EDUCATION AND SCIENCE (1991) *The Parent's Charter: You and Your Child's Education* London, HMSO.

HOCHSCHILD, A. R. (1983) *The Managed Heart: The Commercialisation of Human Feeling*, Berkeley/Los Angeles, University of California Press.

HOCHSCHILD, A. R. (1987) 'The Economy of Gratitude', in DAVIS, D. F. and MCCARTHY, E. D. (Eds) *The Sociology of Emotions: Original Essays and Research Papers*, Greenwich, JAI Press.

HOCHSCHILD, A. R. with MACHUNG, A. (1989) *The Second Shift: Working Parents and the Revolution at Home*, London, Piatkus.

HOGGART, R. (1957) *The Uses of Literacy*, London, Chatto and Windus.

HOLDEN, C., HUGHES, M. and DESFORGES, C. (1994) 'Parents and Entitlement: a fair deal for all?', *Educational Review*, 46:2, pp. 151–158.

HOLLAND, J. and SKOURAS, G. (1977) 'Study of children's views of aspects of the social division of labour: children's aspirations and expectations with respect to work', Social Science Research Council Report, No. 3.

HOLLAND, J. and SKOURAS, G. (1979) 'Study of adolescents' views of aspects of the social division of labour: adolescents' conceptions of features of the social division of labour', Social Science Research Council Report, No. 6.

HOLTON, R. and TURNER, B. (1994) 'Debate and Pseudo-Debate in Class Analysis: Some Unpromising Aspects of Goldthorpe and Marshall's Defence', *Sociology*, 28:3, pp. 799–804.

HOOD-WILLIAMS, J. (1990) 'Patriarchy for Children: On the Stability of Power Relations in Children's Lives', in CHISHOLM, L., BUCHNER, P., KRUGER, H. H. and BROWN, P. (Eds) *Childhood, Youth and Social Change: A Comparative Perspective*, London, Falmer Press.

HOOKS, B. (1984) *Feminist Theory: from margin to centre*, Boston, South End Press.

HOOKS, B. (1989) *Talking Back: Thinking Feminist – Thinking Black*, London, Sheba Feminist Publishers.

HOOKS, B. (1992) *Black Looks: race and representation*, London, Turnaround.

HOPPER, E. (1981) *Social Mobility*, London, Blackwell.

HUGHES, M., WIKELEY, F. and NASH, T. (1994) *Parents and their Children's Schools*, Oxford, Blackwell Publishers.

HUTTON, W. (1995) *The State We're In*, London, Verso.

182

JACKMAN, M. R. and JACKMAN, R. W. (1983) *Class Awareness in the United States*, Berkeley, University of California Press.

JACKSON, B. and MARSDEN, D. (1966) *Education and the Working Class*, Harmondsworth, Penguin.

JACKSON, S. (1993) 'Even Sociologists Fall in Love: An Exploration in the Sociology of Emotions', *Sociology*, 27:2, pp. 201–220.

JAMES, N. (1989) 'Emotional labour: skill and work in the social regulation of feelings', *Sociological Review*, 37:1, pp. 15–42.

JENKINS, R. (1982) 'Pierre Bourdieu and the Reproduction of Determinism', *Sociology*, 16:2, pp. 270–281.

JENKINS, R. (1986) 'Review of "Distinction"', *Sociology*, 20:1, pp. 103–105.

JENKINS, R. (1989) 'Language, Symbolic Power and Communication: Bourdieu's "Homo Academicus"', *Sociology*, 23:4, pp. 639–645.

JENKINS, R. (1992) *Pierre Bourdieu*, London, Routledge.

JOHNSON, D. and RANSOM, E. (1983) *Family and School*, London, Croom Helm.

JORDAN, B., REDLEY, M. and James, S. (1994) *Putting the Family First: Identities, decisions, citizenship*, London, UCL Press.

KERFOOT, D. and KNIGHTS, D. (1994) 'Into the Realm of the Fearful: Identity and the Gender Problematic', in RADKE, H. L. and STAM, H. J. (Eds) *Power/Gender: Social Relations in Theory and Practice*, London, Sage.

KING, R. A. (1978) *All Things Bright and Beautiful? A sociological study of infants' classrooms*, Chichester, John Wiley.

KING, R. A. (1989) *The Best of Primary Education? A sociological study of Junior Middle Schools*, London, Falmer Press.

KRAIS, B. (1993) 'Gender and Symbolic Violence: Female Oppression in the Light of Pierre Bourdieu's Theory of Social Practice', in CALHOUN, C., LiPUMA, E. and POSTONE, M. (Eds) *Bourdieu: Critical Perspectives*, Cambridge, Polity Press.

KRUGER, H.-H. (1990) 'Caught between Homogenization and Disintegration: Changes in the Life-phase "Youth" in West Germany since 1945', in CHISHOLM, L., BUCHNER, P., KRUGER, H.-H. and BROWN, P. (Eds) *Childhood, Youth and Social Change: A Comparative Perspective*, London, Falmer Press.

LAMONT, M. (1992) *Money, Morals and Manners: The Culture of the French and American Upper-Middle Class*, Chicago, University of Chicago Press.

LAMONT, M. and LAREAU, A. (1988) 'Cultural Capital: Allusions, Gaps and Glissandos in Recent Theoretical Developments', *Sociological Theory*, 6:1, pp. 153–168.

LAMPARD, R. (1995) 'Parents' Occupations and Their Children's Occupational Attainment: A Contribution to the Debate on the Class Assignment of Families', *Sociology*, 29: 4, pp. 715–728.

LAREAU, A. (1987) 'Social Class Differences in Family-School Relationships: The Importance of Cultural Capital', *Sociology of Education*, 60:1, pp. 73–85.

LAREAU, A. (1989) *Home Advantage*, London, Falmer Press.

LAREAU, A. (1992) 'Gender Differences in Parent Involvement in Schooling', in WRIGLEY, J. (Ed.) *Education and Gender Equality*, London, Falmer Press.

LASH, S. (1993) 'Pierre Bourdieu: Cultural Economy and Social Change', in CALHOUN, C., LIPUMA, E. and POSTONE, M. (Eds) *Bourdieu: Critical Perspectives*, Cambridge, Polity Press.

LASH, S. and URRY, J. (1993) *Economies of Signs and Space*, London, Sage.

LATHER, P. (1991) *Getting Smart: feminist research and pedagogy within the postmodern*, London, Routledge.

LEIULFSRUD, H. and WOODWARD, A. (1987) 'Women at class crossroads: repudiating conventional theories of family class', *Sociology*, 21, pp. 393–412.

LEIULFSRUD, H. and WOODWARD, A. (1988) 'Women at class crossroads: a critical reply to Erikson and Goldthorpe's note', *Sociology*, 22:4, pp. 555–562.

LEWIS, M. (1988) 'The Construction of Femininity: Embraced in the Work of Caring for Children – Caught Between Aspirations and Reality', *The Journal of Educational Thought*, 22:2A, pp. 259–268.

LIPUMA, E. (1993) 'Culture and the Concept of Culture in a Theory of Practice', in CALHOUN, C., LIPUMA, E. and POSTONE, M. (Eds) *Bourdieu: Critical Perspectives*, Cambridge, Polity Press.

LOCKWOOD, D. (1986) 'Class, Status and Gender', in CROMPTON, R. and MANN, M. (Eds) *Gender and Stratification*, Cambridge, Polity Press.

LUTTRELL, W. (1992) 'Working-Class Women's Ways of Knowing: effects of Gender, Race and Class', in WRIGLEY, J. (Ed.) *Education and Gender Equality*, London, Falmer Press.

LUTTRELL, W. (1993) '"The Teachers, They All Had Their Pets": Concepts of Gender, Knowledge, and Power', *Signs: Journal of Women in Culture and Society*, 18:3, pp. 505–546.

LYNCH, K. and O'NEILL, C. (1994) 'The Colonisation of Social Class in Education', *British Journal of Sociology of Education*, 15:3, pp. 307–324.

MAC AN GHAILL, M. (1994) *The Making of Men: Masculinities, Sexualities and Schooling*, Buckingham, Open University Press.

MACBETH, A. (1995) 'Partnership between parents and teachers in education', in MACBETH, A., MCCREATH, D. and AITCHISON, J. (Eds) *Collaborate or compete: educational partnerships in a market economy*, London, Falmer Press.

McCALL, L. (1992) 'Does gender fit? Bourdieu, feminism and conceptions of social order', *Theory and Society*, 21: 6, pp. 837–868.

McCLELLAND, K. (1990) 'Culmative Disadvantage among the Highly Ambitious', *Sociology of Education*, 63, pp. 102–121.

MACLEOD, F. (Ed.) (1989) *Parents and Schools: The Contemporary Challenge*, London, Falmer Press.

McDONOUGH, P. M. (1996) *Choosing Colleges: How Social Class and Schools Structure Opportunity*, New York, State University of New York Press.

McNay, L. (1996) 'Gender, habitus and the Field: Pierre Bourdieu and the limits of Reflexivity', Paper presented at the Institute of Advanced Legal Studies, May 1996.

McRae, S. (1986) *Cross-Class Families: A Study of Wives' Occupational Superiority*, Oxford, Oxford University Press.

Mahar, C. (1990) 'Pierre Bourdieu: The Intellectual Project', in Harker, R., Mahar, C. and Wilkes, C. (Eds) *An Introduction to the Work of Pierre Bourdieu: The Practice of Theory*, London, Macmillan.

Mahony, P. and Zmroczek, C. (Eds) (1997) *Class Matters: 'Working Class' Women's Perspectives on Social Class*, London, Taylor & Francis.

Manicom, A. (1984) 'Feminist Frameworks and Teacher Education', *Journal of Education*, 166:1, pp. 77–87.

Manicom, A. (1992) 'Feminist Pedagogy: Transformations, Standpoints, and Politics', *Canadian Journal of Education*, 17:3, pp. 365–389.

Marshall, G., Newby, H., Rose, D. and Vogler, C. (1988) *Social Class in Modern Britain*, London, Hutchinson.

Mirza, H. (1992) *Young, Female and Black*, London, Routledge.

Mirza, H. (1995) 'Black Women in Higher Education: Finding a Space, Defining Your Place', in Morley, L. and Walsh, V. (Eds) *Feminist Academics: Creative Agents for Change*, London, Taylor & Francis.

Mirza, H. (1997) (Ed.) *Black British Feminism: A reader*, London, Routledge.

Montandon, C. (1993) 'Parent-teacher relations in Genevan primary schools: the roots of misunderstanding', in Smit, F., van Esch, W. and Walberg, H. J. (Eds) *Parental Involvement in Education*, Nijmegen, University of Nijmegen: Institute for Applied Social Sciences.

Morris, L. (1990) *The Workings of the Household*, Cambridge, Polity Press.

Mouzelis, N. (1995) *Sociological Theory: What went wrong*, London, Routledge.

Nash, R. (1990) 'Bourdieu on Education and Social and Cultural Reproduction', *British Journal of Sociology of Education*, 11:4, pp. 431–447.

Nash, R. (1993) *Succeeding Generations: Family Resources and Access to Education in New Zealand*, Auckland, Oxford University Press.

Nash, R. and Harker, R. (1992) 'Working with Class: the educational expectations and practices of class-resourced families', *New Zealand Journal of Educational Studies*, 27:1, pp. 3–20.

New, C. and David, M. E. (1985) *For the Children's Sake: Making Childcare More Than Women's Business*, Harmondsworth, Penguin.

Nowotny, H. (1981) 'Women in Public Life in Austria', in Epstein, C. F. and Coser, R. L. (Eds) *Access to Power: Cross-National Studies of Women and Elites*, London, George Allen & Unwin.

O'Barr, J., Pope, D. and Wyer, M. (Eds) (1990) *Ties that Bind: Essays on Mothering and Patriarchy*, Chicago, University of Chicago Press.

O'Donnell, L. (1982) 'The Social World of Parents', *Marriage and Family Review*, 5, pp. 9–36.

O'Donnell, L. (1985) *The Unheralded Majority: Contemporary Women as Mothers*, Massachusetts, Lexington Books.

Oakes, J. (1985) *Keeping Track*, New Haven, Yale University Press.

Oakley, A. (1974) *The Sociology of Housework*, Martin Robertson, London.

Oakley, A. (1993) *Social Support and Motherhood: The Natural History of a Research Project*, London, Blackwell.

Oakley, A. and Rajan, L. (1991) 'Social Class and Social Support: The Same or Different?', *Sociology*, 25:1, pp. 31–59.

Opie, A. (1992) 'Qualitative Research, Appropriation of the "Other" and Empowerment', *Feminist Review*, 40, pp. 52–68.

Pahl, R. E. (1989) 'Is the Emperor naked? Some Comments on the Adequacy of Sociological Theory in Urban and Regional Research', *International Journal of Urban and Regional Research*, 13, pp. 709–720.

Payne, G. (1987) *Mobility and Change in Modern Society*, London, Macmillan.

Petrie, P. (1991) 'School-age Child Care and Equal Opportunities', *Women's Studies International Forum*, 14:6, pp. 527–537.

Phoenix, A. and Tizard, B. (1996) 'Thinking through Class: The Place of Social Class in the Lives of Young Londoners', *Feminism and Psychology*, 6:3, pp. 443–456.

Polakow, V. (1993) *Lives on the Edge: Single Mothers and their Children in the Other America*, Chicago, University of Chicago Press.

Porter, M. (1983) *Home, Work and Class Consciousness*, Manchester, Manchester University Press.

Reay, D. (1991) 'Intersections of Gender, Race and Class in the Primary School', *British Journal of Sociology of Education*, 12:2, pp. 163–182.

Reay, D. (1995a) 'Using habitus to look at "race" and class in primary school classrooms', in Griffiths, M. and Troyna, B. (Eds) *Anti-racism, Culture and Social Justice in Education*, Trentham Books.

Reay, D. (1995b) ' "They employ cleaners to do that": Habitus in the primary classroom', *British Journal of Sociology of Education*, 16:3, pp. 353–371.

Reay, D. (1995c) 'The Fallacy of Easy Access', *Women's Studies International Forum*, 18:2, pp. 205–213.

Reay, D. (1996a) 'Insider perspectives or stealing the words out of women's mouths: Interpretation in the research process', *Feminist Review: Speaking out: Researching and representing women*, 53, pp. 55–71.

Reay, D. (1996b) 'Dealing with difficult differences: Reflexivity and Social Class in Feminist Research', in Walkerdine, V. (Ed.) *Feminism and Psychology: Special Issue on Social Class*, 16:3, pp. 443–456.

Reay, D. (1996c) 'Contextualising Choice: Social Power and Parental Involvement', *British Educational Research Journal*, 22:5, pp. 581–596.

Reay, D. (1997a) 'The double-bind of the "working-class" feminist academic: The failure of success or the success of failure', in Mahony, P. and Zmroczek, C. (Eds) *Class Matters: 'Working Class' Women's Perspectives on Social Class*, London, Taylor & Francis.

REAY, D. (1997b) 'Feminist theory, habitus and social class: Disrupting notions of classlessness', *Women's Studies International Forum*, 20:2, pp. 225–233.

REAY, D. (1998) 'Classifying feminist research: Exploring the psychological impact of social class on mothers' involvement in children schooling', *Feminism and Psychology* 8:2.

REAY, D. and BALL, S. J. (1997) ' "Spoilt for choice": the working classes and education markets', *Oxford Review of Education*, 23:1, pp. 89–101.

REAY, D. and MIRZA, H. (1997) 'Genealogies of the margins: Researching black supplementary schooling, *British Journal of Sociology of Education*, 18:4, pp. 477–499.

REID, I. (1986) 'Who's afraid of social class?' *Education and Society*, 4:1, pp. 100–102.

REYNOLDS, D. and CUTTANCE, P. (Eds) (1992) *School Effectiveness: Research, Policy and Practice*, London, Cassell.

RIBBENS, J. (1993) 'Having a Word with the Teacher: Ongoing Negotiations across Home-School Boundaries', in DAVID, M., EDWARDS, R., HUGHES, M. and RIBBENS, J. (Eds) *Mothers and Education: Inside Out?: Exploring Family-Education Policy and Experience*, London, Macmillan.

RIBBENS, J. (1994) *Mothers and Their Children: Towards a Feminist Perspective on Childrearing*, London, Sage.

RITTER, K. V. and HARGENS, L. L. (1975) 'Occupational Positions and Class Identification of Married Working Women: A Test of the Asymmetry Hypothesis', *American Journal of Sociology*, 80, pp. 934–948.

ROBERTS, H. (1993) 'Women and the Class Debate', in MORGAN, D. and STANLEY, L. (Eds) *Debates in Sociology*, Manchester, Manchester University Press.

ROBINSON, R. V. and GARNIER, M. (1985) 'Class Reproduction among Men and Women in France: Reproduction Theory on its Home Ground', *American Journal of Sociology*, 90, pp. 250–280.

ROKER, D. (1993) 'Gaining an edge: Girls at a private school', in BATES, I. and RISEBOROUGH, G. (Eds) *Youth and Inequality*, Buckingham, Open University Press.

ROSS, C. E. and MIROWSKY, J. (1990) 'Women, Work and Family: Changing Gender Roles and Psychological Well-Being', in HALLINAN, M. T., KLEIN, D. M. and GLASS, J. (Eds) *Change in Societal Institutions*, London, Plenum Press.

ROSS, E. (1995) 'New Thoughts on "the Oldest Vocation": Mothers and Motherhood in Recent Feminist Scholarship', *Signs: Journal of Women in Culture and Society*, 20:2, pp. 397–413.

RUBIN, L. (1978) *Worlds of Pain*, New York, Basic Books.

RUDD, E. (1987), 'The Educational Qualifications and Social Class of Students' Parents entering British Universities in 1984', *Journal of The Statistical Society*, 150:4, pp. 346–372.

RUDDICK, S. (1989) *Maternal Thinking*, London, Women's Press.

RUPP, J. C. C. and DE LANGE, R. (1989) 'Social Order, cultural capital and citizenship: An essay concerning educational status and educational power versus comprehensiveness of elementary schools', *Sociological Review*, 37:4, pp. 668–705.

SANDERSON, K. (1989) 'Women's Lives: Social Class and the Oral Historian', *Life Stories*, 1, pp. 27–34.

SAUNDERS, P. (1995) 'Might Britain be a Meritocracy?', *Sociology*, 29:1, pp. 23–42.

SAVAGE, M. (1994) 'Review Article: Class analysis and its futures', *Sociological Review*, 42:3, pp. 531–543.

SCHEERENS, J. (1992) *Effective Schooling: Research, Theory and Practice*, London, Cassell.

SEABROOK, J. (1982) *Working-class Childhood: An oral history*, London, Victor Gollancz.

SEWELL, W. H. (1992), 'The Theory of Structure: Duality, Agency, and Transformation', *American Journal of Sociology*, 98:1, pp. 1–29.

SIEBER, T. R. (1982) 'The Politics of Middle-class Success in an Inner-city Public School', *Boston University Journal of Education*, 164:1, pp. 30–47.

SKEGGS, B. (1994) 'Situating the Production of Feminist Ethnography', in MAYNARD, M. and PURVIS, J. (Eds) *Researching Women's Lives from a Feminist Perspective*, London, Taylor & Francis.

SKEGGS, B. (1996) 'Introduction', in SKEGGS, B. (Ed.) *Feminist Cultural Theory: Process and Production*, Manchester, Manchester University Press.

SKEGGS, B. (1997) *Formations of Class and Gender: Becoming Respectable* London, Sage.

SMITH, D. E. (1983) 'Women, Class and Family', in MILIBAND, R. and SAVILLE, J. (Eds) *The Socialist Register*, London, Merlin Press.

SMITH, D. E. (1988) *The Everyday World as Problematic: a feminist sociology*, Milton Keynes, Open University Press.

SMITH, D. E. (1989a) 'Women's Work as Mothers: A New Look at the Relation of Class, Family and School Achievement', in HOLSTEIN, J. A. and MILLER, G. (Eds) *Perspectives on Social Problems: A Research Annual vol 1*, Greenwich, JAI Press.

SMITH, D. E. (1989b) 'Sociological Theory: Methods of Writing Patriarchy', in WALLACE, R. (Ed.) *Feminism and Sociological Theory*, London, Sage.

SMITH, D. E. (1990) *The Conceptual Practices of Power: A Feminist Sociology of Knowledge*, Toronto, University of Toronto Press.

SMITH, D. E. (1991) 'Writing Women's Experience into Social Science', *Feminism and Psychology*, 1:1, pp. 155–169.

SMITH, D. E. (1992) 'Sociology from Women's Experience: A Reaffirmation', *Sociological Theory*, 10:1, pp. 88–98.

SMITH, D. E. (1993) 'The Standard North American Family: SNAF as an ideological code', *Journal of Family Issues*, 14:1, pp. 50–65.

SMITH, D. E. and GRIFFITH, A. (1990) 'Coordinating the Uncoordinated: Mothering, Schooling and the Family Wage', *Perspectives on Social Problems*, 2:1, pp. 25–43.

SMITH, D. J. and TOMLINSON, S. (1989) *The School Effect: A Study of Multi-Racial Comprehensives*, London, Policy Studies Institute.

SNOW, C. *et al.* (1991) *Unfulfilled Expectations: Home and School Influences on Literacy*, London, Harvard University Press.

SPENDER, D. (1980) *Man Made Language*, London, Routledge and Kegan Paul.

STACEY, J. (1993) 'Untangling feminist theory', in RICHARDSON, D. and ROBINSON, V. (Eds) *Introducing Women's Studies*, London, Macmillan.

STANDING, K. (1995) 'Lone Mothers' unpaid schoolwork as a household issue', Paper presented at the Gender perspectives on household issues Conference, University of Reading, 8–9 April.

STANLEY, L. and WISE, S. (1993) *Breaking Out Again: Feminist Ontology and Epistemology*, London, Routledge.

STANWORTH, M. (1984) 'Women and Class Analysis', *Sociology*, 18:2, pp. 159–170.

STEVENSON, D. L. and BAKER, D. P. (1987) 'The Family-School Relation and the Child's School Performance', *Child Development*, 58:5, pp. 1348–1357.

STEWART, A., PRANDY, K. and BLACKBURN, R. M. (1980) *Social Stratification and Occupations*, London, Macmillan.

SWARTZ, D. (1977) 'Pierre Bourdieu: The Cultural Transmission of Social Inequality', *Harvard Educational Review*, 47:4, pp. 545–553.

SWARTZ, D. (1981) 'Classes, Educational Systems and Labour Markets', *European Journal of Sociology*, 22:2, pp. 325–353.

SZCZELKUN, S. (1993) *The Conspiracy of Good Taste*, London, Working Press.

THOMAS, A. and DENNISON, B. (1991) 'Parental or Pupil Choice – Who Really Decides in Urban Schools?', *Educational Management and Administration*, 19:4, pp. 243–249.

TOOMEY, D. (1989) 'Linking Class and Gender Inequality: the family and schooling', *British Journal of Sociology of Education*, 10:4, pp. 389–402.

TOPPING, K. and WOLFENDALE, S. (Eds) (1986) *Parental Involvement in Children's Reading*, London, Croom Helm.

TOWNSEND, P. (1979) *Poverty in the United Kingdom*, Harmondsworth, Penguin.

ULICH, K. (1989) 'Eltern und schuler: die schule als problem in der familienerziehung', *Zeitschrift fur Sozialisations Forschung und Erzietungssoziologie*, 9:3, pp. 179–194.

VAN GALEN, J. (1987) 'Maintaining Control: The Structuring of Parent Involvement', in NOBLIT, G. W. and PINK, W. T. (Eds) *Schooling in Social Context: Qualitative Studies*, Norwood N.J., Ablex.

VAN MAANEN, J. (1988) *Tales of the Field: On Writing Ethnography*, Chicago, University of Chicago Press.

VINCENT, C. (1992) 'Tolerating intolerance? Parental choice and race relations – the Cleveland case', *Journal of Education Policy*, 7:5, pp. 429–443.

VINCENT, C. (1996) *Parents and Teachers: Power and Participation*, London, Falmer Press.

WACQUANT, L. J. D. (1989) 'Towards a Reflexive Sociology: A Workshop with Pierre Bourdieu', *Sociological Theory*, 7:1, pp. 26–63.

WACQUANT, L. J. D. (1989a) 'The Dark Side of the Classroom in New Caledonia: Ethnic and Class Segregation in Noumea's Primary School System', *Comparative Education Review*, 33:2, pp. 194–212.

WACQUANT, L. J. D. (1991) 'Making Class', in McNALL, S., LEVINE, R. and FANTASIA, R. (Eds) *Bringing Class Back in: Contemporary and Historical Perspectives*, Boulder, West View Press.

WALBY, S. (1986) 'Gender, Class and Stratification: Towards a New Approach', in CROMPTON, R. and MANN, M. (Eds) *Gender and Stratification*, Cambridge, Polity Press.

WALBY, S. (1990) *Theorising Patriarchy*, Oxford, Blackwell.

WALKERDINE, V. (1985), 'On the regulation of Speaking and Silence', in STEEDMAN, C., URWIN, C. and WALKERDINE, V. (Eds) *Language, Gender and Childhood*, London, Routledge and Kegan Paul.

WALKERDINE, V. (1989) *Counting Girls Out*, London, Virago.

WALKERDINE, V. (1990) *Schoolgirl Fictions*, London, Verso.

WALKERDINE, V. and LUCEY, H. (1989) *Democracy in the Kitchen: Regulating Mothers and Socialising Daughters*, London, Virago.

WEBB, S. (1985) *Counter Arguments: an Ethnographic Look at Women and Class*, University of Manchester, Dept of Sociology, Studies in Sexual Politics.

WEIR, A. (1996) *Sacrificial Logics: Feminist Theory and the Critique of Identity*, London, Routledge.

WESTWOOD, S. (1984) *All Day Every Day: Factory and Family in the Making of Women's Lives*, London, Pluto Press.

WILKES, C. (1990) 'Bourdieu's Class', in HARKER, R., MAHAR, C. and WILKES, C. (Eds) *An Introduction to the Work of Pierre Bourdieu*, London, Macmillan.

WILKINSON, R. G. (1996) *Unhealthy Societies: The Afflictions of Inequality*, London, Routledge.

WILLIAMS, R. (1983) *The Year 2000*, New York, Pantheon Books.

WILLIS, P. (1977) *Learning to Labour: How working-class kids get working-class jobs*, Farnborough, Saxon House.

WILLIS, P. (1981) 'Cultural Production is Different from Cultural Reproduction Is Different from Social Reproduction is Different from Reproduction', *Interchange*, 12:2–3, pp. 48–67.

WOLFENDALE, S. (Ed.) (1989) *Parental Involvement – developing networks between school, home and community*, London, Cassell.

WOLPE, A-M. (1988) *Within School Walls: the Role of Discipline, Sexuality and the Curriculum*, London, Routledge.

WOODS, P. (1993a) 'Responding to the Consumer: Parental Choice and School Effectiveness', *School Effectiveness and School Improvement*, 4:3, pp. 205–229.

WOODS, P. (1993b) 'Parental Perspectives on Choice in the United Kingdom: Preliminary Thoughts on Meanings and Realities of Choice in Education', Paper presented at Annual meeting of American Educational Research Association, Atlanta, 12–16 April.

YAO, E. L. (1993) 'Strategies for working effectively with Asian immigrant Parents', in CHAVKIN, N. F. (Ed.) *Families and Schools in a Pluralistic Society*, Albany, State University of New York Press.

Index